D1636301

CRATER LAKE, BRITISH NORTH-WEST TERRITORY, THE SOURCE OF ALASKA'S GREAT RIVER.

A
SUMMER
IN ALASKA
in the 1880s

A POPULAR ACCOUNT OF THE TRAVELS OF AN ALASKA EXPLORING
EXPEDITION ALONG THE GREAT YUKON RIVER,
FROM ITS SOURCE TO ITS MOUTH, IN THE BRITISH NORTH-WEST
TERRITORY, AND IN THE TERRITORY OF ALASKA.

BY
FREDERICK SCHWATKA,
Laureate of the Paris Geographical Society
and of the Imperial Geographical Society of Russia,
Honorary Member Bremen Geographical Socirty, rtc., etc.
Commander of the Expedition.

CASTLE

CONTENTS.

PREFACE.

These pages narrate the travels, in a popular sense, of the latest Alaska exploring expedition. In April the expedition was organized with seven members at Vancouver Barracks, Washington Territory, and left Portland, Oregon, in May, ascending the inland passage to Alaska as far as the Chilkat country; there the party employed over three score of the Chilkat Indians to pack its effects across the glacier-clad pass of the Alaskan coast range of mountains to the head-waters of the Yukon. Here a large raft was constructed, and on this primitive craft, sailing through nearly a hundred and fifty miles of lakes, and shooting a number of rapids, the party floated along the great stream for over thirteen hundred miles, the longest raft journey ever made, in the interest of geographical science. The entire river, over two thousand miles, was traversed, the party returning home by way of Bering's Sea, and touching at the Aleutian Islands.

A SUMMER IN ALASKA.

CHAPTER I.

INTRODUCTORY.

THIS Alaskan exploring expedition was composed of the following members: Lieut. Schwatka, U. S. A., commanding; Dr. George F. Wilson, U. S. A., Surgeon ; Topographical Assistant Charles A. Homan, U.S. Engineers, Topographer and Photographer ; Sergeant Charles A. Gloster, U. S. A., Artist ; Corporal Shircliff, U.S.A., in charge of stores ; Private Roth, assistant, and Citizen J. B. McIntosh, a miner, who had lived in Alaska and was well acquainted with its methods of travel. Indians and others were added and discharged from time to time as hereafter noted.

The main object of the expedition was to acquire such information of the country traversed and its wild inhabitants as would be valuable to the military authorities in the future, and as a map would be needful to illustrate such information well, the party's efforts were rewarded with making the expedition successful in a geographical sense. I had hoped to be able, through qualified subordinates, to extend our scientific knowledge of the country explored, especially in regard to its botany, geology, natural history, etc.; and, although these subjects would not in any event have been adequately discussed in a popular treatise like the present, it must be admitted that little was accomplished in these branches. The explanation of this is as follows: When authority was asked from Congress for a sum of money to make such explorations under military supervision and the request was disapproved by the General of the Army and Secretary of War. This disapproval, combined with the active opposition of government departments which were assigned to work of the same general character and coupled with the reluctance of Congress to make any appropriations whatever that year, was sufficient to kill such an undertaking. When the military were withdrawn from Alaska by the President, about the year 1878, a paragraph appeared at the end of the President's order stating that no further control would be exercised by the army in Alaska; and this proviso was variously interpreted by the friends of the army and its enemies, as a humiliation either to the army or to the President, according to the private belief of the commentator. It was therefore seriously debated whether any military expedition or party sent into that country for any purpose whatever would not be a direct violation of the President's proscriptive order, and when it was decided to waive that consideration, and send in a party, it was considered too much of a responsibility to add any specialists in science, with the disapproval of the General and the Secretary hardly dry on the paper. The expedition was therefore, to avoid being recalled, kept as secret as possible, and when, on May 22d, it departed from Portland, Oregon, upon the *Victoria*, a vessel which had been specially put on the Alaska route, only a two or three line notice had gotten into the Oregon papers announcing the fact; a notice that in spreading was referred to in print by one government official as "a junketing party," by another as a "prospecting" party, while another bitterly acknowledged that had he received another day's intimation he could have had the party recalled by the authorities at Washington. Thus the little expedition which gave the first complete survey to the third * river of our country stole away like a thief in the night and with far less money in its hands to conduct it through its long journey than was afterward appropriated by Congress to publish its report.

Leaving Portland at midnight on the 22d, the *Victoria* arrived at Astoria at the mouth of the Columbia the forenoon of the 23d, the remaining hours of daylight being employed in loading with supplies for a number of salmon canneries in Alaska, the large amount of freight for which had necessitated this extra steamer. That night we crossed the Columbia River bar and next morning entered the Strait of Juan de Fuca, the southern entrance from the Pacific Ocean which leads to the inland passage to Alaska.

---

* The largest river on the North American continent so far as this mighty stream flows within our boundaries. . . . The people of the United States will not be quick to take to the idea that the volume of water in an Alaskan river is greater than that discharged by the mighty Mississippi; but it is entirely within the bounds of honest statement to say that the Yukon river . . . discharges every hour one-third more water than the " Father of Waters."—Petroff's Government Report on Alaska.

CHAPTER II.

THE INLAND PASSAGE TO ALASKA.

 LAND PASSAGE " to Alaska is the fjörd-like channel, resembling a great river, which extends from the northwestern part of Washington Territory, through British Columbia, into southeastern Alaska. Along this coast line for about a thousand miles, stretches a vast archipelago closely hugging the mainland of the Territories named above, the southernmost important island being Vancouver, almost a diminutive continent in itself, while to the north Tchichagoff Island limits it on the seaboard.

From the little town of Olympia at the head of Puget Sound, in Washington Territory, to Chilkat, Alaska, at the head of Lynn Channel, or Canal, one sails as if on a grand river, and it is really hard to comprehend that it is a portion of the ocean unless one can imagine some deep fjörd in Norway or Greenland, so deep that he can sail on its waters for a fortnight, for the fjörd-like character is very prominent in these channels to which the name of " Inland Passage " is usually given.

These channels between the islands and mainland are strikingly uniform in width, and therefore river-like in

appearance as one steams or sails through them. At
occasional points they connect with the Pacific Ocean,
and if there be a storm on the latter, a few rolling swells
may enter at these places and disturb the equilibrium of
sensitive stomachs for a brief hour, but at all other
places the channel is as quiet as any broad river, whatever the weather. On the south we have the Strait of
Juan de Fuca and to the north Cross Sound as the limit-
ing channels, while between the two are found Dixon
Entrance, which separates Alaska from British Columbia, Queen Charlotte Sound, and other less important
outlets.

On the morning of the 24th of May we entered the
Strait of Juan de Fuca, named after an explorer—if
such he may be called—who never entered this beautiful
sheet of water, and who owes his immortality to an
audacious guess, which came so near the truth as to
deceive the scientific world for many a century. To the
left, as we enter, i.e., northward, is the beautiful British
island of Vancouver, the name of which commemorates
one of the world's most famous explorers. Its high
rolling hills are covered with shaggy firs, broken near
the beach into little prairies of brighter green, which are
dotted here and there with pretty little white cottages,
the humblest abodes we see among the industrious,
British or American, who live in the far west.

The American side, to the southward, gives us the
same picture backed by the high range of the Olympian
Mountains, whose tops are covered with perpetual snow,
and upon whose cold sides drifting clouds are condensed.

Through British Columbia the sides of this passage are

covered with firs and spruce to the very tops of the steep
mountains forming them, but as Northing is gained
and Alaska is reached the summits are covered with snow
and ice at all months of the year, and by the time we
cast anchor in Chilkat Inlet, which is about the northernmost point of this great inland salt-water river, we
find in many places these crowns of ice debouching in
the shape of glaciers to the very water's level, and the
tourist beholds, on a regular line of steamboat travel,
glaciers and icebergs, and many of the wonders of arctic
regions, although upon a reduced scale. Alongside the
very banks and edges of these colossal rivers of ice one
can gather the most beautiful of Alpine flowers and
wade up to his waist in grasses that equal in luxuriance
the famed fields of the pampas; while the singing of the
birds from the woods and glens and the fragrance of the
foliage make one easily imagine that the Arctic circle
and equator have been linked together at this point.

Entering Juan de Fuca Strait a few hours were spent
in the pretty little anchorage of Neah Bay, the first
shelter for ships after rounding Cape Flattery, and here
some merchandise was unloaded in the huge Indian
canoes that came alongside, each one holding at least
a ton.

Victoria, the metropolis of British Columbia, was
reached the same day, and as it was the Queen's birth-
day we saw the town in all its bravery of beer, bunting
and banners. Our vessel tooted itself hoarse outside the
harbor to get a pilot over the bar, but none was to be
had till late in the day, when a pilot came out to us
showing plainly by his condition that he knew every bar
in and about Victoria. With the bar pilot on the bridge,

so as to save insurance should an accident occur, we entered the picturesque little harbor in safety, despite the discoveries of our guide that since his last visit all the buoys had been woefully misplaced, and even the granite channel had changed its course. But Victoria has many embellishments more durable than bunting and banners, and most conspicuous among them are her well arranged and well constructed roads, in which she has no equal on the Pacific coast of North America, and but few rivals in any other part of the world.

On the 26th we crossed over to Port Townsend, the port of entry for Puget sound, and on the 27th we headed for Alaska by way of the Inland Passage.

For purposes of description this course should have been designated the "inland passages," in the plural, for its branches are almost innumerable, running in all directions like the streets of an irregular city, although now and then they are reduced to a single channel or fjörd which the steamer is obliged to take or put out to sea. At one point in Discovery Passage leading from the Gulf of Georgia toward Queen Charlotte Sound, the inland passage is so narrow that our long vessel had to steam under a slow bell to avoid accidents, and at this place, called Seymour Narrows, there was much talk of bridging the narrow way in the grand scheme of a Canadian Pacific Railway, which should have its western terminus at Victoria. Through this contracted way the water fairly boils when at its greatest velocity, equaling ten miles an hour in spring tides, and at such times the passage is hazardous even to steamers, while all other craft avoid it until slack water. Jutting rocks increase the danger, and on one of these the United States man-of-war *Saranac* was lost just eight years before we passed through. At the northern end of this picturesque Discovery Passage you see the inland passage trending away to the eastward, with quite a bay on the left around Chatham Point, and while you are wondering in that half soliloquizing way of a traveler in new lands what you will see after you have turned to the right, the great ship swings suddenly to the left, and you find that what you took for a bay is after all the inland passage itself, which stretches once more before you like the Hudson looking upward from West Point, or the Delaware at the Water Gap. For all such little surprises must the tourist be prepared on this singular voyage.

The new bend now becomes Johnstone Strait and so continues to Queen Charlotte Sound, with which it connects by one strait, two passages and a channel, all alike, except in name, and none much over ten miles long. At nearly every point where a new channel diverges both arms take on a new name, and they change as rapidly as the names of a Lisbon street, which seldom holds the same over a few blocks. The south side of Johnstone Strait is particularly high, rising abruptly from the water fully 5,000 feet, and in grandeur not unlike the Yellowstone Cañon. These summits were still covered with snow and probably on northern slopes snow remains the summer through. One noticeable valley was on the Vancouver Island side, with a conspicuous conical hill in its bosom that may have been over a thousand feet in height. These cone-like hills are so common in flat valleys in northwestern America that I thought it worth while to mention the fact in this place. I shall have occasion to do so again at a later point in my narrative. Occasionally windrows occur through the dense coniferous forests of the inland passage, where the trees have been swept or leveled in a remarkable manner. Such as were cut vertically had been caused by an avalanche, and in these instances the work of clearing had been done as faithfully as if by the hands of man. Sometimes the bright green moss or grass had grown up in these narrow ways, and when there was more than one of about the same age there was quite a picturesque effect of stripings of two shades of green, executed on a most colossal plan. These windrows of fallen trees sometimes stretched along horizontally in varying widths, an effect undoubtedly produced by heavy gales rushing through the contracted "passage."

One's notice is attracted by a species of natural beacon which materially assists the navigator. Over almost all the shoals and submerged rocks hang fields of kelp, a growth with which the whole "passage" abounds, thus affording a timely warning badly needed where the channel has been imperfectly charted. As one might surmise the water is very bold, and these submerged and ragged rocks are in general most to be feared. Leaving Johnstone Strait we enter Queen Charlotte Sound, a channel which was named, lacking only three years, a century ago. It widens into capacious waters at once and we again felt the "throbbing of old Neptune's pulse," and those with sensitive stomachs perceived a sort of flickering of their own.

One who is acquainted merely in a general way with the history and geography of this confusing country finds many more Spanish names than he anticipates, and to his surprise, a conscientious investigation shows that even as it is the vigorous old Castilian explorers have not received all the credit to which they are entitled, for many of their discoveries in changing hands changed names as well: the Queen Charlotte Islands, a good day's run to the northwestward of us, were named in 1787 by an Englishman, who gave the group the name of his vessel, an appellation which they still retain, although as Florida Blanca they had known the banner of Castile and Leon thirteen years before. Mount Edgecumbe, so prominent in the beautiful harbor of Sitka, was once Monte San Jacinto, and a list of the same tenor might be given that would prove more voluminous than interesting. American changes in the great northwest have not been so radical. Boca de Quadra Inlet has somehow become Bouquet Inlet to those knowing it best. La Creole has degenerated into Rickreall, and so on: the foreign names have been mangled but not annihilated. We sail across Queen Charlotte Sound as if we were going to bump right into the high land ahead of us, but a little indentation over the bow becomes a valley, then a bay, and in ample time to prevent accidents widens into another salt-water river, about two miles wide and twenty times as long, called Fitzhugh Sound. Near the head of the sound we turn abruptly westward into the Lama Passage, and on its western shores we see nearly the first sign of civilization in the inland passage, the Indian village of Bella Bella, holding probably a dozen native houses and a fair looking church, while a few cattle grazing near the place had a still more civilized air.

As we steamed through Seaforth Channel, a most tortuous affair, Indians were seen paddling in their huge

SCENES IN THE INLAND PASSAGE.

canoes from one island to another or along the high, rocky shores, a cheering sign of habitation not previously noticed.

The great fault of the inland passage as a resort for tourists is in the constant dread of fogs that may at any time during certain months of the year completely obscure the grand scenery that tempted the travelers thither. The waters of the Pacific Ocean on the seaboard of Alaska are but a deflected continuation of the warm equatorial current called the Kuro Siwo of the Japanese ; from these waters the air is laden with moisture, which being thrown by the variable winds against the snow-clad and glacier-covered summits of the higher mountains, is precipitated as fog and light rain, and oftentimes every thing is wrapped for weeks in these most annoying mists. July, with June and August, are by far the most favorable months for the traveler. The winter months are execrable, with storms of rain, snow and sleet constantly occurring, the former along the Pacific frontage, and the latter near the channels of the mainland.

Milbank Sound gave us another taste of the ocean swells which spoiled the flavor of our food completely, for although we were only exposed for less than an hour that hour happened to come just about dinner time ; after which we entered Finlayson Passage, some twenty-five miles long. This is a particularly picturesque and bold channel of water, its shores covered with shaggy conifers as high as the eye can reach, and the mountains, with their crowns of snow and ice, furnishing supplies of spray for innumerable beautiful waterfalls. At many places in the inland passage from here on, come down the

steep timbered mountains the most beautiful waterfalls fed
from the glaciers hidden in the fog.   At every few miles
we pass the mouths of inlets and channels, leading away
into the mountainous country no one knows whither.
There are no charts which show more than the mouths
of these inlets.   Out of or into these an occasional canoe
speeds its silent way perchance in quest of salmon that
here abound, but the secrets of their hidden paths are
locked in the savage mind.   How tempting they must be
for exploration, and how strange that, although so easy
of access, they still remain unknown.   After twisting
around through a few "reaches," channels and passages,
we enter the straightest of them all, Grenville Channel,
so straight that it almost seems to have been mapped by
an Indian.   As you steam through its forty or fifty miles
of mathematically rectilinear exactness you think the
sleepy pilot might tie his wheel, put his heels up in the
spokes, draw his hat over his eyes and take a quiet nap.
In one place it seems to be not over two or three hundred
yards wide, but probably is double that, the high tower-
ing banks giving a deceptive impression.   The windrows
through the timber of former avalanches of snow or land-
slides, now become thicker and their effects occasionally
picturesque in the very devastation created.   Beyond
Grenville Channel the next important stretch of salt
water is Chatham Sound, which is less like a river than
any yet named.   Its connection with Grenville Channel
is by the usual number of three or four irregular water-
ways dodging around fair sized islands, which had at
one time, however, a certain importance because it was
thought that the Canadian Pacific Railway might make
Skeena Inlet off to our right its western terminus.

On the 29th of May, very early in the morning, we crossed Dixon Entrance, and were once more on American soil, that is, in a commercial sense, the United States having drawn a check for its value of $7,200,000, and the check having been honored ; but in regard to government the country may be called no man's land, none existing in the territory. Dixon Entrance bore once a Spanish name in honor of its discoverer, a name which is heard no more, although a few still call the channel by its Indian name, Kaiganee. Broad Dixon Entrance contracts into the narrow Portland Inlet, which, putting back into the mainland for some seventy-five miles, forms the water boundary between Alaska and British Columbia. From here it becomes a thirty mile wide strip drawn " parallel to tide-water," which continues with a few modifications to about Mount St. Elias.

The forenoon of the same day we entered Boca de Quadra Inlet, where a pioneer company had established a salmon cannery, for which we had some freight. The cannery was about half completed and the stores were landed on a raft made of only two logs, which impressed me with the size of the Sitka cedar. The largest log was probably seventy-five feet long and fully eight feet at the butt. It is said to be impervious to the teredo, which makes such sad havoc with all other kinds of wood sunk in salt water. Owing to its fine grain and peculiar odor. handsome chests can be made of it in which that universal pest, the moth, will not live. It is purely an Alaskan tree, and even north of Quadra Inlet it is found in its densest growth. As around all white habitations in frontier lands, we found the usual number of natives, although in this case they were here for the commendable object of seeking employment in catching salmon whenever the run should commence. Their canoes are constructed of the great cedar tree, by the usual Indian method of hollowing them out to a thin shell and then boiling water in them by throwing in red hot stones in the water they hold, producing pliability of the wood by the steaming process, when, by means of braces and ties they are fashioned into nautical "lines." The peaks of the prows are often fantastically carved into various insignia, usually spoken of as " totems," and painted in wild barbaric designs (see page 43,) the body of the boat being covered with deep black made from soot and seal oil. Crawling along under the somber shadows of the dense overhanging trees in the deep dark passages, these canoes can hardly be seen until very near, and when a flash of the water from the paddle reveals their presence, they look more like smugglers or pirates avoiding notice than any thing else. The genial superintendent, Mr. Ward, spoke of his rambles up the picturesque shores of the inlet and his adventures since he had started his new enterprise. A trip of a few days before up one of the diminutive valleys drained by a little Alpine brook, had rewarded him with the sight of no less than eight bears skurrying around through the woods. He had an Indian companion who was armed with a flint-lock, smooth bore Hudson Bay Company musket, while the superintendent had a shot gun for any small game that might happen along, and even with these arms they succeeded in bagging a bear apiece, both being of the black—or small—variety. Hunting the little black bear is not far removed from a good old-fashioned "coon" hunt, and not much more dan-

gerous. The dogs, mostly the sharp-eared, sharp-nosed
and sharp-barking Indian variety, once after a bear,
force him up a tree to save his hamstrings being nipped
uncomfortably, and then he is shot out of it, at the
hunter's leisure, and if wounded is so small and easily
handled by the pack of dogs that he can hardly be
called dangerous. Not so, however, with the great brown
bear, or barren-ground bear of Alaska, so often spoken
of in these parts as the "grizzly" from his similarity
in size and savageness to "the California King of the
Chapparal." Everywhere in his dismal dominions he is
religiously avoided by the native Nimrod, who declares
that his meat is not fit to be eaten, that his robe is almost
worthless, and that he constantly keeps the wrong end
presented to his pursuers. Although he is never hunted
encounters with him are not altogether unknown, as he is
savage enough to become the hunter himself at times,
and over some routes the Indians will never travel unless
armed so as to be fairly protected from this big Bruin.
This Indian fear of the great brown bear I found to be
co-extensive with all my travels in Alaska and the
British North-west Territory. Mr. Ward told me that
wherever the big bear was found, the little black variety
made his presence scarce, as the two in no way affiliate,
and the latter occupies such country as the abundance
of his big brother will allow. These districts may be
intermixed as much as the black and white squares on a
chess-board, but they are as sharply, though not as
mathematically, defined, each one remaining faithfully
on his own color, so to speak. A new repeating rifle
was on our vessel consigned to the sportsman superintendent, and he expected to decrease the bear

census during the summer, so far as his duties would allow.

About noon, after much backing and putting of lines ashore, and working on them from the donkey engines fore and aft, we succeeded in turning our long steamer in the narrow channel, the pilot remarking in reply to the captain's inquiries as to shoals, that he wished he could exchange the depth for the width and he would have no trouble in turning around.

Through this part of the inland passage sea-otters are said to be found, and it was thought that one or two were seen by some of the people on board, but no one could vouch for the discovery.

The everlasting mountain scenery now commences to pall and offers nothing in the way of the picturesque except the same old high mountains, the same dense growth of timber on their steep sides, and the same salt-water canals cutting through them. A valley putting off any where would have been a relief, and breaks in the uniformly high mountains that looked as if they might be ravines, so persistently became other arms and canals of the great networks of passage, that we were any thing but sorry when a fog bank settled down about two hundred feet above our eyes and cut the fjörd as sharply at that height as if it had been the crest line of a fortification extending off into miles of bastions and covered ways.

Early morning on the 30th found us at the little port of Wrangell, named after one of Russia's many famous explorers in northern regions. It was the most tumble-down looking company of cabins I ever saw, the "Chinese quarter" (every place on the Pacific coast has its "Chinese quarter" if it is only a single house) being a wrecked river vessel high and dry on the pebbly beach, which, however, was not much inferior to the rest of the town. Not far from here comes in the Stickeen river, the largest stream that cuts through the south-eastern or "tide-water strip" of Alaska. About its headwaters are the Cassiar mines of British Columbia, and as the Stickeen river is the nearest available way to reach them, although the traveler's course is against the stream of a mountain torrent, the circumstance has made something of a port of Wrangell, which nearly ten years ago was at the height of its glory of gold-dust and excitement. Even at this distance the dark green water of the deep channel is tinged with a white chalky color ground from the flanks of the calcareous hills by the eroding glaciers, then swept into the swift river and by it carried far out into the tortuous passages. Every stream, however small, in this part of the world, with glaciers along its course or upon its tributaries, carries this milk-like water in its current.

With all its rickety appearance there was no small amount of business doing in Wrangell, no less than four or five fair sized backwoods stores being there, all apparently in thrifty circumstances. Indian curiosities of all kinds were to be had, from carved spoons of the mountain goat at "two bits" (twenty-five cents) apiece to the most elaborate idols or totemic carvings. A fair market is found for these articles among the few visitors who travel in this out-of-the-way corner of the earth, and when the supply is exhausted in any line the natives will immediately set to work to satisfy the demand. One huge carved horn spoon was evidently of very ancient make and very fine workmanship, an old pioneer of these regions who had owned it for many years having refused sixty dollars for it from some curiosity collectors only the year before.

From Wrangell we debouched westward by Sumner Strait, the wide salt-water river that continues the narrow fresh-water river of Stickeen to the Pacific Ocean.

Between five and six in the afternoon we are rounding Cape Ommaney, where our pilot tells us it storms eight days in the week. It certainly gave us double rations of wind that day, and many retired early. Even the old Spanish navigators who first laid eyes upon it must have borne it a grudge to have called it *Punta Oeste de la Entrada del Principe;* all its geographical characteristics and relations being shouldered on it for a name.

Early next morning we were in the harbor of Sitka, or New Archangel, as the Russians called it when they had it for their capital of this province. The strong, bold bluffs of the interior passages now give way to gentler elevations along the Pacific seaboard, but the country gradually rises from the coast until but a few miles back the same old cloud-capped, snow-covered peaks recur, and as we stand well out to sea they look as abrupt as ever.

Sitka is a picturesque place when viewed from any point except from within the town limits. From the south-west, looking north-east, Mount Edgecumbe (of Cook) affords a beautiful background against the western sky, and when that is full of low white clouds the abrupt manner in which the point of the mountain is cut off gives it the appearance of being buried in the clouds, thus seeming several times higher than it really is.

SITKA, ALASKA.

From a painting by Captain Cleveland Rockwell, in the possession of J. C. Ainsworth, Esq., Oakland, Cal. (With the kind permission of artist and owner.)

The harbor of Sitka is so full of small islands that looking at it from a height it seems as if it could only be mapped with a pepper-box, and one wonders how any vessel can get to her wharf. Once alongside, the water seems as clear as the atmosphere above, and the smallest objects can be easily identified at the bottom, though there must have been fully thirty or forty feet of water where we made our observations.

On one of the large islands in Sitka harbor, called Japanese Island, an old Niphon junk was cast, early in the present century, and her small crew of Japanese were rescued by the Russians. Sitka has been so often described that it is unnecessary to do more than refer the reader to other accounts of the place.

Ten o'clock in the forenoon of the 31st saw us under way steaming northward, still keeping to the inland passage, and *en route* to deliver wrecking machinery at a point in Peril Straits where the *Eureka*, a small steamer of the same line to which our ship belonged, had formerly run on a submerged rock in the channel, which did not appear upon the charts. The unfortunate boat had just time to reach the shore and beach herself before she filled with water. The Eureka's wreck was reached by two in the afternoon, and as our boat might be detained for some time in assisting the disabled vessel, many of us embraced the opportunity to go ashore in the wilds of the Alexander Archipelago. The walking along the beach between high and low tide was tolerable, and even agreeable for whole stretches, especially after our long confinement on the ship, where the facilities for promenading were poor. To turn inland from the shore was at once to commence the ascent of a slope

that might vary frcm forty to eighty degrees, the climbing of which almost beggars description. The compact
mass of evergreen timber had looked dense enough from
the ship, but at its feet grew a denser mass of tangled
undergrowth of bushes and vines, and at their roots
again was a solid carpeting of moss, lichens, and ferns
that often ran up the trees and underbrush for heights
greater than a man's reach, and all of it moist as a
sponge, the whole being absolutely tropical in luxuriance. This thick carpet of moss extends from the shore
line to the edges of the glaciers on the mountain summits, and the constant melting of the ice through the
warm summer supplies it with water which it absorbs
like a sponge. The air is saturated with moisture from
the warm ocean current, and every thing you see and
touch is like Mr. Mantalini's proposed body, "dem'd
moist and unpleasant." It is almost impossible to conceive how heavily laden with tropical moisture the atmosphere is in this supposed sub-Arctic colony of ours.
It oozes up around your feet as you walk, and drips
from overhead like an April mist, and nothing is exempt
from it. Even the Indians' tall, dead "totem-poles" of
hemlock or spruce, which would make fine kindling
wood any where else, bear huge clumps of dripping moss
and foliage on their tops, at heights varying from ten
to thirty feet above the ground. An occasional stray
seed of a Sitka spruce may get caught in this elevated
tangle, and make its home there just as well as if it were
on the ground. It sprouts, and as its branches run up
in the air, the roots crawl down the "totem-pole" until
the ground is reached, when they bury themselves in it,
and send up fresh sustenance to the trunk and limbs,

which until then have been living a parasitic sort of life
off the decayed moss. This is shown in illustration on
page 19, being a view at Kaigan Village. Imagine a
city boy tossing a walnut from a fourth story window,
and its lodging on top of a telegraph pole, there sprout-
ing next spring, and in the course of a couple of years
extending its roots down the pole, insinuating themselves in the crevices and splitting it open, then piercing
the pavement; the tree continuing to grow for years
until the boy, as a man, can reach out from his window
and pick walnuts every fall, and the idea seems incredible; and yet the equivalent occurs quite often in
the south-eastern portions of our distant colony. Nor
is all this marshy softness confined to the levels or to
almost level slopes, as one would imagine from one's experience at home, but it extends up the steepest places,
where the climbing would be hard enough without this
added obstacle. In precipitous slopes where the foot
tears out a great swath of moist moss, it may reveal underneath a slippery shingle or shale where nothing
but a bird could find a footing in its present
condition. There is wonderful preservative power in all
these conditions, for nothing seems to rot in the ground,
and the accumulated timber of ages, standing and fallen,
stumps, limbs, and trunks, "criss-cross and tumble-
tangled," as the children say, forms a bewildering mass
which, covered and intertwined as it is with a compact
entanglement of underbrush and moss, makes the ascent
of the steep hillsides a formidable undertaking. A
fallen trunk of a tree is only indicated by a ridge of
moss, and should the traveler on this narrow path
deviate a little too far to the right or left, he may sink

up to his arm-pits in a soft mossy trap from which he
can scramble as best he may, according to his activity in
the craft of "backwoodsmanship." Having once reached
the tops of the lower hills—the higher ones are covered
with snow and glacier ice the year round—a few small
openings may be seen, which, if any thing, are more boggy
and treacherous to the feet than the hillsides themselves,
lagoon-like morasses, covered with pond lilies and
aquatic plant life, being connected by a network of
sluggish canals with three or four inches of amber
colored water and as many feet of soft black oozy mud,
with here and there a clump of willow brake or "pussy-
tails" springing above the waste of sedge and flags.
In these bayou openings a hunter may now and then
run across a stray deer, bear, or mountain goat, but, in
general, inland hunting in south-eastern Alaska is a
complete failure, owing to the scarcity of game and the
labor of hunting.

The worst part of Peril Strait being ahead of us,
we backed out with our long unwieldy vessel and turned
westward, passing out late in the evening through
Salisbury Strait to the Pacific Ocean, ours being,
according to the pilot, the first steam vessel to essay
the passage. A last night on the Pacific's rolling water,
and early next morning we rounded Cape Ommaney,
and entered the inland passage of Chatham Strait,
our prow once more pointed northward, the sheet of
water lying as quiet as a mill pond. About 4 P. M. we
reached Killisnoo, a pretty little port in the Strait.
Cod-fish abounding here in unusual numbers, a regular
fishery has been established by a company for the purpose of catching and preserving the cod for the markets

of the Pacific coast. Here I saw many of the Kootznahoo
Indians of the place, who do the principal fishing for
the white men. Their already ugly faces were plastered
over with black, for which, according to the superintendent, there were two causes. A few of the Indians were
clad in mourning, to which this artificial blackness is an
adjunct, while the remainder followed the custom in
order to protect their faces and especially their eyes
from the intense glare of the sun on the water while fishing. Chatham Strait at its northern end subdivides
into Icy Straits and Lynn Canal, the latter being taken
as our course. At its northern end it again branches
into the Chilkat and Chilkoot Inlets, the former being
taken; and at its head, the highest northing we can reach
in this great inland salt-water river, our voyage on the
Victoria terminated. Icy Straits lead off to the westward and unite with the Pacific, by way of Cross Sound,
the most northern of these connecting passages, which
marks the point where the archipelago, and with it the
inland passage, ceases, for from here northward to St.
Elias and beyond a bold bad coast faces the stormy
Pacific, and along its frowning cliffs of rock and ice even
the amphibious Indian seldom ventures.

CHAPTER III.

HILKAT country was reached on the morning of the 2d of June and we dropped anchor in a most picturesque little port called Pyramid Harbor, its name being derived from a conspicuous conical island that the Chilkats call Schlay-hotch, and the few whites, Pyramid Island, shown on page 43. There were two salmon canneries just completed, one on each side of the inlet, awaiting the "run" or coming of salmon, which occurred about two weeks later. Each cannery was manned by about a half dozen white men as directors and workmen in the trades departments, the Chilkats doing the rougher work, as well as furnishing the fish. They differed in no material respect from the salmon canneries of the great Columbia River, so often described. Just above them comes in the Chilkat river, with a broad shallow mouth, which, at low water (sixteen feet below high water) looks like a large sand flat forming part of the shores of the harbor. On these bars the Indians spear the salmon when the water is just deep enough to allow them to wade around readily.

CHILKAT BRACELET MADE FROM SILVER COIN.

Up this Chilkat river are the different villages of the Chilkat Indians, one of fifteen or twenty houses being in sight, on the east bank, the largest, however, which contains four or five times as many houses, called Kluk-wan,

being quite a distance up the river. These Chilkats are
subdivided into a number of smaller clans, named after
the various animals, birds and fishes. At about the time
of my arrival the chief of the Crow clan had died, and as
he was a very important person, a most sumptuous funeral was expected to last about a week or ten days.
These funerals are nothing but a series of feasts, protracted according to the importance of the deceased, and
as they are furnished at the expense of the administra-
tors or executors of the dead man's estate, every Indian
from far and wide, full of veneration for the dead and a
desire for victuals, congregates at the pleasant ceremonies, and gorges to his utmost, being worthless for work
for another week afterward. As I urgently needed some
three or four score of these Indians to carry my effects
on their backs across the Alaskan coast range of mountains to the head waters of the Yukon river, this prolonged funeral threatened seriously to prevent my getting
away in good time. Ranking me as a chief, I was invited
to the obsequies and promised a very conspicuous position therein, especially on the last day when the body
was to be burned on a huge funeral pyre of dry
resinous woods. Cremation is the usual method of dis-
posing of the dead among these people, the priests or
medicine men being the only ones exempt. The latter
claim a sort of infallibility and all of their predictions,
acts, and influences capable of survival, live after them
so long as their bodies exist, but should these be lost by
drowning, devouring, or cremation, this infallibility
ceases. Therefore these defunct doctors of savage witch-
craft inhabit the greatest portion of the few graveyards
that one sees scattered here and there over the shores of

the channels and inlets that penetrate the country. Cre·
mation is not always resorted to, however, with the laity,
for whenever convenience dictates otherwise, they too
may be buried in boxes, and this practice, I understand,
is becoming more common. Cremation is a savage honor,
nevertheless, and slaves were not entitled to the rite. All
the Indians were extremely anxious that I should attend
the obsequies of their dear departed friend, for if I did
they saw that they might also be present and yet feel
sure of employment on my expedition over the
mountains. I declined the invitation, however, and
by being a little bit determined managed to
persuade enough strong sturdy fellows away to do my
proposed packing in two trips over the pass, which had
the effect of inducing the others to come forward in sufficient numbers to accomplish the work in a single journey, and preparations were commenced accordingly.
These preparations consisted mostly in assorting our
effects with reference to every thing that we could
possibly leave behind, taking as little as we could
make our way through with, and putting that little into
convenient bags, boxes, and bundles of about one hundred pounds each, that being the maximum load the Indians could well carry over such Alpine trails. Some
boys, eight or ten, even came forward to solicit a share
in the arduous labor, and one little urchin of not over
fourteen, a son of the Chilkat chief, Shot-rich, manfully
assumed the responsibility of a sixty-eight pound box,
the distance he had to carry it being about thirty miles,
but thirty miles equal to any one hundred and thirty on
the good roads of a civilized country. There were a few
slaves among my numerous Indian packers, slavery

having once flourished extensively among the Chilkats, but having diminished both in vigor and extent, in direct ratio to their contact with the whites. Formerly, slaves were treated in the many barbarous ways common to savage countries, sacrificed at festivals and religious ceremonies, and kept at the severest tasks. They were often tied in huge leathern sacks stretched at full length on the hard stony ground and trodden to death. The murderers, great muscular men, would jump up and down on their bodies, singing a wild death chant, with their fists clinched across their breasts, every cracking of a rib or bone being followed by loud shouts of derisive laughter. Sometimes the slave was bound to huge bowlders at the water's edge at low tide, and as the returning waves came rolling in and slowly drowned the wretch, his cries were deafened by the hideous shouts from the spectators on the land. Of course, as with all slave-holders, an eye was kept open toward mercenary views, and the sacrifices were nearly always of the aged, infirm, or decrepit; those who had ceased to be useful as interpreted by their own savage ideas of usefulness. Entering a Chilkat house nowadays, one can hardly distinguish a slave from the master, unless one is acquainted with the insignificant variations in dress which characterize them, and while the slaves are supposed to do all the work the enforcement of the rule appears to be very lax. Still it is interesting to know that the fourteenth amendment to the United States constitution is not held inviolable in all parts of that vast country. As among nearly all savages, the women are brutalized, but they appear to have one prerogative of the most singular character, that is well worth relat-

ing. Nearly every thing descends on the mother's side,
yet a chattel may be owned, or at least controlled, by the
men, although a traveler will notice many bargains
wherein the woman's consent is first obtained. The
royal succession is most oddly managed with reference
to women's rights. The heir-apparent to the throne is
not the oldest or any other child of the king and queen,
but is the queen's nearest blood relative of the male per-
suasion, although the relationship may be no closer, perhaps, than that of cousin. As this curiously chosen
king may marry any woman of the tribe, it is easy to
see that any one may in this indirect way become the sovereign of the savages, and with the help of luck alone,
may acquire royal honors. One rich Indian woman of
Sitka who took a fancy to a slave, purchased him for the
purpose of converting him into a husband, at a cost of
nearly a thousand dollars in goods and chattels, and if
he was not very expensive thereafter he may have been
cheaper than the usual run of such bargains. When a
couple of Chilkats tie the nuptial knot, they at once, if
possible, adopt a boy and a girl, although these can
hardly be said to stand in the place of adopted children,
when it is understood that they are really a conjugal
reserve corps for the bride and bridegroom in case of
death. Should the man die the boy becomes the widow's
husband without further ceremony, and *vice versa*. Of
course such conjugal mixtures present the most incongruous aspects in the matter of age, but happily these
examples are infrequent.

This Chilkat country is most thoroughly Alpine in
character, and in the quiet, still evenings, far up on the
steep hillsides, where the dense spruce timber is broken

up by natural clearings, one could often see a brown or black bear come out and nose around to get at some of the many roots and berries that there abound, and more than once I was a spectator of a bear hunt, for as soon as Bruin put in an appearance there was always some Indian hunter ambitious enough to toil up the steep mountain sides after him. I have spoken of their extreme fear of the great brown or cinnamon bear, which they seldom attack. So great indeed is the Chilkats' respect for him that the most aristocratic clan is called the Cinnamon Bears. Another high class clan is the Crows, the plebeian divisions being the Wolves and Whales, and the division line is so strong that it leads to feuds between the clans that, in respect of slaughter, are almost entitled to the name of wars, while between the high and low caste intermarriage is almost unknown. As the Brown Bears, or Cinnamon Bears as they are generally called, are the highest clan, so copper is their most highly prized metal. With copper the Chilkats have always been familiar, gold and silver coming with the whites; and therefore a brown bear's head carved in copper is their most venerated charm. In regard to engraving and sculpture it is not too much to say that the Chilkats stand well in the front rank of savage artists. When civilization first came in contact with these people they were in the paleolithic stone age of that material, and their carvings were marvels of design and execution, although subserving the simplest wants of a simple people. Of metals they possessed only copper, and that in such small quantities as to be practically out of the account. With the whites came gold and silver, and the latter from its comparative cheapness became their favorite metal. Coins were hammered out into long slender bars, bent into bracelets, and then beautifully engraved, some of their designs having been borrowed from civilization and copied faithfully in detail, although the old savage ideas of workmanship are for obvious reasons preferred by most purchasers. Some of their women wear a dozen or more bracelets on each arm, covering them up to the elbows and beyond, but this seems to be only a means of preserving them until the arrival of white customers, when they are sold at from one to five or six dollars a pair according to their width. The initial piece of this chapter is sketched from one in the possession of the author and made by one of his hired Indians. Ear-rings, finger-rings, beads and ornamental combs for the hair are made of silver and gold, mostly of silver ; and the Chilkats seem to be as imitative in respect to ideas and designs as the Mongolians, whose talents are so much better known. It is in wood and horn, however, that their best examples of this art have been displayed, and so unique and intricate are they that language is inadequate to describe them. Of wood carvings their "totem" poles show the cleverest workmanship and variety of design. The exact significance of these totem poles remains still undetermined, and the natives themselves seem averse to throwing much light on the subject. This fact alone would appear to indicate a superstitious origin. Some say the totem poles represent family genealogies, life histories, and tribal accounts, all of which conjectures may be well founded. They are simply logs of wood standing on end in front of the houses, and facing the water. This face is covered from top to bottom, for a height of from five to thirty feet, with the most curious carvings, as shown to a limited extent on page 19. The "totem" or tribal symbol, which may be a wolf, a bear, a raven, or a fish, often predominates, while representations of crouching human

PYRAMID HARBOR, CHILKAT INLET.
(Chilkat Indian Canoe in the foreground.)

figures are favorite designs. The making of totem poles has ceased among the Indians, although they carefully preserve those that still exist. Still many of them fall into the clutches of white men in compensation for a few dollars, and hardly a museum of note in the country but displays a Tlinkit totem pole or two, while some possess extensive collections. The best carving is shown in the isolated poles standing in front of the houses, but frequently the houses themselves are fantastically carved in conspicuous places to suit the owner's fancy.

Some of these houses are quite respectable for savage housemaking, the great thick puncheon planks of the floor being often quite well polished, or at any rate neatly covered with white sand. Attempts at civilization are made in the larger and more aristocratic abodes by partitioning the huge hovel into rooms by means of draperies of cloth or canvas. In some the door is made as high as it can be cut in the wall and is reached by steps from the outside, while a similar flight inside gives access to the floor. The fire occupies the center of the room, enough of the floor being removed to allow it to be kindled directly on the ground, the smoke escaping by a huge hole in the roof. The vast majority of the houses are squalid beyond measure, and the dense resinous smoke of the spruce and pine blackens the walls with a funereal tinge, and fills the house with an odor which, when mingled with that of decayed salmon, makes one feel like leaving his card at the door and passing on. It takes no stretch of the imagination to conceive that such architecture provides the maximum of ventilation when least needed, and it is a fact that the winter hours of the Chilkats are cold and cheerless in the extreme. They sit crouched around the fire with their blankets closely folded about them and even drawn over their heads, the house serving indeed as a protection from the fierce wind and deep snow drifts, but no more. They look on all this foolishness, however, with

a sort of Spartan fortitude as necessary to toughen
them and inure them to the rough climate, and at times,
impelled by this belief, they will deliberately expose
themselves with that object in view. When the rivers
and lakes are frozen over the men and boys break great
holes in the ice and plunge in for a limited swim, then
come out, and if a bank of soft snow is convenient roll
around in it like so many polar bears ; and when they
get so cold that they can't tell the truth they wander
leisurely back to the houses and remark that they have
had a nice time, and believe they have done something
toward making themselves robust Chilkat citizens able
to endure every thing. There is no wonder that such
people adopt cremation ; and in fact one interpretation
of its religious significance is based on the idea of future
personal warmth in the happy hunting grounds, which
they regard as a large island, whose shores are unattain-
able except by those whose bodies have been duly consumed by fire. Unless the rite of cremation has been
performed the unhappy shade shivers perpetually in
outer frost. It is the impossibility of cremation which
makes death by drowning so terrible to a Chilkat.

The reason that the *shamans*, or medicine men (whose
bodies are not cremated) have no such dread, is that their
souls do not pass to the celestial island, but are translated into the bodies of infants, and in this way the crop
of medicine men never diminishes, whatever may be the
status of the rest of the population. Dreams and
divinations, or various marks of the child's hair or face,
are relied upon to determine into which infant the
supreme and mysterious power of the defunct doctor of
Tlinkit divinity has entered. To enumerate all of these

signs would consume more of my space than the subject
is worth.   When a Chilkat dies the body is burned at
sunrise, having first been dressed for the ceremony in a
costume more elaborate than any which it ever wore in
life.   The corpse must not be carried out at the door,
which is deemed sacred, a superstition very common
among savage races.   A few boards may be taken from
the rear or side of the hovel, or the body may be hoisted
through the capacious chimney in the roof ; but when the
Chilkat in his last illness sought his house to lie down
and die in it he passed over its threshold for the last
time.   Demons and dark spirits hover around like vul-
tures, and are only kept out of doors by the dreaded
incantations of the medicine men, and these may seize
the corpse as it passes out.   So fiendishly eager are they
to secure and stab their prey that all that is needed is to
lead out a dog from the house, which has been brought
into it at night, when the witches fall upon it and exhaust
their strength in attacking it before they discover their
mistake.   The cremation is seldom perfect, and the
charred bones and remnants are collected and put into a
small box standing on four posts in the nearest graveyard.
In the burial of medicine men, or before cremation with
others, the bodies are bent into half their length, the
knees drawn up to the breast and secured by thongs and
lashings.

A walk into the woods around Chilkat shows the
traveling to be somewhat better than in equally mountainous country near the coast, and where paths had been
cut through the dense timber to the charcoal pits formed
and maintained by the canneries, the walking was exceedingly agreeable and pleasant, especially by way of

contrast. As one recedes from the coast and gets beyond the influence of the warm Japanese current with its ceaseless fogs, rains and precipitation generally, the woods and marshes become more and more susceptible of travel, and by the time the Alaska coast range of mountains is crossed and the interior reached, one finds it but little worse than the tangle-woods and swamps of lower latitudes. The waters swarm with life, which is warmed by this heat-bearing current, and I think I do not exaggerate in saying that Alaska and its numerous outlying islands will alone, in the course of a short time, repay us annually more than the original cost of the great territory. By means of these industries the wedge has begun to enter, and we may hope it will be driven home by means of a wise administration of government, a boon which has been denied to Alaska since the Russians left the territory.

The principal fisheries will always be those of salmon and cod, since these fish are most readily prepared for export, while halibut, Arctic smelt or candle-fish, brook trout, flounders and other species will give ample variety for local use. The salmon has long been the staple fish food of the Chilkats, but this is slowly giving way to the products of civilization which they acquire in return for services at the canneries and for loading and unloading the vessels which visit the port. The salmon season is ushered in with considerable ceremony by the Chilkats, numerous festivals mark its success and its close is celebrated by other feasts. A Chilkat village during the salmon fishing season is a busy place. Near the water, loaded with the fish, their pink sides cut open ready for drying, are the scaffoldings, which are built just high enough to prevent the dogs from investigating too closely ; while out in the shallow water of the shoals or rapids, which often determine the site of a village, may be seen fish-weirs looking like stranded baskets that had served their purpose elsewhere and been thrown away up the stream, and which had lodged here as they floated down.   Many of the salmon are converted into fish-oil, which is used by the Chilkats as food, and resembles a cross between our butter and the blubber of the Eskimo. Taking a canoe that is worn out, yet not so badly damaged as not to be completely water-tight, it is filled some six to eight inches deep with salmon, over which water is poured until the fish are well covered.   This being done on the beach there are always plenty of stones around, and a number of these are heated to as high a temperature as possible in an open fire alongside of the canoe, and are then rapidly thrown into the water, bringing it to a boiling heat, and cooking the mass.   As the oil of the fat fish rises to the surface it is skimmed off with spoons, and after all has been procured that it is possible to obtain by this means, the gelatinous mass is pressed so as to get whatever remains, and all is preserved for winter food.   The salmon to be dried are split open along the back until they are as flat as possible, and then the flesh is split to the skin in horizontal and vertical slices about an inch to an inch and a half apart, which facilitates the drying process.   Each little square contracts in drying and makes a convenient mouthful for them as they scrape it from the skin with their upper canine teeth like a beaver peeling the bark from a cottonwood tree.   In packing over the Alaska coast range of mountains, a task which keeps the Indians absent from three to five days, a single salmon and a quart of flour are considered a sufficient ration per man for even that severe trip. If they are working for white men the employers are supposed to furnish the flour and the Indians the fish. While these Tlinkits of south-eastern Alaska, of which the Chilkats and Chilkoots are the most dreaded and warlike band, are a most jolly, mirth-making, and oftentimes even hilarious crowd of people, yet any thing like a practical joke played upon one of them is seldom appreciated by the recipient with the sheepish satisfaction so common to civilization. An army officer, Lieut. C. E. S. Wood, who spent some time among them sketching and drawing something besides his pay, relates in the Century Magazine the story of an Indian who laboriously crawled up on a band of decoy ducks that somebody had allowed to remain anchored out near the water's edge, and wasted several rounds of ammunition on them before he discovered his mistake. Instead of sneaking back into the brush, dodging through out-of-the-way by-paths to his home, and maintaining a conspicuous silence thereafter, as we of a more civilized country would have done under like circumstances, he sought out the owner of the decoys and demanded direct and indirect damages for the injuries he had suffered and the ammunition he had wasted, and was met by laughter, which only increased his persistency until his demands were satisfied to get rid of him.

At one of the two salmon canneries of which I have spoken as being in Chilkat Inlet, there was also kept a trading store, and here the Indians would bring their furs and peltries and barter for the articles that were so temptingly displayed before their eyes ; and if the skins were numerous and valuable this haggling would often continue for hours, as the Indian never counts time as worth any thing in his bargains. While we were there an Indian brought in a few black fox skins to barter for trading material, a prime skin of this kind being worth about forty dollars in goods from the store, and grading from that down to nearly one-fourth of the amount. At the time when the Chilkats learned the great value of the black fox skins, not many years back, they also learned, in some unaccountable way, the method of making them to order by staining the common red fox or cross fox skin by the application of some native form of blacking, probably made from soot or charcoal. Many such were disposed of before the counterfeit was detected, and even after the cheat was well known the utmost vigilance was needed to prevent natives playing the trick in times of great business activity. The method of detection was simply to place the skin on any hard flat surface like the counter of a trader's store, and rub the clean hand vigorously and with considerable pressure backward and forward over the fur side of the skin, when, if the skin were dyed, the fact would be shown by the blackened hand. This fact had been explained to us by the trader, and the Doctor entering just as the conversation as to the price became animated, and perceiving that the palmar surface of his hand was well soiled and blackened, owing to his having been engaged assorting packs for our Indians, he playfully stepped up to the counter, ran his hand jauntily through the skin once or twice and displayed to the two traders his blackened palm, to the surprise of the white man and absolute consternation of the Indian. The former rapidly but unavailingly tried to verify the Doctor's experiment, when the latter broke out into a hearty laugh, in which the trader joined. Not so with the Indian; when he recovered his senses he was furious at the imputation on his character ; and the best light he could view it in, after all the explanations, was that it had been a conspiracy between the two white men to get the skin at low rates, and the plot having failed, according to their own confession, and he himself having received his own price to quiet him, ought to be satisfied. The Doctor remarked as he finished the story, that he did not believe there was the remotest sense of humor among the whole band of Chilkat or Chilkoot Indians. The constant life of the Tlinkits in their canoes when procuring food or at other occupations on the water has produced, in conformity with the doctrine of natural selection and the survival of the fittest, a most conspicuous preponderating development of the chest and upper limbs over the lower, and their gait on land, resembling that of aquatic birds, is scarcely the poetry of motion as we understand it. The Chilkats, however, are not so confined to a seafaring life, and their long arduous trading journeys inland have assisted to make this physical characteristic much less conspicuous among them than among other tribes of Tlinkits, although even the Chilkats can not be called a race of large men. While they may not compare with the Sioux or Cheyennes, or a few others that might be mentioned, yet there are scores of Indian tribes in the United States proper which are greatly inferior to the Chilkats both in mental, physical, and moral qualities. In warfare they are as brave as the average Indians of the United States, and have managed to conduct their own affairs with considerable order, in spite of governmental interference at times. I quote from a correspondent writing from there as late as August, 1884, to the *New York Times* of November 23d : "The Indians have a great respect for a man-of-war, with its strict discipline and busy steam launches that can follow their canoes to the remote creeks and hiding places in the islands, and naval rule has been most praiseworthy. The army did no good for the country or the natives, and its record is not a creditable one. The Tlinkits sneered openly at the land forces, and snapped their fingers at challenging and forbidding sentries, and paddled away at their pleasure."

CHAPTER IV.

OVER THE MOUNTAIN PASS.

CHILKAT INDIAN PACKER.

Y the 6th of June all of our many arrangements for departure were fully completed, and the next day the party got under way shortly before 10 o'clock in the forenoon. Mr. Carl Spuhn, the Manager of the North-west Trading Company, which owned the western cannery in the Chilkat Inlet, where my party had been disembarked, who had been indefatigable in his efforts to assist me in procuring Indian packers, and in many other ways aiding the expedition, now placed at my disposal the little steam launch of the company, and behind it, tied one to the other by their towing ropes, was a long string of from twelve to twenty canoes, each containing from two to four Chilkat Indians, our prospective packers. Some of the Indians who had selected their packs carried them in the canoes, but the bulk of the material was on the decks of the steam-launch "Louise." They disappeared out of sight in a little while, steaming southward down the Chilkat Inlet, while with a small party in a row-boat I crossed this

channel and then by a good trail walked over to the
Haines Mission, in Chilkoot Inlet, presided over by Mr.
Eugene S. Willard and his wife, with a young lady
assistant, Miss Mathews, and maintained by the Pres-
byterian Board of Missions as a station among the Chilkat and Chilkoot Indians.   Crossing the "mission trail,"
as it was called, we often traversed lanes in the grass, which
here was fully five feet high, while, in whatever direction
the eye might look, wild flowers were growing in the greatest profusion.   Dandelions as big as asters, buttercups
twice the usual size, and violets rivaling the products
of cultivation in lower latitudes were visible around.
It produced a singular and striking contrast to raise the
eyes from this almost tropical luxuriance and allow
them to rest on the Alpine hills, covered, half way down
their shaggy sides, with snow and glacier ice, and with
cold mist condensed on their crowns.   Mosquitoes were
too plentiful not to be called a prominent discomfort,
and small gnats did much to mar the otherwise pleasant
stroll.   Berries and berry blossoms grew in a profusion
and variety which I have never seen equaled within
the same limits in lower latitudes.   A gigantic nettle
was met with in uncomfortable profusion when one
attempted to wander from the beaten trail.   This
nettle has received the appropriate name of "devil-
sticks;" and Mr. Spuhn of the party told me it was
formerly used by the Indian medicine-men as a prophy-
lactic against witch-craft, applied externally, and with
a vigor that would have done credit to the days of old
Salem, a custom which is still kept up among these
Indians.   Gardens have been cultivated upon this narrow peninsula, the only comparatively level track of

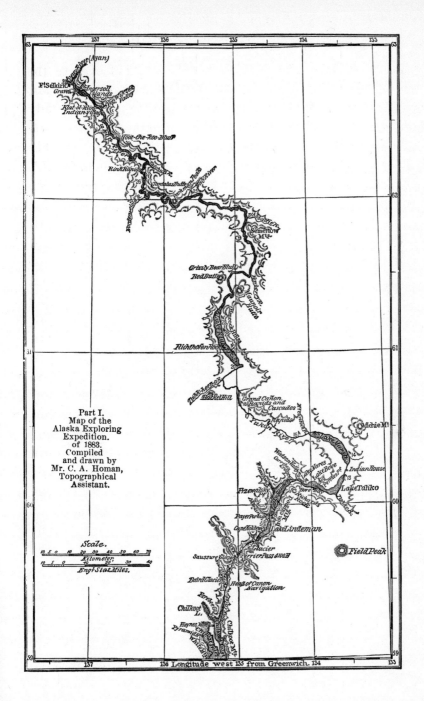

Part I.
Map of the
Alaska Exploring
Expedition.
of 1883.
Compiled
and drawn by
Mr. C. A. Homan,
Topographical
Assistant.

Scale.
Kilometer.
Engl Stat Miles.

considerable size in all south-eastern Alaska, with a success which speaks well for this part of the territory as
far as climate and soil are concerned, although the terribly rough mountainous character of nearly all of this
part of the country will never admit of any broad experiments in agriculture. By strolling leisurely along and
stopping long enough to lunch under the great cedar
trees, while the mosquitoes lunched off us, we arrived at
the mission on Chilkoot Inlet just in time to see the
little launch in the distance followed by its long proces-
sion of canoes, heading for us and puffing away as if it
were towing the Great Eastern. It had gone down the
Chilkat Inlet ten or twelve miles to the southward,
turned around the sharp cape of the peninsula, Point
Seduction, and traveled back northward, parallel to its
old course, some twelve to fifteen miles to where we were
waiting for it, having steamed about twenty-five miles,
while we had come one-fifth the distance to the same
point. Here quite a number of Chilkoot natives and
canoes were added to the already large throng; Mrs.
Schwatka, who had accompanied me thus far, was left in
the kind care of the missionary family of Mr. Willard;
adieus were waved and we once more took our northward course up the Chilkoot Inlet.

After four or five miles the main inlet bears off to the
westward, but a much narrower one still points constantly to the north star, and up the latter we continued
to steam. It is called the Dayay Inlet and gives us
about ten miles of "straight-away course" before coming
to the mouth of the river of the same name. This Dayay
Inlet is of the same general character as the inland passages in this part of Alaska, of which I have already

spoken; a river-like channel between high steep hills, which are covered with pine, cedar and spruce from the water's line nearly to the top, and there capped with bare granite crowns that in gulches and on the summits are covered with snow and glacier ice, which in melting furnish water for innumerable beautiful cascades and mountain torrents, many of them dashing from such dizzy precipitous heights that they are reduced to masses of iridescent spray by the time they reach the deep green waters of the inlet.

With a score of canoes towing behind, the ropes near the launch kept parting so often that we were considerably delayed, and as the Indians were seldom in any great hurry about repairing the damages, and treated it in a most hilarious manner as something of a joke on the launch, the master of that craft, when the rope had parted near the central canoe for about the twentieth time, finally bore on without them, leaving the delinquents to get along as best they could, there being about five miles more to make. Fortunately just then a fair southern breeze sprang up, so that most of the tardy canoes soon displayed canvas, and those that could not, hastily improvised a blanket, a pea-jacket, or even a a broad-shouldered pair of pantaloons, to aid their progress, for the Indian in all sections of the country is much more ingenious than one is apt to suppose, especially if his object be to save manual labor. The mouth of the Dayay river being reached about six in the afternoon, it was found to consist of a series of low swampy mud flats and a very miry delta. Here it is necessary to ascend the swift river at least a mile to find a site that is even half suitable for a camp. During the time when the greatest sediment is brought down by the swift muddy stream, *i. e.*, during the spring freshets and summer high water, the winds are usually from the south, and blow with considerable force, which fact accounts for the presence of soft oozy deposits of great extent so near the mouth of the stream.   Through this shallow water the canoes carried our effects.   The river once reached the canoes proceeded up the stream to camp, the launch whistled us adieu, and as she faded from sight, the last link that bound us to civilization was snapped, and our explorations commenced.   The distance from the Haines' Mission to the mouth of the Dayay where we disembarked was sixteen miles.

At this camp No. 2, we found a small camp of wandering *Tahk-heesh* Indians, or as they are locally called by the few whites of the country, the *Sticks*, a peaceful tribe whose home is over the Alaskan coast range of mountains and along the head-waters of the great Yukon, the very part of the very stream we desired to explore.   It has only been within the last few years that these Tahk-heesh Indians have been allowed to cross over the mountains into the Chilkat country for purposes of trade, the Chilkats and Chilkoots united having from time immemorial completely monopolized the profitable commerce of the interior fur trade, forbidding ingress to the whites and denying egress to the Indians of the interior.   From the former they bought their trading goods and trinkets, and making them into convenient bundles or parcels of about one hundred pounds each, they carried them on their backs across the snow and glacier crowned mountains, exchanging them for furs with the tribes of the interior for many hundreds of miles around.   These furs were again lashed in packs and carried back over the same perilous paths to the coffers of the white traders, and although they realized but a small fractional portion of their value, yet prices were large in comparison with the trifling cost to the venders. When the trade was at its best many years ago, these trips were often made twice a year during the spring and summer, and so great was the commerce in those days, that no less than from eight to ten tons of trading material found its way into the interior by way of these Alpine passes, and was exchanged for its equivalent in furs. As a consequence, the Chilkat nation is the richest tribe of Indians in the great North-west.   Their chief, Shot-rich, alone is worth about ten or twelve thousand dollars in blankets, their standard of wealth, and others in proportion, according to their energy in the trade.   Shot-rich has three large native houses at Klukwan, the main Chilkat town, two of which are filled with blankets worth from two to four dollars apiece.   The trail on which we were now plodding along is known among the Indians as the Chilkoot trail to the interior, and takes from two to four days, packing their goods on their backs, until the headwaters of the Yukon are reached.   It was monopolized solely by the Chilkoots, who had even gone so far as to forbid the Chilkats, almost brothers in blood, from using it, so that the latter were forced to take a longer and far more laborious route. This route of the Chilkats led them up the Chilkat River to near its head, where a long mountain trail that gave them a journey of a week or ten days, packing on their backs, brought them to a tributary of the Yukon, by means of which the interior was gained.   Once on this tributary no serious rapids or other impediments were in their line of travel, while the Yukon, with its shorter trail, had many such obstacles. The great Hudson Bay Company with its well-known indomitable courage, attempted as early as 1850 to tap this rich trading district monopolized by the Chilkat Indians, and Fort Selkirk was established at the junction of the Yukon and Pelly, but so far away from their main base of supplies on Hudson's Bay, that it is said it took them a couple of years to reach it with trading effects. The Indians knew of but one method of competition in business. They went into no intricate inventories for reducing prices of stock, nor did they put bigger advertisements or superior inducements before their customers. They simply organized a war party, rapidly descended the main Yukon for about five hundred miles, burned the buildings and appropriated the goods.

As the Tahk-heesh or *Sticks* were allowed to come abroad so the white men were allowed and, in fact, induced to enter, for the coast Indians found ample compensation in carrying the white men's goods over the trail of about thirty miles at a rate which brought them from ten to twelve dollars per pack of a hundred pounds in weight; and it was my intention to take advantage of this opportunity to reach the head of the river, and then fight my way down it, rather than against its well known rapid current, of which I had heard so much from the accounts of explorers on its lower waters. When it was known, however, that I expected to do my explorations on a raft, the idea was laughed at by the few white men of the country, as evincing the extreme of ignorance, and the Indians seemed to be but little behind them in ridicule of the plan. The latter emphatically affirmed that a hundred and fifty or two hundred miles of lakes stretched before us, and what, they argued, can be more helpless than a raft on a still lake ? Eight or ten miles of boiling rapids occurred at various points in the course of the stream, and these would tear any raft into a shapeless wreck, while it would be hard to find Indians to portage my numerous effects around them. The unwieldiness of a great raft—no small one would serve for us and our stores—in a swift current was constantly pointed out, and I must confess I felt a little discouraged myself when I summed up all these reasons. Why this or the Chilkat route was not attempted long ago by some explorer, who might thereby have traversed the entire river in a single summer, instead of combating its swift current from its mouth, seems singular in the light of the above facts, and I imagine the only explanation is that men who would place sufficient reliance in Indian reports to insert in their maps the gross inaccuracies that we after-ward detected, would rely also upon the Indian reports that from time immemorial have pronounced this part of the river to be unnavigable even for canoes, except for short stretches, and as filled with rapids, cañons, whirl-pools and cascades.

After camping that night on the Dayay, bundles were all assorted and assigned. The packs varied from thirty-six to a hundred and thirty-seven pounds in weight, the men generally carrying a hundred pounds and the boys according to their age and strength. The "Sticks" or Tahk-heesh Indians camped near us were hunting black bear, which were said to be abundant in this locality, an assertion which seemed to be verified by the large num-ber of tracks we saw in the valley. From this band of

Indians we completed our number of packers, a circumstance which irritated the others greatly, for the Chilkats seem to regard the *Sticks* almost in the light of slaves. Here I also secured a stout, sturdy fellow, at half rates, merely to go along in case of sickness among my numerous retinue, in which event he would be put on full wages. His onerous dutes consisted in carrying the guidon, or expedition flag, weighing four or five pounds, and he improvised himself into a ferry for the white men at the numerous fords which the tortuous Dayay River presented as we ascended. As every one gave him a nickel or dime at each ford, and the guidon staff was simply a most convenient alpenstock, he was the envy of all the others as he slowly but surely amassed his gains ; not so slowly either, for the river made so many windings from one side of its high walled valley to the other, that his receipts rivaled a western railroad in the matter of mileage, but the locomotion was scarcely as comfortable as railroad travel.

During the still, quiet evening we could hear many grouse hooting in the spruce woods of the hillsides, this time of day seeming to be their favorite hour for concerts. The weather on this, the first day of our trip, was splendid, with a light southern wind that went down with the sun and gave us a few mist-like sprinkles of rain, serving to cool the air and make slumber after our fatigue doubly agreeable. The head of canoe navigation on the Dayay river, where it terminates abruptly in a huge boiling cascade, is ten miles from the mouth of the stream, although fully fifteen are traveled by the canoemen in ascending its tortuous course, which is accomplished by the usual Indian method of "tracking," with ropes and poles from the bank of the river. I observed that they "tracked" their canoes against the current in two ways, each method requiring two men to one canoe. The diagrams given

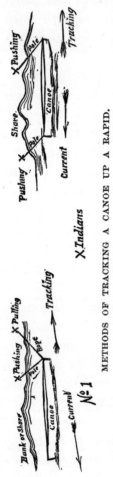

will show these methods ; in No. 1, an Indian pulls the canoe with a rope, while a companion just in his rear and following in his steps keeps the head of the canoe in the stream, with a long pole, at just such distance as he may desire according to the obstacles that are presented. If the water from the bank for some distance out, say twelve or fifteen feet, is clear of all obstacles, his companion will fall to the rear as far as his pole will allow and assist the ropeman by pushing up stream, but in shallow, swift places he has all he can do to regulate the canoe's course through the projecting stones, and the burden of the draft falls on the ropeman. In the other mode both the men use poles and all the motive power is furnished by pushing. The advantage over the first is that in "boiling" water full of stones, the bowman may steer his end clear of all of these, only to have the seething waters throw the stern against a sharp corner of a rock and tear a hole in that part, an accident which can only be avoided by placing a poleman at the stern. It is readily apparent, however, that there is much more power expended in this method of making headway

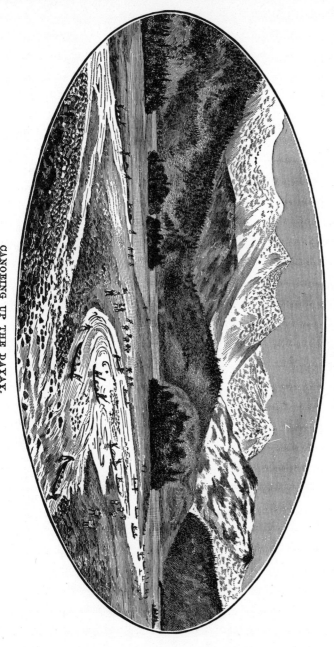

CANOEING UP THE DAYAY.

against the current than in the other. Some few of the Indians judiciously vary the two methods to suit the circumstances. On long stretches of only moderately swift water the tired trackers would take turns in resting in the canoe, using a paddle to hold the bow out from the shore. The current of the Dayay is very swift, and two days' "tracking" is often required to traverse the navigable part of the stream. Every few hundred yards or so the river needs to be crossed, wherever the timber on the banks is dense, or where the circuitous river cuts deep into the high hillsides that form the boundaries of its narrow valley. In these crossings from fifty to a hundred yards would often be lost. The Indians seemed to make no effort whatever to stem the swift current in crossing, but pointed the canoe straight across for the other bank and paddled away as if dear life depended on the result.

The march of the 8th to Camp 3, brought us within a half mile or a mile of the head of canoe navigation on the river, and here the Indians desired to camp, as at that particular spot there is no dry wood with which to cook their meals ; although all they had to cook was the little flour that I had issued, the salmon being dried and eaten without further preparation. The Dayay Valley is well wooded in its bottom with poplar and several varieties of willow, and where these small forests did not exist were endless ridges of sand, gravel and even huge bowlders cutting across each other at all angles, evidently the work of water, assisted at times by the more powerful agency of moving or stranded ice. All day we had been crossing bear tracks of different ages, and after camping some of the white men paddled across the river (here thirty-five or forty yards wide) to take a stroll up the valley ; and while returning a large black bear was seen perched on a conspicuous granite ridge of the western mountain wall, probably four hundred yards away and at an angle of twenty degrees above our position in the river bottom.   A member of the party got two shots at him, but he disappeared in the dense underbrush, evidently afraid that the sportsman might aim at something else and so hit him.   Dr. Wilson and Mr. Homan fished with bait and flies for a long distance up and down the different channels of the river, but could not get a single "rise" or "bite," although the Indians catch mountain trout in their peculiar fish-weirs, having offered us that very day a number thus captured.   Like all streams rising in glacier bearing lands of calcareous structure, its waters are very white and chalky, which may account for the apparent reluctance of the fish to rise to a fly.   The pretty waterfalls on the sides of the mountains still continued and the glaciers of the summits became more numerous and strongly marked, and descended nearer to the bed of the stream.

I could not but observe the peculiar manifestations of surprise characteristic of the Chilkats.   Whenever one uttered a shout over some trifle, such as a comrade's slipping on a slimy stone into the water, or tumbling over the root of a log, or any mishap, comical or otherwise, every one within hearing, from two to two hundred, would immediately chime in, and such a cry would ensue as to strike us with astonishment.   This may be repeated several times in a minute, and the abruptness with which it would begin and end, so that not a single distinct voice can be heard at either beginning or ending, reminds one somewhat of a gang of coyotes howling around a frontier camp or the bayings of Indian dogs on moonlight serenades, from which one would be strongly tempted to believe they had borrowed it.   Withal they are a most happy, merry-hearted and jovial race, laughing hilariously at every thing with the least shadow of comicality about it, and "guying" every trifling mishap of a companion in which the sufferer is expected to join, just as the man who chases his hat in a muddy street on a windy day must laugh with the crowd.   Such characteristics of good nature are generally supposed to be accompanied by a generous disposition, especially as toward men of the same blood, but I was compelled to notice an almost cruel piece of selfishness which they exhibited in one point, and which told strongly against any such theory as applied to Indians, or at least this particular band of them.   When we got to the mouth of the Dayay river, many of the packers had no canoes in which to track their bundles or packs to the head of canoe navigation, and their companions who owned such craft flatly and decisively refused to take their packs, although, as far as I could see, it would have caused them no inconvenience whatever.   In many cases this selfishness was the effect of caste, to which I have already alluded and which with them is carried to an extreme hardly equaled in the social distinctions of any other savage people.   Nor was this the only conspicuous instance of selfishness displayed.   As I have already said, the Dayay is very tortuous, wide and swift, and therefore has very few fords, and these at inconvenient intervals for travelers carrying a hundred pounds apiece on their backs, yet the slight service of ferrying the packers and their packs across the stream was refused by the canoemen as rigidly as the other favor, and where the river cut deep into some high projecting bank of the mountain flanks, these unfortunate packers would be forced to carry burdens up over some precipitous mountain spur, or at least to make a long detour in search of available fords. My readers can rest assured that I congratulated myself on having taken along a spare packer in the event of sickness among my numerous throng, for even in such a case I found them as disobliging and unaccommodating as before, utterly refusing to touch a sick man's load until he had promised them the lion's share of his wages and I had ratified the contract.

Every afternoon or evening after getting into camp, no matter how fatiguing the march had been, as soon as their simple meal was cooked and consumed, they would gather here and there in little parties for the purpose of gambling, and oftentimes their orgies would run far into the small hours of the night. The gambling game which they called *la-hell* was the favorite during the trip over the Chilkoot trail, although I understand that they have others not so complicated. This game requires an even number of players, generally from four to twelve, divided into two parties which face each other. These "teams" continue sitting about two or three feet apart, with their legs drawn up under them, *à la Turque*, the place selected being usually in sandy ground under the shade of a grove of poplar or willow trees. Each man lays a wager with the person directly opposite him, with whom alone he gambles as far as the gain or loss of his stake is concerned, although such loss or gain is determined by the success of the team as a whole. In other words, when a game terminates one team of course is the winner, but each player wins only the stake put up by his vis-à-vis. A handful of willow sticks, three or four inches long, and from a dozen to a score in number, are thrust in the sand or soft earth, between the two rows of squatting gamblers, and by means of these a sort of running record or tally of the game is kept. The implements actually employed in gambling are merely a couple of small bone-bobbins, as shown on page 227, of about the size of a lady's pen-knife, one of which has one or more bands of black cut around it near its center and is called the king, the other being pure white. At the commencement of the game, one of the players picks up the bone-bobbins, changes them rapidly from one hand to the other, sometimes behind his back, then again under an apron or hat resting on his lap, during all of which time the whole assembly are singing in a low measured melody the words, "Oh! oh! oh! Oh, ker-shoo, ker-shoo!—" which is kept up with their elbows flapping against their sides and their heads swaying to the tune, until some player of the opposite row, thinking he is inspired, and singing with unusual vehemence, suddenly points out the hand of the juggler that, in his belief, contains "the king." If his guess is correct, his team picks up one of the willow sticks and places it on their side, or, if the juggler's team has gained, any one of their sticks must be replaced in the reserve at the center. If he is wrong then, the other side tallies one in the same way. The bone "king and queen" are then handed to an Indian in the other row, and the same performance repeated, although it may be twice as long, or half as short, as no native attempts to discern the whereabouts of the "king" until he feels he has a revelation to that effect, produced by the incantation. A game will last any where from half an hour to three hours. Whenever the game is nearly concluded and one party has gained almost all the willow sticks, or at any other exciting point of the game, they have methods of "doubling up" on the wagers, by not exchanging the bobbins but holding both in one hand or leaving one or both on the ground under a hat or apron, and the guesses are about both and count double, treble or quadruple, for loss or gain. They wager the caps off their heads, their shirts off their backs, and with many of them no doubt, their prospective pay for the trip was all gone before it was half earned. Men and boys alike entered the contest, and from half a dozen places at once, in the woods near by, could be heard the everlasting refrain, the never-ceasing chant of "Oh! oh! oh! Oh! ker-shoo, ker-shoo!" They used also to improvise hats of birch-bark (wherever that tree grew near the evening camp) with pictures upon them that would prohibit their passing through the mails. These habits do not indicate any great moral improvement thus far produced by contact with civilization.

Two miles and a half beyond the head of canoe navigation, the *Kut-lah-cook-ah* River of the Chilkats comes in from the west. This is really larger in volume and width than the Dayay, the two averaging respectively fifty and forty yards in width by estimation. I shortened its name, and called it after Professor Nourse of the United States Naval Observatory. Large glaciers feed its sources by numerous waterfalls, and its cañon-like bed is very picturesque. Like all such streams its

DAYAY VALLEY, LOOKING UP THE NOURSE RIVER VALLEY.

A glimpse of Baird Glacier covered with fog is given. The mountains holding the glacier being twice as high as the one shown on the left, their crests, if they had been visible, would not have been shown in the photograph from which this illustration is made, being above the line where it is cut off. It is only at night that the fog-banks lift, when it is too late to take photographs.

waters were conspicuously white and milk-like, and the most diligent fisherman was unrewarded. At the head of the Nourse River the Indians say there is a very large lake. The mountains that bound its course on the west are capped by an immense glacier, which might be traced along their summits for probably ten or twelve miles, and was then lost in the lowering clouds of their icy crests. These light fogs are frequent on warm days, when the difference of temperature at the upper and lower levels is more marked, but they disappear at night as the temperatures approach each other. This glacier, a glimpse of which is given on page 73, was named after Professor Baird, of the Smithsonian Institute at Washington. The march of the 9th of June took us three miles and a half up the Dayay River, and while resting, about noon, I was astonished to hear the Indians declare this was their expected camp for the night, for we had really accomplished so little. I was much inclined to anticipate that the rest of the journey was not much worse, and would give a forcible example of the maxim that "dangers disappear as they are approached." The rough manner in which my illusions were dispelled will appear further on. Another inducement to stop at this particular point was found in a small grove of spruce saplings just across the river, which was so dense that each tree trunk tapered as regularly as if it had been turned from a lathe. These they desired for salmon-spears, cutting them on their way over the trail, and collecting them as they returned, so as to give the poles a few days to season, thus rendering them lighter for the dextrous work required. These peculiar kinds of fish-spears are so common over all the districts of Arctic and sub-Arctic America that I think them worthy of description. The pole is from eight to twelve feet in length, extending from P to P, as shown in the figure on this page. Two arms A A are made of elastic wood, and 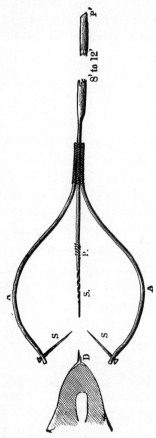 at their ends they carry incurved spikes of iron or steel, S S, which act as barbs on a fish-hook. Another sharpened spike projects from the tip of the pole P, and the three together make the prongs of the spear or gig. When the fish is speared the arms A A bend out as the spikes "ride" over its back, and these insert themselves in its sides, the pole spike penetrating its back. In the figure there is represented the cross-section of a fish (its dorsal-fin D) just before the spear strikes. Among the Eskimo of King William's Land I found the spear-handles made of driftwood thrown on the beach, the arms A A made of very elastic musk-ox horn, and the spikes of copper taken from the abandoned ships of Sir John Franklin's ill-fated expedition. Again at this camp (No. 4), the fishing-tackle of various kinds was employed vigilantly, but although the water seemed much clearer there were no results, the doctor advancing the theory that trout will not rise

A VIEW IN THE DAYAY VALLEY. (FROM CAMP 4.)

A finger of the Saussure Glacier is seen peeping round the mountain, the rest being covered with fog.

to a fly in streams where salmon are spawning, as they then live on the salmon roe to the exclusion of every thing else.

At this camp I saw the Chilkat boy packers wrestling in a very singular manner, different from any thing in that branch of athletics with which I am acquainted. The two wrestlers lie flat on their backs upon the ground or sand and against each other, but head to foot, or in opposite directions. Their inner legs, *i.e.*, those touching their opponents, are raised high in the air, carried past each other, and then locked together at the knee. They then rise to a sitting posture, or as nearly as possible, and with their nearest arms locked into a firm hold at the elbows, the contest commences. It evidently requires no mean amount of strength to get on top of an equal adversary, and the game seems to demand considerable agility, although the efforts of the contestants, as they rolled around like two angle worms tied together, appeared more awkward than graceful.

Northward from this camp (No. 4), lying between the Nourse and Dayay Rivers, was the southern terminal spur of a large glacier, whose upper end was lost in the cold drifting fog that clung to it, and which can be seen on page 77. I called it the Saussure Glacier, after Professor Henri de Saussure, of Geneva, Switzerland. The travels in the Dayay Inlet and up the valley of the river had been reasonably pleasant, but on the 10th of June our course lay over the rough mountain spurs of the east side for ten or twelve miles, upon a trail fully equal to forty or fifty miles over a good road for a day's walking. Short as the march was in actual measurement, it consumed from 7:30 in the morning until 7:15 in the evening ; nearly half the time, however, being occupied in resting from the extreme fatigue of the journey. In fact, in many places it was a terrible scramble up and down hill, over huge trunks and bristling limbs of fallen timber too far apart to leap from one to the other, while between was a boggy swamp that did not increase the pleasure of carrying a hundred pounds on one's back. Sometimes we would sink in almost to our knees, while every now and then this agony was supplemented by the recurrences of long high ridges of rough bowlders of trachyte with a splintery fracture. The latter felt like hot iron under the wet moccasins after walking on them and jumping from one to the other for awhile. Some of these great ridges of bowlders on the steep hillsides must have been of quite recent origin, and from the size of the

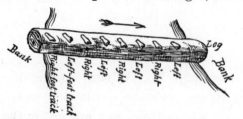

POSITION OF THE FEET IN WALKING A LOG, AS PRACTICED BY THE CHILKAT INDIANS.

big rocks, often ten or twelve feet in diameter, I infer that the force employed must have been enormous, and I could only account for it on the theory that ice had been an important agent in the result. So recent were some of the ridges that trees thirty and forty feet high were embedded in the debris, and where they were not cut off and crushed by the action of the rocks they were growing as if nothing had happened, although half the length of their trunks in some cases was below the tops of the ridges. I hardly thought that any of the trees could be over forty or fifty years old. Where these ridges of great bowlders were very wide one would be obliged to follow close behind some Indian packer acquainted with the trail, which might easily be lost before re-entering the brush.

That day I noticed that all my Indians, in crossing logs over a stream, always turned the toes of both feet in the same direction (to the right), although they kept the body square to the front, or nearly so, and each foot passed the other at every step, as in ordinary walking. The advantage to be gained was not obvious to the author; as the novice, in attempting it, feels much more unsafe than in walking over the log as usual. Nearing Camp 5, we passed over two or three hundred yards of snow from three to fifteen feet deep. This day's march of the 10th of June brought us to the head of the Dayay river at a place the Indians call the "stone-houses." These *stone-houses*, however, are only a loose mass of huge bowlders piled over each other, projecting high above the deep snow, and into the cave-like crevices the natives crawl for protection whenever the snow has buried all other tracts, or the cold wind from the glaciers is too severe to permit of sleep in the open. All around us was snow or the clear blue ice of the glacier fronts, while directly northward, and seemingly impassable, there loomed up for nearly four thousand feet the precipitous pass through the mountains, a blank mass of steep white, which we were to essay on the morrow.

Shortly after camping I was told that the Indians had seen a mountain goat nearly on the summit of the western mountain wall, and I was able to make out his presence with the aid of field-glasses. The Indians had detected him with their unaided eyes, in spite of his white coat

being against a background of snow. Had the goat
been on the summit of a mountain in the moon I should
not have regarded him as any safer than where he was,
if the Indians were even half as fatigued as I felt, and

CHASING A MOUNTAIN GOAT IN THE PERRIER PASS.

they had carried a hundred pounds over the trail and I
had not. But the identity of the goat was not fully
established before an Indian, the only one who carried a
gun, an old flint-lock, smooth bore, Hudson Bay musket, made preparations for the chase. He ran across the
valley and soon commenced the ascent of the mount-

ains, in a little while almost disappearing on the white
sides, looking like a fly crawling over the front of a
house. The Indian, a "Stick," finally could be seen
above the mountain goat and would have secured him,
but that a little black cur dog which had started to follow him when he was almost at the summit, made its
appearance on the scene just in time to frighten the animal and started him running down the mountain side
toward the pass, the "Stick" closely following in pur-
suit, assisted by the dog. Just as every one expected
to see the goat disappear through the pass, he wheeled
directly around and started straight for the camp, producing great excitement. Every one grabbed the first
gun he could get his hands on and waited for the animal's approach. A shot from camp sent him flying up
the eastern mountains, which were higher than those of
the west, closely followed almost to the summit by the
indefatigable "Stick," who finally lost him. I thought
it showed excellent endurance for the mountain goat,
but the Indian's pluck was beyond all praise, and as he
returned with a jovial shake of the head, as if he met
such disappointments every day, I felt sure that I would
not have undertaken his hunt for all the goat meat in
the country, even with starvation at hand.

On the morning of the next day about five o'clock, we
commenced the toilsome ascent of this coast range pass,
called by the Indians Kotusk Mountains, and by seven
o'clock all my long pack train was strung up the precipitous pass, making one of the prettiest Alpine sights
that I have ever witnessed, and as seen from a distance
strangely resembling a row of bowlders projecting from
the snow. Up banks almost perpendicular they scram-

bled on their hands and knees, helping themselves by
every projecting rock and clump of juniper and dwarf
spruce, not even refusing to use their teeth on them at
the worst places. Along the steep snow banks and the
icy fronts of glaciers steps were cut with knives, while
rough alpenstocks from the valley helped them to
maintain their footing. In some such places the incline
was so steep that those having boxes on their backs cut
scratches in the icy crust with the corners as they passed
along, and oftentimes it was possible to steady one's self
by the open palm of the hand resting against the snow.
In some of these places a single mis-step, or the caving
in of a foot-hold would have sent the unfortunate traveler many hundred feet headlong to certain destruction. Yet not the slightest accident happened, and
about ten o'clock, almost exhausted, we stood on the
top of the pass, enveloped in a cold drifting fog, 4,240
feet above the level of the sea (a small portion of the
party having found a lower crossing at 4,100 feet above
sea-level). How these small Indians, not apparently
averaging over one hundred and forty pounds in weight,
could carry one hundred pounds up such a precipitous
mountain of ice and snow, seems marvelous beyond
measure. One man carried one hundred and thirty-
seven pounds, while boys from twelve to fourteen carried from fifty to seventy pounds. I called this the
Perrier Pass after Colonel J. Perrier of the French Geographical Society.

Once on top of the Pass the trail leads northward and
the descent is very rapid for a few hundred yards to a
lake of about a hundred acres in extent, which was yet
frozen over and the ice covered with snow, although

ASCENDING THE PERRIER PASS.

drainage from the slopes had made the snow very slushy. Over the level tracks of snow many of the Indians wore their snow-shoes, which in the ascent and steep descent had been lashed to their packs. These Indians have two kinds of snow-shoes, a very broad pair used while packing, as with my party, and a narrower and neater kind employed while hunting. The two kinds are figured below. This small lake, abruptly walled in, greatly resembled an extinct crater, and such it may well have been. From this re-semblance it received its name of Crater Lake, a view of which figures as the frontis-piece. Here there was no timber, not even brush, to be seen; while the gullies of the granite hills, and the valleys deeply covered with snow, gave the whole scene a decid-edly Arctic appear-ance. I noticed that my Indian packers,

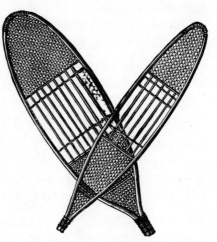

CHILKAT HUNTING AND PACKING SNOW-SHOES.

The usual thongs are used to fasten them to the feet, but are not shown in the illustration.

in following a trail on snow, whether it was up hill, on a level, or even a slight descent, always stepped in each other's tracks, and hence our large party made a trail that at first glance looked as if only five or six had passed over; but when going down a steep descent, especially on soft snow, each one made his own trail, and they scattered out over many yards in width. I could not but be

impressed with the idea that this was worth considering
should it ever be necessary to estimate their numbers.
From the little crater-like lake at the very head of the
Yukon, the trail leads through a valley that converges to
a gorge ; and while crossing the snow in this ravine we
could hear the running water gurgling under the snow
bridge on which we were walking. Further down the little valley, as it opened at a point where these snow-
arches were too wide to support their weight, they had
tumbled into the stream, showing in many places abutments of deep perpendicular snow-banks often twenty to
twenty-five feet in height. Where the river banks were
of stone and perpendicular the packers were forced to
pass over the projecting abutments of snow, undermined
by the swift stream. It was hazardous for many to
attempt the passage over the frail structure at the same
time. Passing by a few small picturesque lakes on our
left, some still containing floating cakes of ice, we caught
sight of the main lake in the afternoon, and in a few
hours were upon its banks at a point where a beautiful
mountain stream came tumbling in, with enough swift
water to necessitate crossing on a log. Near the Crater
Lake a curlew and a swallow were seen, and a small black
bear cub was the only other living thing visible,
although mountain goats were abundant a short distance
back in the high hills. We had gotten into camp quite
late in the evening and here the contracts with our Indian
packers expired.

Imagine my surprise, after a fatiguing march of thirteen miles that had required fourteen hours to accomplish, and was fully equal to forty or fifty on any good
road, at having the majority of my packers, men and

boys, demand payment at once with the view of an immediate return. Some of them assured me they would make the mouth of the Dayay before stopping, and would then only stay for a short rest. It should be remembered that we were so far north and the sun so near his northern solstice that it was light enough even at midnight, for traveling purposes, especially on the white snow of the worst portion of the journey, Perrier Pass. I had no reason to doubt their assurances, and afterward learned that one of them went through to the mission without stopping, in spite of a furious gale which was raging on the Dayay and Chilkoot Inlets.

CHAPTER V.

ALONG THE LAKES.

large lake near the head of the Yukon I named in honor of Dr. Lindeman, of the Bremen Geographical Society. The country thus far, including the lake, had already received a most thorough exploration at the hands of Dr. Aurel Krause and Dr. Arthur Krause, two German scientists, heretofore sent out by the above named society, but I was not aware of the fact at that time. Looking out upon Lake Lindeman a most beautiful Alpine-like sheet of water was presented to our view. The scene was made more picturesque by the mountain creek, of which I have spoken, and over which a green willow tree was supposed to do duty as a foot-log. My first attempt to pass over this tree caused it to sink down into the rushing waters and was much more interesting to the spectators than to me. Lake Lindeman is about ten miles long, and from one to one and a-half wide, and in appearance is not unlike a portion of one of the broad inland passages of south-eastern Alaska already described. Fish were absent from these glacier-fed streams and lakes, or at least they were not to be enticed by any of the standard allurements of the fishermen's

wiles, but we managed to kill a few dusky grouse and
green-winged teal ducks to vary the usual government
ration; though all were tough beyond measure, it being
so near their breeding season.

Over the lake, on quiet days, were seen many gulls,
and the graceful little Arctic tern, which I recognized as
an old companion on the Atlantic side. A ramble among
the woods next day to search for raft timber revealed a
number of bear, caribou and other game tracks, but
nothing could be seen of their authors. A small flock
of pretty harlequin ducks gave us a long but unsuccessful shot. The lakes of the interior, of which there were
many, bordered by swampy tracts, supplied Roth, our
cook, with a couple of green-winged teal, duck and drake,
as the reward of a late evening stroll, for, as I have said,
it was light enough at midnight to allow us to shoot, at
any rate with a shot-gun.

While the lakes were in many places bordered with
swampy tracts, the land away from them was quite pas-
sable for walking, the great obstacle being the large
amount of fallen timber that covered the ground in all
directions. The area of bog, ubiquitous beyond the
Kotusk range, was now confined to the shores of the lakes
and to streams emerging from or emptying into them,
and while these were numerous enough to a person desir-
ing to hold a straight course for a considerable distance,
the walking was bearable compared with previous experience.

Two of the *Tahk-heesh* or "Stick" Indians, who had
come with us as packers, had stored away in this vicinity
under the willows of the lake's beach, a couple of the
most dilapidated looking craft that ever were seen. To

call them canoes, indeed, was a strain upon our consciences. The only theory to account for their keeping afloat at all was that of the Irishman in the story, "that for every hole where the water could come in there were a half a dozen where it could run out." These canoes are made of a species of poplar, and are generally called "cottonwood canoes;" and as the trees from which they are made are not very large, the material "runs out" so to speak, along the waist or middle of the canoe, where a greater quantity is required to reach around, and this deficiency is made up by substituting batten-like strips of thin wood tacked or sewed on as gunwales, and calking the crevices well with gum. At bow and stern some rude attempt is made to warp them into canoe lines, and in doing this many cracks are developed, all of which are smeared with spruce gum. The thin bottom is a perfect gridiron of slits, all closed with gum, and the proportion of gum increases with the canoe's age. These were the fragile craft that were brought to me with a tender to transport my effects (nearly three tons besides the *personnel* of the expedition) almost the whole length of the lake, fully seven or eight miles, and the owners had the assurance to offer to do it in two days. I had no idea how far it was to the northern end or outlet of Lake Lindeman, as I had spent too many years of my life among Indians to attempt to deduce even an approximate estimate from the assurances of the two "Sticks" that "it was just around the point of land" to which they pointed and which may have been four or five miles distant. I gave them, however, a couple of loads of material that could be lost without serious damage, weighing three hundred to four hundred pounds, and as

LAKE LINDEMAN. CAPE KOLDEWEY ON THE RIGHT.

The view is taken from the upper (southern) end of Payer Portage, looking (south) toward Kotusk Mountains. Perier Pass is on the extreme left wrapped in fog. Named after Captain Koldewey of the German Navy.

I did not know the length of the lake I thought I would
await their return before attempting further progress.
Even if they could accomplish the bargain in double the
time they proposed I was quite willing to let them proceed, as I understood the outlet of the lake was a narrow
river full of cascades and rocks through which, according
to Indian reports, no raft of more than a few logs could
possibly float. I did not feel disposed to build a couple
of such cumbersome craft to traverse so short a distance.
A southern gale setting in shortly after their departure,
with waves running on the lake a foot or two high, was
too terrible a storm for the rickety little boats, and we
did not see any thing of them or their owners until three
days later, when the men came creeping back overland—
the gale still raging—to explain matters which required
no explanation.

In the meantime, having surmised the failure of our
Indian contractors, the best logs available, which were
rather small ones of stunted spruce and contorted pine,
had been floated down the little stream and had been
tracked up and down along the shores of the lake, and
a raft made of the somewhat formidable dimensions of
fifteen by thirty feet, with an elevated deck amidships.
The rope lashings used on the loads of the Indian packers were put to duty in binding the logs together, but
the greatest reliance was placed in stout wooden pins
which united them by auger holes bored through both,
the logs being cut or "saddled out" where they joined,
as is done at the corners of log cabins. A deck was made
on the corduroy plan of light seasoned pine poles, and
high enough to prevent ordinary sized waves from wetting
the effects, while a pole was rigged by mortising it into

one of the central logs at the bottom and supporting it by four guy ropes from the top, and from this was suspended a wall tent as a sail, the ridge pole being the yard arm, with tackling arranged to raise and lower it. A large bow and stern oar with which to do the steering completed the rude craft. On the evening of the 14th of June the raft was finished, when we found that, as a number of us had surmised, it was not of sufficient buoyancy to hold all our effects as well as the whole party of whites and natives.

The next day only three white men, Mr. Homan, Mr. McIntosh and Corporal Shircliff, were placed in charge. About half the stores were put on the deck, the raft swung by ropes into the swift current of the stream so as to float it well out into the lake, and as the rude sail was spread to the increasing wind, the primitive craft commenced a journey that was destined to measure over thirteen hundred miles before the rough ribs of knots and bark were laid to rest on the great river, nearly half a thousand miles of whose secrets were given up to geographical science through the medium of her staunch and trusty bones. As she slowly obeyed her motive power, the wind began blowing harder and harder, until the craft was pitching like a vessel laboring in an ocean storm ; but despite this the middle of the afternoon saw her rough journey across the angry lake safely completed, and this without any damage to her load worth noticing. The three men had had an extremely hard time of it, and had been compelled to take down their wall tent sail, for when this was lashed down over the stores on the deck to protect them from the deluge of flying spray breaking up over the stern there was ample

surface presented to the furious gale to drive them along
at a good round pace, especially when near the bold
rocky shores, where all their vigilance and muscle were
needed to keep them from being dashed to pieces in the
rolling breakers. They had started with a half dozen or
so good stout poles, but in using them over the rocks on
the bottom one would occasionally cramp between a
couple of submerged stones and be wrested violently
from their hands as the raft swept swiftly by before it
could be extricated. The remainder of the *personnel*,
white and native, scrambled over the rough precipitous
mountain spurs on the eastern side of the lake, wading
through bog and tangled underbrush, then up steep
slippery granite rocks on to the ridge tops bristling with
fallen burned timber, or occasionally steadying themselves
on some slight log that crossed a deep cañon, whose bed
held a rushing stream where nothing less than a trout
could live for a minute, the one common suffering every
where being from the mosquitoes. The rest of the stores
not taken on the raft found their way along slowly by
means of the two dilapidated canoes, previously described,
in the hands of our own Indians.

As we neared Camp 7, at the outlet of Lake Lindeman, on the overland trail we occasionally met with little
openings that might be described by an imaginative person as *prairies*, and for long stretches, that is, two and
three hundred yards, the walking would really be pleasant.

An inspection of the locality showed that the lake we
had just passed was drained by a small river averaging
from fifty to seventy-five feet in width and a little over a
mile long. It was for nearly the whole length a repeti-

tion of shallow rapids, shoals, cascades, ugly-looking bowlders, bars and network of drift-timber. At about the middle of its course the worst cascade was split by a huge projecting bowlder, just at a sudden bend of the stream, and either channel was barely large enough to allow the raft to pass if it came end on, and remained so while going through, otherwise it would be sure to jam. Through this narrow chute of water the raft was "shot" the next day—June 16th—and although our predictions were verified at this cascade, a few minutes' energetic work sufficed to clear it, with the loss of a side-log or two, and all were glad to see it towed and anchored alongside the gravelly beach on the new lake, with so little damage received. Here we at once commenced enlarging its dimensions on a scale commensurate with the carrying of our entire load, both *personnel* and *materiel*. Around this unnavigable and short river the Indian packers and traders portage their goods when making their way into the interior, there being a good trail on the eastern side of the stream, which, barring a few sandy stretches, connects the two lakes. I called these rapids and the portage Payer Portage, after Lieutenant Payer, of the Austro-Hungarian expedition of 1872–74.

By the 17th of June, at midnight, it was light enough to read print, of the size of that before my readers, and so continued throughout the month, except on very cloudy nights. Many bands of pretty harlequin ducks were noticed in the Payer Rapids, which seemed to be their favorite resort, the birds rarely appearing in the lakes, and always near the point at which some swift stream entered the smoother water. Black and brown bears and caribou tracks were seen in the valley of a small stream that here came in from the west. This valley was a most picturesque one as viewed from the Payer Portage looking westward, and was quite typical of the little Alpine valleys of this locality. I named it after Mr. Homan, the topographer of the expedition. We were quite fortunate in finding a number of fallen logs, sound and seasoned, which were much larger than any in our raft, the only trouble being that they were not long enough. All of the large trees tapered rapidly, and at the height of twenty or twenty-five feet a tree was reduced to the size of the largest of its numerous limbs, so that it did not offer surface enough at the small end to use with safety as the side-log or bottom-log of a well-constructed craft. We soon had a goodly number of them sawed in proper lengths, or, at any rate, as long as we could get them, their numerous limbs hacked off, and then, with much labor, we made log-ways through the brush and network of trunks, by means of which we plunged them into the swift river when they were floated down to the raft's position. One of the delights of this raft-making was our having to stand a greater part of the day in ice-water just off the mountain tops, and in strange contrast with this annoyance, the mosquitoes would come buzzing around and making work almost impossible by their attacks upon our heads, while at the same time our feet would be freezing. When the larger logs were secured, they were built into the raft on a plan of fifteen by forty feet; but, taking into account the projections outside of the corner pins, the actual dimensions were sixteen by forty-two. These were never afterward changed.

Two elevated decks were now constructed, separated by a lower central space, where two cumbersome oars might be rigged, that made it possible to row the ponderous craft at the rate of nearly a mile an hour, and these side-oars were afterward used quite often to reach some camping place on the beach of a lake when the wind had failed us or set in ahead. The bow and stern steering-oars were still retained, and we thus had surplus oars for either service, in case of accident, for the two services were never employed at once under any circumstances. There was only one fault with the new construction, and that was that none of the logs extended the whole length of the raft, and the affair rather resembled a pair of rafts, slightly dove-tailed at the point of union, than a single raft of substantial build.

The new lake on which we found ourselves was named Lake Bennett, after Mr. James Gordon Bennett, a well-known patron of American geographical research. While we were here a couple of canoes of the same dilapidated kind as those we saw on Lake Lindeman came down Lake Bennett, holding twice as many Tahk-heesh Indians who begged for work, and whom we put to use in various ways. I noticed that one of them stammered considerably, the first Indian I ever met with an impediment in his speech.

Among my Chilkat packers I also noticed one that was deaf and dumb, and several who were afflicted with cataract in the eye, but none were affected with the latter disease to the extent I had observed among the Eskimo, with whom I believe it is caused by repeated attacks of snow-blindness.

On the summits of high mountains to the right, or

LAKE BENNETT FROM PAYER PORTAGE.

Iron-capped mountains on the right, covered with fog.

eastward of Lake Bennett, were the familiar blue-ice glaciers, but in charming relief to these were the red rocks and ridges that protruded amid them. Specimens of rocks very similar in color were found on the lake beach and in the terminal moraines of the little glaciers that came down the gulches, and these having shown iron as their coloring matter, I gave to this bold range the name of the Iron-capped Mountains.

On the morning of the 19th of June the constructors reported that their work was done, and the raft was immediately hauled in closer to shore, the load put on and carefully adjusted with reference to an equitable weight, the bow and stern lines cast loose, and after rowing through a winding channel to get past the shallow mud-flats deposited by the two streams which emptied themselves near here, the old wall tent was again spread from its ridge-pole, lashed to the top of the rude mast, and our journey was resumed.

The scenery along this part of Lake Bennett is very much like the inland passages of Alaska, except that there is much less timber on the hills.

I had started with four Chilkat Indians, who were to go over the whole length of the Yukon with me. One of them was always complaining of severe illness, with such a wonderful adaptation to the amount of labor on hand that I discharged him at Lake Bennett as the only method of breaking up the coincidence. The best workman among them discharged himself by disappearing with a hatchet and an ax, and I was left with but two, neither of whom, properly speaking, could be called a Chilkat Indian ; in fact one was a half-breed Tlinkit interpreter, "Billy" Dickinson by name, whose mother had been a

Tsimpsean Indian woman and whose father kept the
store of the North-west Trading Company in Chilkat
Inlet. "Billy," as we always called him, was a rather
good-looking young fellow of about twenty-five years,
who understood the Tlinkit language thoroughly, but
had the fault of nearly all interpreters of mixed blood,
that when called on for duty he considered himself as
one of the high contracting parties to the bargain to be
made ; a sort of agent instead of an interpreter, and being
a wonderfully poor agent he became still worse as an
interpreter. He was as strong as two or three ordinary men of his build and in any sort of an emergency
with a sprinkle of dangerous excitement about it he put
all his strength to use and proved invaluable, but in the
hum-drum, monotonous work of the trip, such as the
steering of the raft or other continuous labor, his Indian
nature came to the front, and he did every thing in the
world on the outskirts of the work required, but would
not be brought down to the main issue until compelled
to do so by the application of strong language. Our
other native companion was named *Indianne*, a Chilkat
Tahk-heesh Indian, whose familiarity with the latter
language, through his mother, a Tahk-heesh squaw,
made him invaluable to us as an interpreter while in the
country of this tribe, which stretches to the site of
old Fort Selkirk at the mouth of the Pelly River.
Physically, Indianne was not all that might be required
in an Indian, for they are generally supposed to do twice
as much out-of-door work as a white man, but he was
well past fifty years and such activity was hardly to be
expected of him. Besides being a Tahk-heesh, or Stick
interpreter, he was fairly familiar with the ground as a

guide, having traveled over parts of it much oftener than most Indians, owing to the demand for his services as an interpreter among the Sticks. Through the medium of our two interpreters, and the knowledge found in each tribe of the language of their neighbors, we managed to get along on the river until English and Russian were again encountered, although we occasionally had to use four or five interpreters at once.

There was a fair wind in our favor as we started, but it was accompanied with a disagreeable rain which made things very unpleasant, as we had no sign of a cover on our open boat, nor could we raise one in a strong wind. Under this wind we made about a mile and a half an hour, and as it kept slowly increasing we dashed along at the noble rate of two or two and a half miles an hour. This increasing wind, however, also had its disadvantages, for on long, unprotected stretches of the lake the water was swelling into waves that gave us no small apprehension for our vessel. Not that we feared she might strike a rock, or spring a leak, but that in her peculiar explorations she might spread herself over the lake, and her crew and cargo over its bottom. By three in the afternoon the waves were dashing high over the stern, and the raft having no logs running its entire length, was working in the center like an accordion, and with as much distraction to us. Still it was important to take advantage of every possible breath of wind in the right direction while on the lakes; and we held the raft rigidly to the north for about two hours longer, at which time a perfect hurricane was howling, the high waves sweeping the rowing space so that no one could stand on his feet in that part, much less sit down to the oars, and as a few of the faithful pins commenced snapping, we headed the vessel for the eastern shore at as sharp an angle as it was possible to make running before the wind, and which I do not think was over two points of the compass, equal to an angle of about twenty degrees.

This course brought us in time to a rough, rocky beach strewn with big bowlders along the water's edge, over which the waves were dashing in a boiling sheet of water that looked threatening enough; but a line was gotten ashore through the surf with the aid of a canoe, and while a number of the crew kept the raft off the rocks with poles, the remainder of the party tracked it back about a half a mile along the slippery stones of the beach, to a crescent-shaped cove sheltered from the waves and wind, where it was anchored near the beach. We at once began looking around for a sufficient number of long logs to run the whole length of the raft, a search in which we were conspicuously successful, for the timber skirting the little cove was the largest and best adapted for raft repairing of any we saw for many hundred miles along the lakes. Four quite large trees were found, and all the next day, the 20th, was occupied in cutting them down, clearing a way for them through the timber to the shore of the lake, and prying, pulling, and pushing them there, and then incorporating them into the raft. Two were used for the side logs and two for the center, and when we had finished our task it was evident that a much needed improvement had been made. It was just made in time, too, for many of our tools were rapidly going to pieces; the last auger had slipped the nut that held it in the handle, so that it could not be withdrawn from the logs to clear it of the shavings, but a small hand-vise was firmly screwed on as a substitute, and this too lost its hold and fell overboard on the outer edge of the raft in eight or ten feet of water, and ice-water at that. A magnet of fair size was lashed on the end of a long pole, and we fished for the invisible implement, but without avail. "Billy" Dickinson, our half-breed Chilkat interpreter, of his own free will and accord, then stripped himself and dived down into the ice-cold water and discovered that near the spot where it had sunk was a precipitous bank of an unknown depth, down which it had probably rolled, otherwise the magnet would have secured it. Other means were employed and we got along without it.

The day we spent in repairing the raft a good, strong, steady wind from the south kept us all day in a state of perfect irritation at the loss of so much good motive power, but we consoled ourselves by observing that it did us one service at least—no mean one, however—in keeping the mosquitoes quiet during our labors.

Across Lake Bennett to the north-westward was a very prominent cape, brought out in bold relief by the valley of a picturesque stream, which emptied itself just beyond. I called it Prejevalsky Point after the well-known Russian explorer, while the stream was called Wheaton River after Brevet Major-General Frank Wheaton, U. S. Army, at the time commanding the Military Department (of the Columbia) in which Alaska is comprised, and to whose efforts and generosity the ample outfit of the expedition was due.

On the 21st we again started early, with a good breeze

behind us that on the long stretches gave us quite heavy
seas, which tested the raft very thoroughly, and with a
result much to our satisfaction. It no longer conformed to
the surface of the long swelling waves, but remained rigidly
intact, the helmsman at the steering oar getting considerably splashed as a consequence. The red rocks and
ridges of the ice-covered mountain tops that I have mentioned finally culminated in one bold, beetling pinnacle,
well isolated from the rest, and quite noticeable for
many miles along the lake from either direction. This
I named Richards' Rock, after Vice-Admiral Richards,
of the Royal Navy. The country was becoming a little
more open as we neared the northern end of Lake Bennett, and, indeed, more picturesque in its relief to the
monotonous grandeur of the mountain scenery. Lake
Bennett is thirty miles long. At its north-western extremity a couple of streams disembogue, forming a wide,
flat and conspicuous valley that, as we approached it, we
all anticipated would prove our outlet. Several well
marked conical buttes spring from this valley, and these
with the distant mountains give it a very picturesque
appearance, its largest river being sixty to seventy-five
yards wide, but quite shallow. It received the name of
Watson Valley, for Professor Sereno Watson, of Harvard University.

About five o'clock the northern end or outlet of the
lake was reached. As the sail was lowered, and we
entered a river from one hundred to two hundred yards
wide, and started forward at a speed of three or four miles
an hour—a pace which seemed ten times as fast as our
progress upon the lake, since, from our proximity to the
shore, our relative motion was more clearly indicated,

our spirits ascended, and the prospects of our future journey when we should be rid of the lakes were joyfully discussed, and the subject was not exhausted when we grounded and ran upon a mud flat that took us two hours of hard work to get clear of. This short stretch of the draining river of Lake Bennett, nearly two miles long, is called by the natives of the country "the place where the caribou cross," and appears on the map as Caribou Crossing.

At certain seasons of the year, so the Tahk-heesh Indians say, these caribou—the woodland reindeer—pass over this part of the river in large numbers in their migrations to the different feeding grounds, supplied and withdrawn in turn by the changing seasons, and ford its wide shallow current, passing backward and forward through Watson Valley. Unfortunately for our party neither of these crossings occurred at this time of the year, although a dejected camp of two Tahk-heesh families not far away from ours (No. 10) had a very ancient reindeer ham hanging in front of their brush tent, which, however, we did not care to buy. The numerous tracks of the animals, some apparently as large as oxen, confirmed the Indian stories, and as I looked at our skeleton game score and our provisions of Government bacon, I wished sincerely that June was one of the months of the reindeers' migration, and the 21st or 22d about the period of its culmination.

The very few Indians living in this part of the country—the "Sticks"—subsist mostly on these animals and on mountain goats, with now and then a wandering moose, and more frequently a black bear. One would expect to find such followers of the chase the very hardiest of all Indians, in compliance with the rule that prevails in most countries, by which the hunter excels the fisherman, but this does not seem to be the case along this great river. Here, indeed, it appears that the further down the stream the Indian lives, and the more he subsists on fish, the hardier, the more robust, the more self-asserting and impudent he becomes.

After prying our raft off the soft mud flat we again spread our sail for the beach of the little lake and went into camp, after having been on the water (or in it) for over thirteen hours.

The country was now decidedly more open, and it was evident that we were getting out of the mountains. Many level spots appeared, the hills were less steep and the snow was melting from their tops. Pretty wild rose-blossoms were found along the banks of the beach, with many wild onions with which we stuffed the wrought-iron grouse that we killed, and altogether there was a general change of verdure for the better. There were even a number of rheumatic grasshoppers which feebly jumped along in the cold Alpine air, as if to tempt us to go fishing, in remembrance of the methods of our boy-hood's days, and in fact every thing that we needed for that recreation was to be had except the fish. Although this lake (Lake Nares, after Sir George Nares) was but three or four miles long, its eastern trend delayed us three days before we got a favorable wind, the banks not being good for tracking the raft. Our old friend, the steady summer south wind, still continued, but was really a hindrance to our progress on an eastern course. Although small, Lake Nares was one of the prettiest in the lacustrine chain, owing to the greater openness of country on its banks. Grand terraces stretching in beautiful symmetry along each side of the lake plainly showed its ancient levels, these terraces reaching nearly to the tops of the hills, and looking as if some huge giant had used them as stairways over the mountains. Similar but less conspicuous terraces had been noticed on the northern shores of Lake Bennett.

Although we could catch no fish while fishing with bait or flies, yet a number of trout lines put out over night in Lake Nares rewarded us with a large salmon trout, the first fish we had caught on the trip. I have spoken of the delay on this little lake on account of its eastward trend, and the next lake kept up the unfavorable course, and we did not get off this short eastern stretch of ten or fifteen miles for five or six days, so baffling was the wind. Of course, these protracted delays gave us many chances for rambles around the country, some of which we improved.

Everywhere we came in contact with the grouse of these regions, all of them with broods of varying numbers, and while the little chicks went scurrying through the grass and brush in search of a hiding place, the old ones walked along in front of the intruder, often but a few feet away, seemingly less devoid of fear than the common barn fowls, although probably they had never heard a shot fired.

The Doctor and I sat down to rest on a large rock with a perturbed mother grouse on another not over three yards away, and we could inspect her plumage and study her actions as well as if she had been in a cage. The temptation to kill them was very great after having been so long without fresh meat, a subsistence the appetite loudly demands in the rough out-of-door life of an explorer. A mess of them ruthlessly destroyed by our Indian hunters, who had no fears of the game law, no sportsman's qualms of conscience, nor in fact compassion of any sort, lowered our desire to zero, for they were tougher than leather, and as tasteless as shavings ; and after that first mess we were perfectly willing to allow them all the rights guaranteed by the game laws of lower latitudes.

Quite a number of marmots were seen by our Indians, and the hillsides were dotted with their holes. The Indians catch them for fur and food (in fact, every thing living is used by the Indians for the latter purpose) by means of running nooses put over their holes, which choke the little animal to death as he tries to quit his underground home. A

CARVED PINS FOR FASTENING MAR-
MOT SNARES.

finely split raven quill, running the whole length of the rib of the feather, is used for the noose proper and the instant this is sprung it closes by its own flexibility. The rest is a sinew string tied to a bush near the hole if one be convenient, otherwise to a peg driven in the ground. Sometimes they employ a little of the large amount of leisure time they have on their hands in cutting these pegs into fanciful and totemic designs, although in this respect the Sticks, as in every thing else pertaining to the savage arts, are usually much inferior to the Chilkats in these displays, and the illustrations give on page 112 are characteristic rather of the latter tribe than of the former. Nearly all the blankets of this Tahk-heesh tribe of Indians are made from these marmot skins, and they are exceedingly light considering their warmth. Much of the warmth, however, is lost by the ventilated condition in which the wearers maintain them, as it costs labor to mend them, but none to sit around and shiver.

The few Tahk-heesh who had been camped near us at Caribou Crossing suddenly disappeared the night after we camped on the little lake, and as our "gum canoe" that we towed along behind the raft and used for emergencies, faded from view at the same eclipse, we were forced to associate the events together and set these fellows down as subject to kleptomania. Nor should I be too severe either, for the canoe had been picked up by us on Lake Lindeman as a vagrant, and it certainly looked the character in every respect, therefore we could not show the clearest title in the world to the dilapidated craft. It was a very fortunate circumstance that we were not worried for the use of a canoe afterward until we could purchase a substitute, although we hardly thought such a thing possible at the time, so much had we used the one that ran away with our friends.

The 23d of June we got across the little lake (Nares), the wind dying down as we went through its short draining river, having made only three miles.

The next day, the 24th, the wind seemed to keep swinging around in a circle, and although we made five miles, I think we made as many landings, so often did the wind fail us or set in ahead.

This new lake I called after Lieutenant Bove of the Italian navy. Here too, the mountainous shores were carved into a series of terraces rising one above the other, which probably indicated the ancient beaches of the lake when its outlet was closed at a much higher level than at present, and when great bodies of ice on their surface plowed up the beach into these terraces. This new lake was nine miles long. The next day again we had the same fight with a battling wind from half past six in the morning until after nine at night, nearly seventeen hours, but we managed to make twelve miles, and better than all, regain our old course pointing northward. During one of these temporary landings on the shores of Lake Bove our Indians amused themselves in wasting government matches, articles which they had never seen in such profusion before, and in a little while they succeeded in getting some dead and fallen spruce trees on fire, and these communicating to the living ones above them, soon sent up great billows of dense resinous smoke that must have been visible for miles, and which lasted for a number of minutes after we had left. Before camping that evening we could see a very distant smoke, apparently six or seven miles ahead, but really ten or twenty, which our Indians told us was an answering smoke to them, the Tahk-heesh, who kindled the second fire, evidently thinking that they were Chilkat traders in their country, this being a frequent signal among them as a means of announcing their approach, when engaged in trading. It was worthy of note as marking the existence of this primitive method of signaling, so common among some of the Indian tribes of the plains, among these far-off savages, but I was unable to ascertain whether they carried it to such a degree of intricacy with respect to the different meanings of compound smokes either as to number or relative intervals of time or space. It is very doubtful if they do, as the necessity for such complex signals can hardly arise.

This new lake on which we had taken up our northward course, and which is about eighteen miles long, is called by the Indians of the country Tahk-o (each lake and connecting length of river has a different name with them), and, I understand, receives a river coming in from the south, which, followed up to one of its sources, gives a mountain pass to another river emptying into the inland estuaries of the Pacific Ocean. It is said by the Indians to be smaller than the one we had just come over, and therefore we might consider that we were on the Yukon proper thus far.

Lake Tahk-o and Lake Bove are almost a single sheet, separated only by a narrow strait formed by a point of remarkable length (Point Perthes, after Justus Perthes of Gotha), which juts nearly across to the opposite shore. It is almost covered with limestones, some of them almost true marble in their whiteness, a circumstance which gives a decided hue to the cape even when seen at a distance.

Leaving the raft alongside the beach of Lake Tahk-o at our only camping place on it (Camp No. 13), a short stroll along its shores revealed a great number of long, well-trimmed logs that strongly resembled telegraph poles, and would have sold for those necessary nuisances in a civilized country. They were finally made out to be the logs used by the Indians in rafting down the stream, and well-trimmed by constant attrition on the rough rocky beaches while held there by the storms. Most of these were observed on the northern shores of the lakes, to which the current through them, slight as it was, coupled with the prevailing south wind, naturally drifts them. I afterward ascertained that rafting was

LOOKING ACROSS LAKE BOVE FROM PERTHES POINT.
Field Peak in the far distance. (Named for Hon. David Dudley Field.)

quite a usual thing along the head waters of the Yukon, and that we were not pioneers in this rude art by any means, although we had thought so from the direful prognostications they were continually making as to our probable success with our own. The "cottonwood" canoes already referred to are very scarce, there probably not existing over ten or twelve along the whole length of the upper river as far as old Fort Selkirk. Many of their journeys up the swift stream are performed

by the natives on foot, carrying their limited necessities
on their backs. Upon their return a small raft of from
two to six or eight logs is made, and they float down
with the current in the streams, and pole and sail
across the lakes. By comparing these logs with telegraph poles one has a good idea of the usual size of the
timber of these districts. The scarcity of good wooden
canoes is also partially explained by this smallness of the
logs; while birch bark canoes are unknown on the Yukon
until the neighborhood of old Fort Selkirk is reached.

This same Lake Tahk-o, or probably some lake very
near it, had been reached by an intrepid miner, a Mr.
Byrnes, then in the employ of the Western Union Telegraph Company. Many of my readers are probably
not acquainted with the fact that this corporation, at
about the close of our civil war, conceived the grand idea
of uniting civilization in the eastern and western conti-
nents by a telegraph line running by way of Bering's
Straits, and that a great deal of the preliminary surveys and even a vast amount of the actual work had
been completed when the success of the Atlantic cable
put a stop to the project. The Yukon River had been
carefully examined from its mouth as far as old Fort
Yukon (then a flourishing Hudson Bay Company post),
some one thousand miles from the mouth, and even
roughly beyond, in their interest, although it had previously been more or less known to the Russian-American
and Hudson Bay trading companies. Mr. Byrnes, a
practical miner from the Caribou mines of British
Columbia, crossed the Tahk-o Pass, already cited, got on
one of the sources of the Yukon, and as near as can
be made out, descended it to the vicinity of the lake

of which I am writing. Here it appears he was recalled
by a courier sent on his trail and dispatched by the
telegraph company, who were now mournfully assisting in the jubilee of the Atlantic cable's success, and he
retraced his steps over the river and lakes, and returned
to his former occupation of mining.

Whether he ever furnished a map and a description of
his journey, so that it could be called an exploration,
I do not know, but from the books which purport to
give a description of the country as deduced from his
travels, I should say not, considering their great inac-
curacy. One book, noticing his travels, and purporting
to be a faithful record of the telegraph explorers on the
American side, said that had Mr. Byrnes continued his
trip only a day and a half further in the light birch-
bark canoes of the country, he would have reached old
Fort Selkirk, and thus completed the exploration of the
Yukon. Had he reached the site of old Fort Selkirk,
he certainly would have had the credit, had he recorded
it, however rough his notes may have been, but he
would never have done so in the light birch-bark
canoes of the country, for the conclusive reason that
they do not exist, as already stated ; and as to doing
it in a day and a half, our measurements from Lake
Tahk-o to Fort Selkirk show nearly four hundred and
fifty miles, and observations proved that the Indians
seldom exceed a journey of six hours in their cramped
wooden craft, so that his progress would necessarily
have demanded a speed of nearly fifty miles an hour.
At this rate of canoeing along the whole river, across
Bering Sea and up the Amoor River, the telegraph company need not have completed their line along this part,

but might simply have turned their dispatch over to these rapid couriers, and they would have only been a few hours behind the telegraph dispatch if it had been worked as slowly as it is now in the interest of the public.

We passed out of Lake Tahko a little after two o'clock in the afternoon of the 26th of June, and entered the first considerable stretch of river that we had yet met with on the trip, about nine miles long. We quitted the river at five o'clock, which was quite an improvement on our lake traveling even at its best. The first part of this short river stretch is full of dangerous rocks and bowlders, as is also the lower portion of Tahko Lake.

On the right bank of the river, about four miles from the entrance, we saw a tolerably well-built "Stick" Indian house. Near it in the water was a swamped Indian canoe which one of our natives bailed out in a manner as novel as it was effectual. Grasping it on one side, and about the center, a rocking motion, fore and aft, was kept up, the bailer waiting until the recurrent wave was just striking the depressed end of the boat, and as this was repeated the canoe was slowly lifted until it stood at his waist with not enough water in it to sink an oyster can. This occupied a space of time not much greater than it has taken to relate it. This house was deserted, but evidently only for a while, as a great deal of its owner's material of the chase and the fishery was still to be seen hanging inside on the rafters. Among these were a great number of dried salmon, one of the staple articles of food that now begin to appear on this part of the great river, nearly two thousand miles from its mouth. This salmon, when dried before putrefaction sets in, is tolerable, ranking somewhere between Limburger cheese and walrus hide. Collecting some of it occasionally from Indian fishermen as we floated by, we would use it as a lunch in homeopathic quantities until some of us got so far as to imagine that we really liked it. If smoked, this salmon is quite good, but by far the larger amount is dried in the open air, and, Indian like, the best is first served and soon disappears.

Floating down the river, and coming near any of the low marshy points, we were at once visited by myriads of small black gnats which formed a very unsolicited addition to the millions of mosquitoes, the number of which did not diminish in the least as we descended the river. The only protection from them was in being well out from land, with a good wind blowing, or when forced to camp on shore a heavy resinous smoke would often disperse a large part of them.

When we camped that evening on the new lake the signal smoke of the Tahk-heesh Indians—if it was one— was still burning, at least some six or seven miles ahead of us, which showed how much we had been mistaken in estimating its distance the day before. A tree has something definite in its size, and even a butte or mountain peak has something tangible on which a person can base a calculation for distance, but when one comes down to a distant smoke I think the greatest indefiniteness has been reached, especially when one wants to estimate its distance. I had often observed this before, when on the plains, where it is still worse than in a hilly country, where one can at least perceive that the smoke is beyond the hill, back of which it rises, but when often looking down an open river valley no such indications are to be had. I remember when traveling through the sand hills of western Nebraska that a smoke which was variously estimated to be from eight to twelve or possibly fifteen miles away took us two days' long traveling in an army ambulance, making thirty-five or forty miles a day, as the winding road ran, to reach its site.

The shores of the new lake—which I named Lake Marsh, after Professor O. C. Marsh, a well-known scientist of our country—was composed of all sizes of

LOOKING SOUTHWARD FROM CAMP 14 ON LAKE MARSH

On the left is the Tahko Pass, on the right the Yukon Pass in the mountains, directly over the point of land. Between this point and the Yukon Pass can be seen the Yukon River coming into the lake.

clay stones jumbled together in confusion, and where the water had reached and beat upon them it had reduced them to a sticky clay of the consistency of thick mortar, not at all easy to walk through. This mire, accompanied by a vast quantity of mud brought down by the streams that emanated from grinding glaciers, and which could be distinguished by the whiter color and impalpable character of its ingredients, nearly filled the new lake, at least for wide strips along the shores where it had been driven by the storms. Although drawing a little

less than two feet of water, the raft struck several times
at distances from the shore of from fifty to a hundred
yards, and the only alternative was to wade ashore in
our rubber boots (the soft mud being deeper than the
water itself) and tie the raft by a long line whenever we
wanted to camp.

One night, while on this lake, a strong inshore breeze
coming up, our raft, while unloaded, was gradually
lifted by the incoming high waves, and brought a few
inches further at a time, until a number of yards had
been made. The next morning when loaded and sunk
deep into the mud, the work we had to pry it off is more
easily imagined than described, but it taught us a lesson
that we took to heart, and thereafter a friendly prod or
two with a bar was generally given at the ends of the
cumbersome craft to pry it gradually into deeper water
as the load slowly weighed it down. When the wind
was blowing vigorously from some quarter—and it was
only when it was blowing that we could set sail and
make any progress—these shallow mud banks would
tinge the water over them with a dirty white color that
was in strong contrast with the clear blue water over the
deeper portion, and by closely watching this well-defined
line of demarcation when under sail, we could make out
the most favorable points at which to reach the bank, or
approach it as nearly as possible. This clear-cut outline
between the whitened water within its exterior edges
and the deep blue water beyond, showed in many places
an extension of the deposits of from four hundred to
five hundred yards from the beach. It is probable that
the areas of water may vary in Lake Marsh at different
seasons sufficiently to lay bare these mud banks, or cover

them so as to be navigable for small boats ; but at the time of our visit there seemed to be a most wonderful uniformity in the depth of the water over them in every part of the lake, it being about eighteen inches.

Camping on the lakes was generally quite an easy affair. There was always plenty of wood, and, of course, water everywhere, the clear, cold mountain springs occurring every few hundred yards if the lake water was too muddy ; so that about all that we needed was a dry place large enough to pitch a couple of tents for the white people and a tent fly for the Indians, but simple as the latter seemed, it was very often quite difficult to obtain. It was seldom that we found places where tent pins could be driven in the ground, and when rocks large enough to do duty as pins, or fallen timber or brush for the same purpose could not be had, we generally put the tent under us, spread our blankets upon it, crawled in and went to sleep. The greatest comfort in pitching our tent was in keeping out the mosquitoes, for then we could spread our mosquito bars with some show of success, although the constantly recurring light rains made us often regret that we had made a bivouac, not particularly on account of the slight wettings we got, but because of our constant fear that the rain was going to be much worse in reality than it ever proved to be. I defy any one to sleep in the open air with only a blanket or two over him and have a great black cloud sprinkle a dozen drops of rain or so in his face and not imagine the deluge was coming next. I have tried it off and on for nearly twenty years, and have not got over the feeling yet. If, after camping, a storm threatened, a couple of stout skids were placed fore and aft under the logs of the raft nearest the shore to prevent their breaking off as they bumped on the beach in the waves of the surf, a monotonous music that lulled us to sleep on many a stormy night. The baggage on the raft, like that in an army wagon or upon a pack train of mules, in a few days so assorted itself that the part necessary for the night's camping was always the handiest, and but a few minutes were required after landing until the evening meal was ready.

So important was it to make the entire length of the river (over 2000 miles) within the short interval between the date of our starting and the probable date of departure of the last vessel from St. Michaels, near the mouth of the river, that but little time was left for rambles through the country, and much as I desired to take a hunt inland, and still more to make an examination of the country at various points along the great river, I constantly feared that by so doing I might be compromising our chances of getting out of the country before winter should effectually forbid it. Therefore, from the very start it was one constant fight against time to avoid such an unwished for contingency, and thus we could avail ourselves of but few opportunities for exploring the interior.

On the 28th of June a fair breeze on Lake Marsh continuing past sunset (an unusual occurrence), we kept on our way until well after midnight before the wind died out. At midnight it was light enough to read common print and I spent some time about then in working out certain astronomical observations. Venus was the only star that was dimly visible in the unclouded sky. Lake Marsh was the first water that we could trust in which to take a bath, and even there—and for that matter it was the same along the entire river—bathing was only possible on still, warm, sunny days.

Below old Fort Selkirk on the Yukon, at the mouth of the White River (so-called on account of its white muddy water), bathing is almost undesirable on account of the large amount of sediment contained in the water ; its swift current allowing it to hold much more than any river of the western slope known to me, while its muddy banks furnish a ready base of supplies. Its temperature also seldom reaches the point that will allow one to plunge in all over with any degree of comfort. One annoyance in bathing in Lake Marsh during the warmer hours of the day was the presence of a large fly, somewhat resembling the "horse-fly," but much larger and inflicting a bite that was proportionately more severe. These flies made it necessary to keep constantly swinging a towel in the air, and a momentary cessation of this exertion might be punished by having a piece bitten out of one that a few days later would look like an incipient boil. One of the party so bitten was completely disabled for a week, and at the moment of infliction it was hard to believe that one was not disabled for life. With these "horse" flies, gnats and mosquitoes in such dense profusion, the Yukon Valley is not held up as a paradise to future tourists.

The southern winds which had been blowing almost continuously since we first spread our sail on Lake Lindeman, and which had been our salvation while on the lakes, must prevail chiefly in this region, as witness the manner in which the spruce and pine trees invariably lean to the northward, especially where their isolated condition and exposure on flat level tracts give the winds full play, to influence their position. Near Lake Lindeman a dwarfed, contorted pine was noticed, the fibers of which were not only twisted around its heart two or three times, in a height of fifteen or twenty feet, but the heart itself was twisted in a spiral like a corkscrew that made two or three turns in its length, after which, as if to add confusion to disorder, it was bent in a graceful sweep to the north to conform to the general leaning of all the trees similarly exposed to the action of the winds. There was a general brash condition of all the wood which was very apparent when we started to make pins for binding the raft, while it was seldom that a log was found large enough for cutting timber. The little cove into which we put on the 19th of June, when chased by a gale, by a singular freak of good fortune had just the logs we needed, both as to length and size, to repair our raft, and I do not think we saw a good chance again on the upper waters of the Yukon. Further down, every island—and the Yukon has probably as many islands as any half-dozen rivers of the same size in the world put together—has its upper end covered with enough timber to build all the rafts a lively party could construct in a summer.

Lake Marsh also had a few terraces visible on the eastern hillsides, but they were nearer together and not so well marked as those we observed on some of the lakes further back. Along these, however, were pretty open prairies, covered with the dried, yellow grass of last year, this summer's growth having evidently not yet forced its way through the dense mass. More than one of us compared these prairies, irregular as they seemed, with the stubble fields of wheat or oats in more civilized climes. I have no doubt that they furnish good grazing to mountain goats, caribou and moose, and would be sufficient for cattle if they could keep on friendly terms with the mosquitoes. According to the general terms of the survival of the fittest and the growth of muscles the most used to the detriment of others, a band of cattle inhabiting this district in the far future would be all

TYPICAL TAHK-HEESH OR "STICK" INDIANS.
From sketches by Sergeant Gloster.

tail and no body unless the mosquitoes should experience a change of numbers.

At Marsh a few miserable "Stick" Indians put in an appearance, but not a single thing could be obtained from them by our curiosity hunters. A rough-looking pair of shell ear-rings in a small boy's possession he instantly refused to exchange for the great consideration of a jack-knife offered by a member of the party, who sup-

posed the ornaments to be purely local in character and
of savage manufacture. Another trinket was added to
the jack-knife and still refused, and additions were made
to the original offer, until just to see if there was any
limit to the acquisitiveness of these people, a final offer
was made, I believe, of a double-barreled shot-gun with
a thousand rounds of ammunition, a gold watch, two
sacks of flour and a camp stove, and in refusing this the
boy generously added the information that its value to
him was based on the fact that it had been received from
the Chilkats, who, in turn, had obtained it from the
white traders.

A few scraggy half-starved dogs accompanied the
party. An unconquerable pugnacity was the principal
characteristic of these animals, two of them fighting
until they were so exhausted that they had to lean
up against each other to rest. A dirty group of children of assorted sizes completed the picture of one of the
most dejected races of people on the face of the earth.
They visited their fish lines at the mouth of the incoming river at the head of Lake Marsh, and caught enough
fish to keep body and soul together after a fashion.
This method of fishing is quite common in this part of
the country, and at the mouth of a number of streams,
or where the main stream debouches into a lake, long
willow poles driven far enough into the mud to prevent
their washing away are often seen projecting upward
and swayed back and forth by the force of the current.
On closer examination they reveal a sinew string tied to
them at about the water-line or a little above. They
occasionally did us good service as buoys, indicating the
mud flats, which we could thereby avoid, but the num-

ber of fish we ever saw taken off them was not alarming.
The majority of those caught are secured by means of
the double-pronged fish-spears, which were described on
page 76. I never observed any nets in the possession
of the Tahk-heesh or "Sticks," but my investigations in
this respect were so slight that I might easily have over-
looked them. Among my trading material to be used
for hiring native help, fish-hooks were eagerly sought by
all of the Indians, until after White River was passed,
at which point the Yukon becomes too muddy for any
kind of fishing with hook and line. Lines they were not
so eager to obtain, the common ones of sinew sufficiently
serving the purpose. No good bows or arrows were seen
among them, their only weapons being the stereotyped
Hudson Bay Company flintlock smooth-bore musket,
the only kind of gun, I believe, throwing a ball that this
great trading company has ever issued since its foundation. They also sell a cheap variety of double-barreled
percussion-capped shotgun, which the natives buy, and
loading them with ball—being about No. 12 or 14 guage
—find them superior to the muskets. Singular as it may
appear, these Indians, like the Eskimo I found around
the northern part of Hudson's Bay, prefer the flintlock
to the percussion-cap gun, probably for the reason that
the latter depends on three articles of trade—caps, powder and lead—while the former depends on but two of
these, and the chances of running short of ammunition
when perhaps at a distance of many weeks' journey from
these supplies, are thereby lessened. These old muskets
are tolerably good at sixty to seventy yards, and even
reasonably dangerous at twice that distance. In all
their huntings these Indians contrive by that tact pecu-

liar to savages to get within this distance of moose, black
bear and caribou, and thus to earn a pretty fair subsistence the year round, having for summer a diet of salmon
with a few berries and roots.

The 28th we had on Lake Marsh a brisk rain and
thunder shower, lasting from 12.45 P. M. to 2.15 P. M.,
directly overhead, which was, I believe, the first thun-
derstorm recorded on the Yukon, thunder being unknown on the lower river, according to all accounts.
Our Camp 15 was on a soft, boggy shore covered with
reeds, where a tent could not be pitched and blankets
could not be spread. The raft lay far out in the lake, a
hundred yards from the shore, across soft white mud,
through which one might sink in the water to one's
middle. When to this predicament the inevitable mosquitoes and a few rain showers are added, I judge that
our plight was about as disagreeable as could well be
imagined. Such features of the explorer's life, however,
are seldom dwelt upon. The northern shores of the lake
are unusually flat and boggy. Our primitive mode of
navigation suffered also from the large banks of "glacier
mud" as we approached the lake's outlet. Most of this
mud was probably deposited by a large river, the
McClintock (in honor of Vice-Admiral Sir Leopold
McClintock, R. N.), that here comes in from the north-
east—a river so large that we were in some doubt as to
its being the outlet, until its current settled the matter
by carrying us into the proper channel. A very conspicuous hill, bearing north-east from Lake Marsh, was
named Michie Mountain after Professor Michie of West
Point.

CHAPTER VI.

A CHAPTER ABOUT RAFTING.

"SNUBBING" THE RAFT.

AKE Marsh gave us four days of variable sailing on its waters, when, on the 29th of June, we emerged from it and once more felt the exhilaration of a rapid course on a swift river, an exhilaration that was not allowed to die rapidly away, by reason of the great amount of exercise we had to go through in managing the raft in its many eccentric phases of navigation. On the lakes, whether in storm or still weather, one man stationed at the stern oar of the raft had been sufficient, as long as he kept awake, nor was any great harm done if he fell asleep in a quiet breeze, but once on the river an additional oarsman at the bow sweep was imperatively needed, for at short turns or sudden bends, or when nearing half-sunken bowlders or tangled masses of driftwood, or bars of sand, mud or gravel, or while steering clear of eddies and slack water, it was often necessary to do some very lively work at both ends of the raft in swinging the ponderous contrivance around to avoid these obstacles, and in the worst cases two or three other men assisted the oarsmen in their difficult task. Just how much strength a couple of strong men could put on a steering sweep was a delicate matter to gauge, and too often in the most trying places our experiments in testing the questions were failures, and with a sharp snap the oar would part, a man or two would sit down violently without stopping to pick out the most luxurious places, and the craft like a wild animal unshackled would go plowing through the fallen timber that lined the banks, or bring up on the bar or bowlder we had been working hard to avoid. We slowly became practical oar makers, however, and toward the latter part of the journey had some crude but effective implements that defied annihilation.

As we leisurely and lazily crept along the lakes somebody would be driving away *ennui* by dressing down pins with a hatchet, boring holes with an auger and driving pins with an ax, until by the time the lakes were all passed I believe that no two logs crossed each other in the raft that were not securely pinned at the point of juncture with at least one pin, and if the logs were large ones with two or three. In this manner our vessel was as solid as it was possible to make such a craft, and would bring up against a bowlder with a shock and swing dizzily around in a six or seven mile current with no more concern than if it were a slab in a mill race.

I believe I have made the remark in a previous chapter that managing a raft—at least our method of managing a raft—on a lake was a tolerably simple affair, especially with a favorable wind, and to tell the truth, one can not manage it at all except with a favorable wind. It was certainly the height of simplicity when compared with its navigation upon a river, although at first sight one might perhaps think the reverse; at least I had thought so, and from the conversation of the whites and Indians of south-eastern Alaska, I knew that their opinions coincided with mine; but I was at length compelled to hold differently from them in this matter, as in many others. Especially was this navigation difficult on a swift river like the Yukon, and I know of none that can maintain a flow of more even rapidity from source to mouth than this great stream. It is not very hard to keep a raft or any floating object in the center of the current of a stream, even if left alone at times, but the number of things which present themselves from time to time to drag it out of this channel seems marvelous.

Old watermen and rafting lumbermen know that while a river is rising it is hard to keep the channel, even the driftwood created by the rise clinging to the shores of the stream. Accordingly they are anxious for the moment when this driftwood begins to float along the main current and out in the middle of the stream, for then they know the water is subsiding, and from that point it requires very little effort to keep in the swiftest current. Should this drift matter be equally distributed over the running water it is inferred that the river is at "a stand-still," as they say. An adept can closely judge of the variations and stage of water by this means.

In a river with soft or earthy banks (and in going the whole length of the Yukon, over two thousand miles, we saw several varieties of shores), the swift current, in which one desires to keep when the current is the motive power, nears the shores only at points or curves, where it digs out the ground into steep perpendicular banks, which if at all high make it impossible to find a camping place for the night, and out of this swift current the raft had to be rowed to secure a camp at evening, while breaking camp next morning we had to work it back into the current again.   Nothing could be more aggra-

AMONG THE SWEEPERS.

vating than after leaving this swift current to find a camp, as evening fell, to see no possible chance for such a place on the side we had chosen and to go crawling along in slack water while trees and brushes swept rapidly past borne on the swift waters we had quitted.

If the banks of a river are wooded—and no stream can show much denser growth on its shores than the Yukon— the trees that are constantly tumbling in from these places that are being undermined, and yet hanging on by their roots, form a series of *chevaux de frise* or *abatis*, to which is given the backwoods cognomen of "sweepers," and a man on the upper side of a raft plunging through them in a swift current almost wishes himself a beaver or a muskrat so that he can dive out and escape.

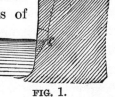

Not only is the Yukon equally wooded on its banks with the average rivers of the world, but this fringe of fallen timber is much greater in quantity and more formidable in aspect than any found in the temperate

FIG. 1.

zones. I think I can explain this fact to the satisfaction of my readers. Taking fig. 1 on this page as representing a cross-section perpendicular to the trend of a bank of a river in our own climate, the stumps *ss* representing

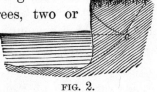

trees which if undermined by the water as far as *c* will generally fall in along the line *cd*, and carry away a few trees, two or three at most, then, as the roots of no more than one such tree are capable of holding it so as to form an *abatis*

FIG. 2.

along the bank, trees so held will lean obliquely down stream and any floating object will merely brush along on their tips without receiving serious damage. Figure

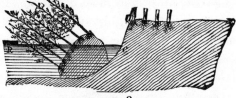

2, above, represents a similar sketch of a cross-section on the banks of the Yukon, especi-

FIG. 3.

ially along its numerous islands, these banks, as we saw them, being generally from six to eight feet above the level of the water. This is also about the depth to

which the moist marshy ground freezes solid during the
intense cold of the Alaskan winter in the interior districts, and the banks therefore have the tenacity of ice
to support them ; and it is not until the water has excavated as far as c (five or six times as far as in Figure 1),
that the overhanging mass csd becomes heavy enough to
break off the projecting bank along cd.   This as a solid
frozen body falls downward around the axis c, being too
heavy for the water to sweep away, it remains until
thawed out by the river water already but little above
freezing, by reason of the constant influx of glacier
streams and from running between frozen banks.   I
have roughly attempted to show this process in Fig. 3.
I think any one will acknowledge that the raft R, carried
by a swift current sweeping toward c is not in a very
desirable position.   Such a position is bad enough on
any river which has but a single line of trees along its
scarp and trending down stream, but on the Yukon it is
unfortunately worse, with every branch and twig fero-
ciously standing at "charge bayonets," to resist any
thing that floats that way.   In Fig. 3, the maximum is
depicted just as the bank falls or shortly after ; and it
requires but a few days, possibly a week or a fortnight,
for all the outer and most dangerous looking trees to be
more or less thoroughly swept away by the swift current,
and a less bristling aspect presented, the great half
frozen mass acting somewhat as a breakwater to further
undermining of the bank for a long while.   In many
places along the river, these excavations had gone so far
that the bank seemed full of deep gloomy caves ; and as
we drifted close by, we could see, and, on quiet days
hear, the dripping from the thawing surface, $c s$ (fig. 2).

In other places the half polished surface of the ice in the frozen ground could be seen in recent fractures as late as July, or even August.

Often when camped in some desolate spot or floating lazily along, having seen no inhabitants for days, we would be startled by the sound of a distant gun-shot on the banks, which would excite our curiosity to see the savage sportsman ; but we soon came to trace these reports to the right cause, that of falling banks, although not until after we had several times been deceived. Once or twice we actually saw these tremendous cavings in of the banks quite near us, and more frequently than we wanted we floated almost underneath some that were not far from the crisis of their fate, a fate which we thought might be precipitated by some accidental collision of our making. By far the most critical moment was when both the current and a strong wind set in against one of these banks. On such occasions we were often compelled to tie up to the bank and wait for better times, or if the danger was confined to a short stretch we would fight it out until either the whole party was exhausted or our object was attained.

Whenever an island was made out ahead and it appeared to be near the course of our drifting, the conflicting guesses we indulged in as to which shore of the island we should skirt would indicate the difficulty of making a correct estimate. It takes a peculiarly well practiced eye to follow with certainty the line of the current of the stream from the bow of the raft beyond any obstruction in sight a fair distance ahead, and on more than one occasion our hardest work with the oars and poles was rewarded by finding ourselves on the very bar or flat we had been striving to avoid. The position of the sun, both vertical and horizontal, its brightness and the character of the clouds, the clearness and swiftness of the water, the nature and strength of the wind, however lightly it might be blowing, and a dozen other circumstances had to be taken into account in order to solve this apparently simple problem. If we could determine at what point in the upper end of the island the current was parted upon either side (and at any great distance this was often quite as difficult a problem as the other), one could often make a correct guess by projecting a tree directly beyond and over this point against the distant hills. If the tree crept along these hills to the right, the raft might pass to the left of the island, and vice versâ ; this would certainly happen if the current was not deflected by some bar or shoal between the raft and the island. And such shoals and bars of gravel, sand and mud are very frequent obstructions in front of an island —at least it was so on the Yukon—indeed the coincidence was too frequent to be without significance. These bars and shoals were not merely prolongations from the upper point of the island, but submerged islands, so to speak, just in front of them, and between the two a steamboat could probably pass. Using tall trees as guides to indicate on which side of the island the raft might pass was, as I have said, not so easy as appears at first sight, for unless the tree could be made out directly over the dividing point of the current, all surmises were of little value. The tall spruce trees on the right and left flanks of the island in sight were always the most conspicuous, being fewer in number, and more prominent in their isolation, than the dense growth of the center of the island, as it was seen "end on" from above. People were very prone to use these convenient reference marks in making their calculations, and one can readily perceive when the trees were near and the island fairly wide, both of the outer trees would appear to diverge in approaching, and according as one selected the right or the left of the two trees, one would infer that our course was to the left or right of the island. As one stood on the bow—as we always called the down-stream end of the raft, although it was shaped no differently from the stern—and looked forward on the water flowing along, the imagination easily conceives that one can follow up from that position to almost any thing ahead and see the direction of the current leading straight for it. Eddies and slack currents, into which a raft is very liable to swing as it rounds a point with an abrupt turn in the axis of the current, are all great nuisances, for though one may not get into the very heart of any of them, yet the sum total of delay in a day's drift is often considerable, and by a little careful management in steering the raft these troubles may nearly always be avoided. Of course, one is often called upon to choose between these and other impediments, more or less aggravating, so that one's attention is constantly active as the raft drifts along.

In a canal-like stream of uniform width, which gives little chance for eddies or slack water—and the upper Yukon has many long stretches that answer to this description—every thing goes along smoothly enough until along toward evening, when the party wishes to go into camp while the river is tearing along at four or five miles an hour. I defy any one who has never been similarly situated, to have any adequate conception of the way in which a ponderous vessel like our raft, constructed of large logs and loaded with four or five tons of cargo and crew, will bring up against any obstacle while going at this rate. If there are no eddies into which it can be rowed or steered and its progress thereby stopped or at least slackened, it is very hard work indeed to go into camp, for should the raft strike end on, a side log or two may be torn out and the vessel transformed by the shock into a lozenge-shaped affair. Usually, under these circumstances, we would bring the raft close in shore, and with the bow oar hold its head

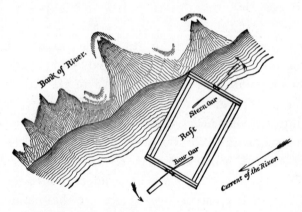

well out into the stream, while with the steering oar the stern end would be thrown against the bank and there held, scraping along as firmly as two or three men could do it (see diagram above), and this frictional brake would be kept up steadily until we slowed down a little, when one or two, or even half-a-dozen persons would jump ashore at a favorable spot, and with a rope complete the slackening until it would warrant our twisting the rope around a tree on the bank and a cross log on the raft, when from both places the long rope would be slowly allowed to pay out under strong and increasing friction, or "snubbing" as logmen call it, and this would bring the craft to a standstill in water so swift as to boil up over the stern logs, whereupon it would receive a series of snug lashings. If the position was not favorable for camping we would slowly "drop" the craft down stream by means of the rope to some better site, never allowing her to proceed at a rate of speed that we could not readily control. If, however, we were unsuccessful in making our chosen camping ground and had drifted below it, there was not sufficient power in our party, nor even in the strongest rope we had, ever to get the craft up stream in the average current, whether by tracking or any other means, to the intended spot.

Good camping places were not to be had in every stretch of the river, and worse than all, they had to be selected a long way ahead in order to be able to make them, with our slow means of navigation, from the middle of the broad river where we usually were.

Oftentimes a most acceptable place would be seen just abreast of it, having until then been concealed by some heavily wooded spur or point, and then of course it would be too late to reach it with our slow craft, while to saunter along near shore, so as to take immediate advantage of such a possible spot, was to sacrifice a good deal of our rapid progress. To run from swift into slacker water could readily be accomplished by simply pointing the craft in the direction one wanted to go, but the reverse process was not so easy, at least by the same method. I suppose the proper way to manage so clumsy a concern as a raft, would be by means of side oars and rowing it end on (and this we did on the lakes in making a camp or in gaining the shore when a head wind set in), but as our two oars at bow and stern were the most convenient for the greater part of the work, we used them entirely, always rowing our bundle of logs broadside on to the point desired, provided that no bars or other obstacles interfered. We generally kept the bow end inclined to the shore that we were trying to reach, a plan that was of service, as I have shown, in passing from swift to slack water, and in a three mile current by using our oars rowing broadside on we could keep at an angle of about thirty degrees from the axis of the stream as we made shoreward in this position. The knowledge of this fact enabled us to make a rough calculation as to the point at which we should touch the bank. The greater or less swiftness of the current would of course vary this angle and our calculations accordingly.

Our bundles of effects on the two corduroy decks made quite high piles fore and aft, and when a good strong wind was blowing—and Alaska in the summer is the land of wind—we had by way of sail power a spread of broadside area that was incapable of being lowered. More frequently than was pleasant the breeze carried us along under "sweepers" or dragged us over bars or drove us down unwelcome channels of slack water. In violent gales we were often actually held against the bank, all movement in advance being effectually checked. A mild wind was always welcome, for in the absence of a breeze when approaching the shore the musquitoes made existence burdensome.

During hot days on the wide open river—singular as it may seem so near the Arctic Circle—the sun would strike down from overhead with a blistering effect and a bronzing effect from its reflection in the dancing waters that made one feel as though he were floating on the Nile, Congo or Amazon, or any where except in the very shadow of the Arctic Circle. Roughly improvised tent flies and flaps helped us to screen ourselves to a limited extent from the tropical torment, but if hung too high, the stern oarsman, who had charge of the "ship," could see nothing ahead on his course, and the curtain would have to come down. No annoyance could seem more singular in the Arctic and sub-Arctic zones than a blistering sun or a swarm of mosquitoes, and yet I believe my greatest discomforts in those regions came from these same causes, certainly from the latter. Several times our thermometer registered but little below 100° Fahrenheit in the shade, and the weather seemed much warmer even than that, owing to the bright reflections that gleamed from the water upon our faces.

"Cut offs" through channels that led straight across were often most deceptive affairs, the swifter currents nearly always swinging around the great bends of the river. Especially bad was a peculiarly seductive "cut-off" with a tempting by swift current as you entered it, caused by its flowing over a shallow bar, whereupon the current would rapidly and almost immediately deepen and would consequently slow down to a rate that was provoking beyond measure, especially as one saw one's self overtaken by piece after piece of drift-timber that by keeping to the main channel had "taken the longest way around as the shortest way home," and beaten us by long odds in the race. And worse than all it was not always possible to avoid getting in these side "sloughs of despond," even when we had learned their tempting little tricks of offering us a swifter current at the entrance, for this very swiftness produced a sort of suction on the surface water that drew in every thing that passed within a distance of the width of its entrance.

Of submerged obstructions, snags were of little account, for the great ponderous craft would go plowing through and casting aside some of the most formidable of them. I doubt very much if snags did us as much harm as benefit, for as they always indicated shoal water, and were easily visible, especially with glasses, they often served us as beacons. I saw very few of the huge snags which have received the appellation of "sawyers" on the Mississippi and Missouri, and are so much dreaded by the navigators of those waters.

Sand, mud and gravel bars were by far the worst obstruction we had to contend with, and I think I have given them in the order of their general perversity in raft navigation, sand being certainly the worst and gravel the slightest.

Sand bars and spits were particularly aggravating, and when the great gridiron of logs ran up on one of them in a swift current there was "fun ahead," to use a western expression of negation. Sometimes the mere jumping overboard of all the crew would lighten the craft so that she would float forward a few yards, and in lucky instances might clear the obstruction ; but this was not often the case, and those who made preparations for hard work were seldom disappointed. In a swift current the running water would sweep out the sand around the logs of the raft until its buoyancy would prevent its sinking any deeper, and out of this rut the great bulky thing would

PRYING THE RAFT OFF A BAR.

have to be lifted before it would budge an inch in a
lateral direction, and when this was accomplished, and,
completely fagged out, we would stop to take a breath
or two, we would often be gratified by seeing our noble
craft sink down again, necessitating a repetition of the
process. The simplest way to get off a sand bar was to
find (by sounding with a stick or simply wading around),
the point nearest to a deep navigable channel and then to
swing the raft, end for end, up stream, even against the
swiftest current that might come boiling over the upper
logs, until that channel was reached. There was no more
happy moment in a day's history than when, after an
hour or so had been spent in prying the vessel inch by
inch against the current, we could finally see the current
catch it on the same side upon which we were working
and perform the last half of our task in a few seconds,
where perhaps we had spent as many hours upon our
portion of the work. At one bad place, on the upper
end of an island, we had to swing our forty-two foot
corvette around four times. Our longest detention by a
sand bar was three hours and fifty minutes.

Mud bars were not nearly so bad, unless the material
was of a clayey consistency, when a little adhesiveness
would be added to the other impediments, and again, as
we always endeavored to keep in the swift water we seldom encountered a mud bar. But when one occurred
near to a camping place, it materially interfered with our
wading ashore with our heavy camping effects on our
backs, and would reduce our rubber boots to a deplora-
ble looking condition. Elsewhere, it was possible to pry
the raft right through a mud bank, by dint of muscle
and patience, and then we could sit down on the outer

logs of the deck and wash our boots in the water at leisure as we floated along.   Our raft drew from twenty to
twenty-two inches of water, and of course it could not
ground in any thing deeper, so that good rubber boots
coming up over the thighs kept our feet comparatively
dry when overboard ; but there were times when we were
compelled to get in almost to our middle ; and when the
water was so swift that it boiled up over their tops and
filled them they were about as useless an article as
can be imagined, so that we went into all such places
barefooted.

The best of all the bars were those of gravel, and the
larger and coarser the pebbles the better. When the
pebbles were well cemented into a firm bed by a binding
of clay almost as solid and unyielding as rock, we could
ask nothing better, and in such cases we always went to
work with cheerful prospects of a speedy release. By
simply lifting the raft with pries the swift current throws
it forward, and since it does not settle as in sand, every
exertion tells.   By turning the raft broadside to the current and prying or "biting" at each end of the "boat"
alternately, with our whole force of pries, leaving the
swift water to throw her forward, we passed over gravel
bars on which I do not think the water was over ten or
eleven inches deep, although the raft drew twice as much.
One of the gravel bars over which we passed in this manner was fully thirty or forty yards in length.

In aggravated cases of whatever nature the load would
have to be taken off, carried on our backs through the
water and placed on the shore, and when the raft was
cleared or freed from the obstruction it would be brought
alongside the bank at the very first favorable spot for

reloading.   Such cases occurred fully a score of times during our voyage.   When the raft stranded on a bar with the water on each side so deep that we could not wade ashore, the canoe was used for "lightering the load," an extremely slow process which, fortunately, we were obliged to employ only once on the whole raft journey, although several times in wading the water came up to our waists before we could get to shore.   In fact, with a heavy load on one's back or shoulders, it is evidently much easier to wade through water of that depth and proportional current than through very swift water over shallow bars.

Looking back, it seems almost miraculous that a raft could make a voyage of over thirteen hundred miles, the most difficult part of which was unknown, starting at the very head where the stream was so narrow that the raft would have been brought at a standstill if it swung out of a straight course end on (as it did in the Payer Rapids), and covering nearly two months of daily encounters with snags and bowlders, sticking on bars and shooting rapids, and yet get through almost unscathed. When I started to build this one on Lake Lindeman I had anticipated constructing two or three of these primitive craft before I could exchange to good and sufficient native or civilized transportation.

The raft is undoubtedly the oldest form of navigation extant, and undoubtedly the worst; it is interesting to know just how useful the raft can be as an auxiliary to geographical exploration, and certainly my raft journey was long enough to test it in this respect.

The raft, of course, can move in one direction only, viz. : with the current, and therefore its use must be restricted to streams whose upper waters can be reached by the explorer. The traveler must be able to escape by the mouth of the stream or by some divergent trail lower down, unless his explorations prove the river to be navigable for such craft as he finds on its lower waters, when he may use these for returning. The building of a raft requires the presence of good, fair-sized timber along the stream. The river too, must offer no falls of any great size. My journey, however, has demonstrated that a well constructed raft can go any where, subject to the above restrictions, that a boat can, at least such a boat as is usually employed by explorers.

I know of nothing that can give an explorer a better opportunity to delineate the topography of the surrounding country with such instruments as are commonly used in assisting dead reckoning, than is afforded by floating down a river. I believe the steady movement with the current makes "dead reckoning" much more exact than with a boat, where the rate of progress is variable, where one hour is spent in drifting as a raft, another in rowing, and a third in sailing with a changeable wind, and where each mode of progress is so abruptly exchanged for another. Any steady pace, such as the walking of a man or a horse, or the floating of a raft carefully kept in the axis of the current, makes dead reckoning so exact, if long practiced, as often to astonish the surveyor himself, but every thing depends upon this steadiness of motion. The errors in dead reckoning of Mr. Homan, my topographer, in running from Pyramid Harbor in Chil kat Inlet to Fort Yukon, both carefully determined by astronomical observations and over a thousand miles apart, was less than one per cent., a fact which proves that rafting as a means of surveying may be ranked with any method that requires walking or riding, and far exceeds any method in use by explorers ascending a stream, as witness any map of the Yukon River that attempts to show the position of Fort Yukon, before it was astronomically determined by Captain Raymond. Meridian observations of the sun for latitude are hard to obtain, for the reader already knows what a task it is to get a raft into camp. This difficulty of course will vary with the size of the raft, for one as large as ours would not always be needed and a small one can be more readily handled in exploration. While rafting, field photography, now so much used by explorers, is very difficult, as it can only be achieved at camping places unless the apparatus is carried ashore in a canoe, if the raftsmen have one ; and the ease with which separated persons can lose each other along a river full of islands makes this kind of work a little uncertain, and the services of a good artist more valuable.

This summary covers nearly all the main points that are strictly connected with geographical exploration, in the meaning ordinarily accepted ; but on expeditions where this exploration is the main object there are often other matters of a scientific nature to be taken into account, such as the geology, botany, and zoölogy of the districts traversed, to which the question of geographical distribution is important, and for all these objects researches by means of a raft are at considerable disadvantage.

Also in rafting there is a slight tendency to over-estimate the length of the stream, although the map may be perfectly accurate. In the figure on page 152, the axis

AA' is undoubtedly the accepted line on which to estimate and measure the length of the stream between those
two points, and it is equally evident to one familiar with
the currents of a river that some such line as RR' would
represent the course of a floating raft, and the excess of
RR' over AA', both being developed, would be the error
mentioned. In this figure the relative curves are exaggerated to show the principle more clearly. Again, every
island and shoal would materially affect this somewhat

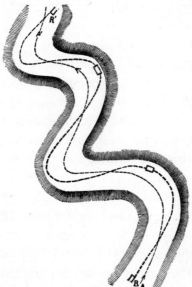

mathematical plan, but I
think even these would
tend to produce an over-
estimate.

Drifting close along the
shores of an island, and
nearing its lower termination, we occasionally were
delayed in a singular manner, unless prompt to
avoid it. A long, nar-
row island, with tapering
ends, and lying directly
in the course of the cur-
rent, gave us no trouble ;
but oftentimes these
lower ends were very blunt, and the currents at the
two sides came at all angles with respect to the
island and each other, and this was especially true of
large groupings of islands situated in abrupt bends of
the river. To take about the worst case of this nature
that we met, imagine a blunted island with the current
at either side coming in at an angle of about forty-five

degrees to the shore line, or at right angles to each other, as I have tried to show in figure on this page, the arrows showing the current. At some point below the island the recurving and ex-curving waters neutralize each other in a huge whirlpool (W). Between W and the island the waters, if swift, would pour back in strong, dancing waves like tide-rips, and in some places with such force as to cut a channel (C) into the island. It is

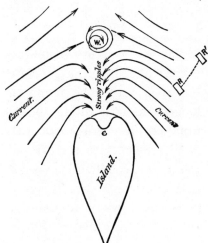

evident that with the raft at R, it is necessary to row to starboard as far as R′ before W is reached, as otherwise it would be carried back against the island. We got caught in one violent whirlpool that turned the huge raft around ˙so rapidly that I believe the tender stomachs of those prone to sea-sickness would soon have weakened if we had not escaped by vigorous efforts. At great angles of the swift water and broad-based islands I have seen the whirlpool when nearly half a mile from the island, and they were usually visible for three or four hundred yards if worth noticing. So many conditions were required for the creation of these obstacles that they were not common.

CHAPTER VII.

THE GRAND CAÑON OF THE YUKON.

GRAYLING.

WE slowly floated out of Lake Marsh it was known to us by Indian reports that somewhere not far ahead on the course of the river would be found the longest and most formidable rapid on the entire length of the great stream. At these rapids the Indians confidently expected that our raft would go to pieces, and we were therefore extremely anxious to inspect them. By some form of improper interpretation, or in some other way, we got the idea into our heads that these rapids, "rushing," as the natives described them, "through a dark cañon," would be reached very soon, that is, within two or three miles, or four or five at the furthest. Accordingly I had the raft beached at the river's entrance, and undertook, with the doctor, the task of walking on ahead along the river bank to inspect them before making any further forward movement, after which one or both of us might return. After a short distance I continued the journey alone, the doctor returning to start the raft. I hoped to be at the upper end of the rapids by the time she came in sight so as to signal her in ample time for her to reach the bank from the swiftest current in the center, as the river was now five or six hundred yards wide in places. It turned out afterward that the great rapids were more than fifty miles further on.

I now observed that this new stretch of river much more closely resembled some of the streams in temperate climes than any we had yet encountered. Its flanking hillsides of rolling ground were covered with spruce and pine, here and there breaking into pleasant-looking grassy prairies, while its own picturesque valley was densely wooded with poplar and willows of several varieties. These latter, in fact, encroached so closely upon the water's edge, and in such impenetrable confusion, that camping places were hard to find, unless a friendly spur from the hills, covered with evergreens, under which a little elbow room might be had, wedged its way down to the river, so as to break the continuity of these willowy barriers to a night's good camping place. The raft's corduroy deck of pine poles often served for a rough night's lodging to some of the party.

Muskrats were plentiful in this part of the river, and I could hear them "plumping" into the water from the banks, every minute or two, as I walked along them ; and afterward, in the quiet evenings, these animals might at once be traced by the wedge-shaped ripples they made on the surface of the water as they swam around us.

I had not walked more than two or three miles, fighting great swarms of mosquitoes all the way, when I came to a peculiar kind of creek distinctive of this portion of the river, and worth describing. It was not very wide, but altogether too wide to jump, with slopes of slippery clay, and so deep that I could not see bottom nor touch it with any pole that I could find. These singular streams have a current seemingly as slow as that of a glacier, and the one that stopped me—and I suppose all the rest—had the same unvarying canal-like width for over half a mile from its mouth. Beyond this distance I dared not prolong my rambles to find a crossing place for fear the raft might pass me on the river, so I returned to its mouth and waited, fighting mosquitoes, for the raft to come along, when the canoe would pick me up. In my walks along the creek I found many moose and caribou tracks, some of them looking large enough to belong to prize cattle, but all of them were old. Probably they had been made before the mosquitoes became so numerous.

The first traveler along the river was one of our old Tahk-heesh friends, who came down the stream paddling his "cottonwood" canoe with his family, a squaw and three children, wedged in the bottom. He partially comprehended my situation, and I tried hard to make him understand by signs that I wanted simply to cross the canal-like creek in his canoe, while he, evidently remembering a number of trifles he had received from members of the party at a few camps back, thought it incumbent upon him to take me a short way down the river, by way of a *quid pro quo*, to which I did not object, especially after seeing several more of those wide slack-water tributaries, and as I still supposed that the rapids were but a short distance ahead, and that my Indian guide expected to camp near them. The rain was falling in a persistent drizzle, which, coupled with my cramped position in the rickety canoe, made me feel any thing but comfortable.   My Indian patron, a good natured looking old fellow of about fifty, was evidently feeling worried and harassed at not meeting other Indians of his tribe—for he had previously promised me that he would have a number of them at the rapids to portage my effects around it if my raft went to pieces in shooting them, as they were all confident it would, or if I determined to build another forthwith at a point below the dangerous portion of the rapids—and he ceased the not unmusical strokes of his paddle every minute or two in order to scan with a keen eye the river banks or the hillsides beyond, or to listen for signals in reply to the prolonged shouts he occasionally emitted from his vigorous lungs.   After a voyage of three or four miles, he became discouraged, and diving down into a mass of dirty rags and strong-scented Indian bric-a brac of all sorts in the bottom of the canoe, he fished out an old brass-mounted Hudson Bay Company flintlock horse-pistol, an object occasionally found in the possession of a well-to-do Yukon River savage.   He took out the bullet, which he did not desire to lose, and held it in his teeth, and pointing the unstable weapon most uncomfortably close to my head, pulled the trigger, although from all I have seen of these weapons of destruction (to powder) I imagine the butt end of the pistol was the most dangerous.   The report resounded through the hills and valleys with a thundering vibration, as if the weapon had been a small cannon, but awakened no reply of any kind, and as it was getting well along into the evening my "Stick" friend pointed his canoe for an old camping place on the east bank of the river (although the boat was so warped and its nose so broken that one might almost have testified to its pointing in any other direction), and with a few strokes of his paddle he was soon on shore. Thereupon I went into the simplest camp I had ever occupied, for all that was done was to pull an old piece of riddled canvas over a leaning pole and crawl under it and imagine that it kept out the rain, which it did about as effectually as if it had been a huge crochet tidy. My companions, however, did not seem to mind the rain very much, their only apparent objection to it being that it prevented their kindling a fire with their usual apparatus of steel and damp tinder ; and when I gave them a couple of matches they were so profuse in their thanks and their gratitude seemed so genuine, that I gave them all I had with me, probably a couple of dozen, when they overwhelmed me with their grateful appreciation, until I was glad to change the subject to a passing muskrat and a few ducks that were swimming by. I could not help contrasting their behavior with that of the more arrogant Chilkats. They seemed much more like Eskimo in their rude hospitality and docility of nature, although I doubt if they equal them in personal bravery.

There is certainly one good thing about a rain-storm in Alaska, however, and that is the repulsion that exists between a moving drop of rain and a comparatively stationary mosquito when the two come in contact, and which beats down the latter with a most comforting degree of pertinacity. Mosquitoes evidently know how to protect themselves from the pelting rain under the broad deciduous leaves, or under the lee of trees and branches, for the instant it ceases they are all out, apparently more voracious than ever. All along this bank near the Indians' camp, the dense willow brake crawled up and leaned over the water, and I feared there was no camping place to be found for my approaching party, until after walking back about half a mile I espied a place where a little spur of spruce-clad hillocks infringed on the shore. Here I halted the raft and we made an uncomfortable camp. Fish of some kind kept jumping in the river, but the most seductive "flies" were unrewarded with a single bite, although the weather was not of the kind to tempt one either to hunt or fish.

The next day, the 30th of June, was but little better as far as the weather was concerned, and we got away late from our camp, having overslept ourselves. Our Tahkheesh friend, with his family, now preceded us in his canoe for the purpose of indicating the rapids in good season; but of course he disappeared ahead of us around every bend and island, so as to keep us feeling more anxious about it. At one time, about eight o'clock in the evening—our Tahkheesh guide out of sight for the last half hour—we plainly heard a dull roaring ahead of us as we swung around a high broken clay bluff, and were clearly conscious of the fact that we were shooting forward at a more rapid pace. Thinking that discretion was the better part of valor, the raft was rapidly swung inshore with a bump that almost upset the whole crew, and a prospecting party were sent down stream to walk along the bank until they found out the cause of the sound, a plan which very soon revealed that there were noisy, shallow rapids extending a short distance out into the bend of the river, but they were not serious enough to have stopped us; at least they would have been of no consequence if we had not landed in the first place, but, as matters stood, they were directly in front of our position on the shore, and so swift was the current that we could not get out fast enough into the stream with our two oars to avoid sticking on the rough bar of gravel and bowlders. Shortly after the crew had jumped off, and just as they were preparing to pry the raft around into the deeper water of the stream, the most violent splashing and floundering was heard on the outer side of the craft, and it was soon found that a goodly-sized and beautifully-spotted grayling had hooked himself to a fish-line that some one had allowed to trail over the outer logs in the excitement of attending to the more important duties connected with the supposed rapids. He was rapidly taken from the hook, and when the line was again thrown over into the ripples another immediately repeated the operation, and it soon became evident that we were getting into the very best of fishing waters, the first we had discovered of that character on the river. After the raft was swung clear of the outer bowlders of the reef and had started once more on its way down stream, several lines, poles and flies were gotten out, and it was quite entertaining to see the long casts that were attempted as we rushed by distant ripples near the curve of the banks. More than one of these casts, however, proved successful in landing a fine grayling. A jump and a splash and a miss, and there was no more chance at that ripple for the same fish, for by the time a recover and a cast could be made the raft was nearly alongside of another tempting place, so swift was the river and so numerous the clean

gravel bars jutting into it at every bend. Many a pretty
grayling would come sailing through the air like a flying squirrel and unhooking himself *en route*, with a
quick splash would disappear through the logs of the
raft, with no other injury than a good bump of his nose
against the rough bark, and no doubt ready to thank his
stars that his captors were not on land. Passing over
shallow bottoms covered with white pebbles, especially
those shoaling down stream from the little bars of which
I have spoken, a quick eye could often detect great
numbers of fish, evidently grayling, with their heads
up stream and propelling their tails just enough to
remain over the same spot on the bottom, in the swift
current. That evening we camped very late—about 10
P. M.—having hopes to the last that we might reach the
upper end of the Grand Canon. Our Stick guide had
told us that when we saw the mouth of a small stream
coming in from the west and spreading out in a mass of
foam over the rocks at the point of confluence, we could
be sure of finding the great canon within half a mile. An
accurate census of small creeks answering exactly to
that description having been taken, gave a total of about
two dozen, with another still in view ahead of us as we
camped. Knowing the *penchant* of our fishy friends
for half-submerged gravel bars, our camp was picked
with reference to them, and near it there were two of
such bars running out into the stream. Some fifty or
sixty grayling were harvested by the three lines that
were kept going until about eleven o'clock, by which
time it was too dark to fish with any comfort, for the
heavy banked clouds in the sky brought on darkness
much earlier than usual. Red and white mixed flies

were eagerly snapped by the voracious and active creatures, and as the evening shadows deepened, a resort to more white in the mixture kept up the exhilarating sport until it was too dark for the fisherman to see his fly on the water. The grayling caught that evening seemed to be of two very distinct sizes, without any great number of intermediate sizes, the larger averaging about a pound in weight, the smaller about one-fourth as much. So numerous and voracious were they that two or three flies were kept on one line, and two at a cast were several times caught, and triplets once.

On the morning of July 1st, we approached the great rapids of the Grand Cañon of the Yukon. Just as I had expected, our Tahkheesh guide in his cottonwood canoe was *non est*, until we were within sight of the upper end of the cañon and its boiling waters, and tearing along at six or seven miles an hour, when we caught sight of him frantically gesticulating to us that the rapids were in sight, which was plainly evident, even to us. He probably thought that our ponderous raft was as manageable in the seething current as his own light craft, or he never would have allowed us to get so near. In the twinkling of an eye we got ashore the first line that came to hand, and there was barely time to make both ends fast, one on the raft and the other to a convenient tree on the bank, before the spinning raft came suddenly to the end of her tether with a snappish twang that made the little rope sing like a musical string. Why that little quarter-inch manilla did not part seems a mystery, even yet,—it was a mere government flagstaff lanyard that we had brought along for packing purposes, etc.—but it held on as if it knew the importance of its task, and with the swift

VIEW IN GRAND CAÑON FROM ITS SOUTHERN ENTRANCE.

The only cañon on the Yukon, 1870 miles from Aphoon mouth.

water pouring in a sheet of foam over the stern of the shackled raft, she slowly swung into an eddy under the lee of a gravel bar where she was soon securely fastened, whereupon we prepared to make an inspection of our chief impediment. A laborious survey of three or four hours' duration, exposed to heat and mosquitoes, revealed that the rapids were about five miles long and in appearance formidable enough to repel any one who might contemplate making the passage even in a good boat, while such an attempt seemed out of the question with an unmanageable raft like ours.

The Yukon River, which had previously been about three hundred or three hundred and fifty yards in width, gradually contracts as it nears the upper gate of the cañon and at the point where the stream enters it in a high white-capped wave of rolling water, I do not believe its width exceeds one-tenth of that distance. The walls of the cañon are perpendicular columns of basalt, not unlike a diminutive Fingal's cave in appearance, and nearly a mile in length, the center of this mile stretch being broken into a huge basin of about twice the usual width of the stream in the cañon, and which is full of seething whirlpools and eddies where nothing but a fish could live for a minute. On the western rim of this basin it seems as though one might descend to the water's edge with a little Alpine work. Through this narrow chute of corrugated rock the wild waters of the great river rush in a perfect mass of milk-like foam, with a reverberation that is audible for a considerable distance, the roar being intensified by the rocky walls which act like so many sounding boards. Huge spruce trees in somber files overshadow the dark cañon, and it resembles a deep black thoroughfare paved with the whitest of marble.   At the northern outlet of the cañon, the rushing river spreads rapidly into its former width, but abates not a jot of its swiftness, and flows in a white and shallow sheet over reefs of bowlders and bars thickly studded with intertwining drifts of huge timber, ten times more dangerous for a boat or raft than the narrow cañon itself, although perhaps not so in appearance. This state of things continues for about four miles further, offering every possible variety of obstacle in turn, when the river again contracts, hemmed in by low basaltic banks, and becomes even narrower than before. So swift is it, so great the volume of water, and so contracted the channel, that half its water ascends the sloping banks, runs over them for nearly a score of yards, and then falls into the narrow chute below, making a veritable horseshoe funnel of boiling cascades, not much wider than the length of our raft, and as high at the end as her mast.   Through this funnel of foam the waves ran three or four feet high, and this fact, added to the boiling that often forced up columns of water like small geysers quite a considerable distance into the air, made matters very uninviting for navigation in any sort of craft.

Every thing being in readiness, our inspection made, and our resolution formed, in the forenoon of the second of July, we prepared to "shoot" the raft though the rapids of the grand cañon, and at 11:25 the bow and stern lines were cast loose and after a few minutes' hard work at shoving the craft out of the little eddy where she lay, the poor vessel resisting as if she knew all that was ahead of her and was loth to go, she finally swung

clear of the point and like a racer at the start made
almost a leap forward and the die was cast. A moment's
hesitation at the cañon's brink, and quick as a flash the
whirling craft plunged into the foam, and before twenty
yards were made had collided with the western wall of
columnar rock with a shock as loud as a blast, tearing
off the inner side log and throwing the outer one far into
the stream. The raft swung around this as upon a hinge,
just as if it had been a straw in a gale of wind, and
again resumed its rapid career. In the whirlpool basin
of the cañon the craft, for a brief second or two, seemed
actually buried out of sight in the foam. Had there
been a dozen giants on board they could have had no
more influence in directing her course than as many
spiders. It was a very simple matter to trust the rude
vessel entirely to fate, and work out its own salvation.
I was most afraid of the four miles of shallow rapids
below after the cañon, but she only received a dozen or a
score of smart bumps that started a log here and there, but
tore none from the structure, and nothing remained ahead
of her but the cascades. These reached, in a few minutes
the craft was caught at the bow by the first high wave in the
funnel-like chute and lifted into the air until it stood
almost at an angle of thirty degrees, when it went through
the cascades like a charge of fixed bayonets, and almost
as swiftly as a flash of light, burying its nose in the foam
beyond as it subsided. Those on board of the raft now
got hold of a line from their friends on shore, and after
breaking it several times they finally brought the craft
alongside the bank and commenced repairing the damage with a light heart, for our greatest obstacle was now
at our backs.

Near the spot where we camped, just below the cascades that terminated the long rapids, was found a small grove of sapling spruce through which the fire had swept a year or two before, and the trees were thoroughly seasoned and sound, the black burned bark peeling as freely from them as the hull of a chestnut, leaving excellent light and tough poles with which we renewed our two decks, our constant walking over the old ones having converted them into somewhat unsatisfactory places for promenades unless one carefully watched his footsteps. Evidences of conflagration in the dense coniferous forests were everywhere frequent, the fires arising from the carelessness of the Indian campers, and from the making of signal smokes, and even it is said, from design, with the idea of clearing the district of mosquitoes. While waiting at the cascades of the rapids to repair our raft, our fishing tackle was kept busy to such an extent that we landed between four and five hundred fine grayling, a fishing ground that excelled any we afterward found on the Yukon River.

Our favorite fishing place was just below the cascades, where a number of the disintegrating columns of basalt had fallen in, forming a talus along which we could walk between the water and the wall. A little beyond the wall itself sloped down and ran close beside the little ripples where we were always sure of a "rise" when the grayling would bite. This was nearly always in the cool of the mornings or evenings, or in the middle of the day when even a few light fleecy clouds floated over the sun. Yet there were times when they would cease biting as suddenly as if they were disciplined and under orders, and that without any apparent reason, returning to the

bait just as suddenly and as mysteriously. Light
northern winds brought fine sunny weather, and with it
a perfect deluge of light brown millers or moths migrat-
ing southward, thousands of which tumbled in the
waters of the river and filled every eddy with their floating bodies. These kept the grayling busy snapping at

THE CASCADES AT THE END OF THE GREAT RAPIDS.
Head of Navigation on the Yukon, 1866 miles from Aphoon mouth.

them, and indicated to a certain degree when to go fishing,
but still it was remarkable that our efforts should be so
well rewarded when there were so many living, struggling
bait to tempt them away from our flies. Strangest of all
we were most successful when casting with brown flies.
The millers caught by the water and drifted into eddies
would not be touched, and it was only when a solitary
moth came floating along beating its wings and fluttering

on the surface around the swiftest corners that a spring
for it was at all certain, and even then a brown hackle
dancing around in the same place would monopolize
every rise within the radius of a fish's eyesight. Our
Tahk-heesh friends, who had been made useful by us in
several ways, such as carrying effects over the portage,
helping with poles and logs, and so on, were as much
surprised at this novel mode of fishing as the grayling
themselves, and expressed their astonishment, in guttural
grunts. They regarded themselves as admitted to high
favor when we gave them a few of the flies as presents.
They ate all the spare grayling we chose to give them,
which was often nearly a dozen apiece, and, in fact, during the three or four days we were together their subsistence was almost altogether derived from this source, as
we had no provisions to spare them. The largest grayling we caught weighed two pounds and a quarter, but
we had the same invariable two sizes already mentioned,
with here and there a slight deviation in grade. These
grayling were the most persistent biters I ever saw rise
to a fly, and more uncertain than these uncertain fish
usually are in grasping for a bait, for there were times
when I really believe we got fifty or sixty rises from a
single fish before he was hooked or the contest abandoned.

The portage made by the Indians around the cañon
and rapids was over quite a high ridge just the length of
the cañon, and then descended abruptly with a dizzy
incline into a valley which, after continuing nearly down
to the cascades, again ascended a sandy hill that was
very difficult to climb. The hilly part around the cañon
was pretty thoroughly covered with small pines and

spruce, and all along the portage trail some miners who had been over it had cut these down near the path and felled them across it, and had then barked them on their upper sides, forming stationary skids along which they could drag their whip-sawed boats. Two large logs placed together on the steep declivity, and well trimmed of their limbs and bark, made good inclines on which the boat or boats could be lowered into the valley below. Here they had floated their boats by towlines down to the cascades, around which point they had again dragged them. It may readily be imagined that such a chapparal of felled brush and poles across our path did not improve the walking in the least. It was a continued case of hurdle walking the whole distance. The day we walked over the trail on the eastern side of the cañon and rapids was one of the hottest and most insufferable I ever experienced, and every time we sat down it was only to have "a regular down-east fog" of mosquitoes come buzzing around, and the steady swaying of arms and the constant slapping of the face was an exercise fully as vigorous as that of traveling. Our only safe plan was to walk along brandishing a great handful of evergreens from shoulder to shoulder. As we advanced the mosquitoes invariably kept the same distance ahead, as if they had not the remotest idea we were coming toward them. An occasional vicious reach forward through the mass with the evergreens would have about as much effect in removing them as it would in dispersing the same amount of fog, for it seemed as if they could dodge a streak of lightning. Nothing was better than a good strong wind in one's face, and as one emerged from the brush or timber it was simply delicious to feel the cool breeze on one's peppered face and to see the rascals disappear. Our backs, however, were even then spotted with them, still crawling along and testing every thread in one's coat to see if they could not find a thin hole where they might bore through. Once in the breeze, it was comical to turn around slowly and see their efforts to keep under the lee of one's hunting shirt, as one by one they lose their hold and are wafted away in the wind. If these pests had been almost unbearable before, they now became simply fiendish while we were repairing our raft; nothing could be done unless a wind was blowing or unless we stood in a smoke from the resinous pine or spruce so thick that the eyes remained in an acute state of inflammation. Mosquito netting over the hat was not an infallible remedy and was greatly in the way when at work.

A fair wind one day made me think it possible to take a hunt inland, but, to my disgust, it died down after I had proceeded two or three miles, and my fight back to camp with the mosquitoes I shall always remember as one of the salient points of my life. It seemed as if there was an upward rain of insects from the grass that became a deluge over marshy tracts, and more than half the ground was marshy. Of course not a sign of any game was seen except a few old tracks; and the tracks of an animal are about the only part of it that could exist here in the mosquito season, which lasts from the time the snow is half off the ground until the first severe frost, a period of some three or four months. During that time every living creature that can leave the valleys ascends the mountains, closely following the snow line, and even there peace is not completely attained, the exposure to the winds being of far more benefit than the coolness due to the altitude, while the mosquitoes are left undisputed masters of the valleys, except for a few straggling animals on their way from one range of mountains to the other. Had there been any game, and had I obtained a fair shot, I honestly doubt if I could have secured it owing to these pests, not altogether on account of their ravenous attacks upon my face, and especially the eyes, but for the reason that they were absolutely so dense that it was impossible to see clearly through the mass in taking aim. When I got back to camp I was thoroughly exhausted with my incessant fight and completely out of breath, which I had to regain as best I could in a stifling smoke from dry resinous pine knots. A traveler who had spent a summer on the Lower Yukon, where I did not find the pests so bad on my journey as on the upper river, was of opinion that a nervous person without a mask would soon be killed by nervous prostration, unless he were to take refuge in mid-stream. I know that the native dogs are killed by the mosquitoes under certain circumstances, and I heard reports, which I believe to be well founded, both from Indians and trustworthy white persons, that the great brown bear—erroneously but commonly called the grizzly—of these regions is at times compelled to succumb to these insects. The statement seems almost preposterous, but the explanation is com- paratively simple. Bruin having exhausted all the roots and berries on one mountain, or finding them scarce, thinks he will cross the valley to another range, or per- haps it is the odor of salmon washed up along the river's banks that attracts him. Covered with a heavy fur on his body, his eyes, nose and ears are the vulnerable points for mosquitoes, and here of course they congregate in the greatest numbers. At last when he reaches a swampy stretch they rise in myriads until his forepaws are kept so busy as he strives to keep his eyes

ALASKA BROWN BEAR FIGHTING MOSQUITOES.

clear of them that he can not walk, whereupon he becomes enraged, and bear-like, rises on his haunches to fight. It is now a mere question of time until the bear's eyes become so swollen from innumerable bites as to render him perfectly blind, when he wanders helplessly about until he gets mired in the marsh, and so starves to death.

CHAPTER VIII.

DOWN THE RIVER TO SELKIRK.

IN THE RINK RAPIDS.

NE evening about eight o'clock, while encamped below the cascades, we could hear dull, heavy concussions occurring at intervals of two or three minutes. The sound did not at all resemble that of distant thunder, and moreover, the sky was cloudless. Earthquakes were suggested, but the theory did not seem plausible, and we were compelled to attribute it to the cascades, which, I believe, have been known to cause earth tremblings and analogous phenomena.

I noticed that a Tahk-heesh Indian in arranging his head and breast bands for a load to be carried on his back, adjusted them as follows: The breast-band was grasped in the center by the palm of the hand, and when pulled out taut if the elbow of the packer just touched the load,—box, bag or bundle,—it was considered to be in proper condition to carry. The breast band adjusted, the head band is also pulled out, and between the two there must be the width of the packer's hand; the head-band, which is not always used, being the longer. I had hitherto noticed this manner of arranging the load when among my Chilkat packers; the most singular feature of it being that the breast band passes over the arms so as to pinion them to the sides, making them apparently useless when the most needed.

CLAY BLUFFS ON THE UPPER YUKON.

On the 5th of July we again got under way on our raft. For the first few miles, eight or ten, the river is very swift and occasionally breaks into light rapids, although I believe a powerful light-draft river steamer, such as are used on the shallow western rivers, could easily surmount all the bad places we saw below the cascades of the great rapids. If I am right in my conjectures upon this point, the Yukon River is navigable for 1866 miles from the Aphoon or northernmost mouth of its delta.

Shortly after noon we passed the mouth of the Tahk-heen'-a or Tahk River coming in from the west, which is about two-thirds the size of the Yukon. By following it to its head, where the Indians say is a large lake, the traveler arrives at the Chilkat portage, the relation of which with the Chilkoot trail has already been noticed. From this point on my Chilkat guide, Indianne, was much more familiar with the country, having been over the Chilkat trail many times, and over the Chilkoot portage but once when a small boy. From the cascades to the Tahk River, a distance of nearly twenty-five miles, the banks of the Yukon are quite high and often broken into perpendicular bluffs of white clay, whose rolling crescent-shaped crowns were densely covered with pine and spruce. While the Tahk-heen'-a is the smaller stream, its bed and valley apparently determine the general characteristics of the river beyond its confluence, the high bold bluffs of clay just mentioned being from this point succeeded by lower shores wooded to the water's edge.

The Tahk-heen'-a, like all streams not interspersed with lakes on its upper course, carries quite muddy water, and we all felt a little uneasy about our fine grayling fisheries, a foreboding well founded, for they diminished with an exasperating suddenness, our evenings seldom being rewarded with more than two or three.

The last of the chain of lakes was reached the same day at 5 p. m., and we were prevented from taking advantage of a good wind by a three hours' detention on a sand-bar that stretched almost entirely across the river's mouth. This bar had a deep channel on either side of it, and when our most strenuous efforts completely failed to get the raft off, there was nothing to be done but to put the load ashore, and as wading was impossible, the cottonwood canoe was brought into action, slow as the method was. Not having been used much lately its condition was unknown, and as soon as we launched it, the water came pouring in from a dozen cracks where the gum had scaled off. One very vicious looking hole was suddenly developed in the bow as the first load went ashore, and "Billy" undertook to overcome this difficulty by putting most of the load in the stern, taking his own place there so as to allow the bow to stand well out of the water. With every load the leak grew worse, and about the fourth or fifth trip there was a most desperate struggle between the canoeman and the leak to see which would conquer before they reached the shore, the result being a partial victory for both, the canoe's head going under water just as it reached the shore, upon which there was a hurried scramble to unload it without damage.

This lake was called by the Indians Kluk-tas'-si ; and, as it was one of the very few pronounceable names of Indian derivation in this section of the country, I retained it, although it is possible that this may be the Lake Labarge of some books, the fact that it is the first lake above the site of old Fort Selkirk being the only geographical datum in its favor, while all its other relations to equal points of importance are opposed to the theory. In fact, it had evidently been mapped by the merest guesswork from vague Indian reports.

I hope I shall be excused for again reviving the subject of conjectural geography, so uncertain in its results and

so prevalent in Alaskan charts, especially those relating
to the interior, even when they are of an official character. If the self-satisfaction of these parlor map-makers
has been gratified in following unknown rivers and
mountains wherever their fancy and imagination led
them, and no other harm resulted, one conversant with
the facts might dismiss the manifold errors that occur
in their charts with a contemptuous smile at the method
pursued. But that harm of the most serious nature can
result from these geographical conjectures is evident
from the following true story told me by the person in-
terested. A party of miners had crossed the Chilkoot
trail and were on a " prospecting tour " down the river
and lakes. Discouraged at the outlook as to finding
gold or silver in paying quantities, there was considerable diversity of opinion in regard to the propriety of
any further advance in such a wild unexplored country,
the majority advocating a return. Among their number
was a young lawyer, a graduate of an eastern college, I
believe, who had joined the party in the hope of finding
adventures and of repairing his health, which had suffered
from too close an application to his professional studies.
Having in his possession an official government chart
which pretended to map the route over which he had
come as well as that ahead of him, although he had received proof of its untrustworthiness in the past, he resolved to trust it once more. Numerous Indian villages
and towns were shown upon the chart at convenient intervals along the remainder of the route. He thought
the villages might not be just where they were marked,
but believed that in the main their number and positions
were at least approximately correct. Basing his expect-

ations on the help to be obtained from these numerous Indian villages, he announced to the party his determination to continue his travels, whatever might be the
conclusion to which the others should come, pointing out
the hospitality which they had received from the Indians
they had previously met, and expressing his expectation
of meeting many others as friendly. Whether his reasoning influenced them or not I have forgotten, and it
matters but little, but at any rate the party gave up the
idea of returning and continued on drifting down the river
and prospecting wherever the conditions seemed favorable, until old Fort Selkirk was reached, when they ascended the Pelly, upon the bars of which stream the prospect of finding gold was greatest. During all this long
journey not a single Indian was seen by the party, and
only one deserted house, with an occasional peeled spruce
pole at long intervals that marked the temporary camps
of the few wandering natives. Young C—— took the
jokes of his companions upon his chart and its Indian
towns good-naturedly enough, and the map was nailed
to a big spruce tree and used for a target for rifle practice, but he often spoke to me in a far different strain as
he recounted the chances of his taking the journey alone
aided solely by this worthless map. In fact there is not
an official or government map of Alaska, that, taken as
a whole, is worth the ink with which it is printed. Limited explorations and surveys in this vast territory, such
as those of Captain Raymond on the Yukon, Lieutenant,
Ray on the Arctic Coast, Lieutenant Stoney on the Put-
nam river, and many others, are undoubtedly excellent,
second to none in the world made under similar circumstances, and confined strictly to the country actually

traversed by each, with broken line delineations in surrounding districts, indicating conjectures; but as soon as
these or such portions of them as the Washington com-
piler may see fit to take, are dumped into a great map of
Alaska, they are so mixed with conjectural topography
and map work that one must know the history of
Alaskan exploration about as well as the history of his
own life to be able to discriminate between the good and
the worthless.

Like Lake Marsh, Kluk-tas-si is full of mudbanks
along its shores; its issuing waters being clear as a
mountain stream, while its incoming tributaries are
loaded with earthy deposits. So full of these is Kluk-
tas-si, and so much more contracted is the waterway
through them, that we thought we could detect a slight
current when making our way along in the blue water.
This was especially noticeable when the wind died down
to a calm. In spite of all this, Kluk-tas-si offered fewer
difficulties in the way of making landings than Lake
Marsh. It seemed to me that but a brief geological
period must elapse before these lakes are filled with
deposits, their new shores covered with timber, and
their beds contracted to the dimensions of the river.
Such ancient lakes appear to occur in the course of the
stream further on.

We started at seven in the morning and were occupied
until eight in rowing and sailing through the tortuous
channel which led to blue water in the deep portion of
the lake. To keep this channel readily we sent the
Indians ahead in the canoe, who sounded with their
long paddles, and by signals indicated the deepest parts.
In spite of their exertions we stuck a couple of times,

and had to lower sail and jump overboard. The wind kept slowly increasing and by the time we set the full spread of our sail in bold water, we were forging along at such a rate that we put out a trolling spoon, but nothing was caught, the huge craft probably frightening every thing away. The wind died down and sprang up again several times during the day, but every time it arose it was in our favor. That evening by the time we reached Camp 21, on the eastern shore of the lake, we had scored about thirteen miles, a very good reckoning for lake travel any time.

The west bank of this lake is very picturesque about fourteen or fifteen miles from its southern entrance, large towers and bastion-like projections of red rock upheaving their huge flanks upon what seems to be a well-marked island, but which is in reality a part of the mainland, as our Indians assured us. According to the same authorities a river comes in here at this point, having shores of the same formation, and called by them the Red River. The frequency of this name in American geographical nomenclature was to me sufficient reason for abandoning it ; and I gave the name of Richthofen to the rocks and river (the latter, however, not having been seen by us), after Freiherr von Richthofen of Leipsic, well known in geographical science. The next evening was a still and beautiful one, with the lake's surface like a mirror, and the reflection of the red rocks in the quiet water made the most striking scene on our trip ; two warm pictures of rosy red in the sinking sun joined base to base by a thread of silver, at the edge of the other shore. The eastern shores of the lake seem to be formed of high rounded hills of light gray limestone,

picturesquely striped with the foliage of the dark evergreen growing in the ravines. From the lake the contrast was very pretty, and showed a regularity that
scarcely seemed the work of nature. I named them
the Hancock Hills after General Hancock of the army.
A number of salmon-trout were caught in this lake (the
first one was caught in Lake Nares), the largest of which
weighed over eight pounds, that being the limit of the
pocket scales of the doctor. Saturday the 7th gave us
the most conflicting winds, and although we were upon
the waters of Kluk-tas-si, for twelve hours we made but
nine miles, a head wind driving us into Camp 22.

We did not allow the 8th to tempt us on the lake so
readily, and the day was employed in taking astronomical observations, arranging our photographic apparatus
and similar work, until early afternoon. At 1.30 P.M.
a favorable breeze from the south sprang up, and by 2
o'clock was raging in a gale, blowing over the tent where
we were eating our midday meal, filling the coffee and
eatables with sand and gravel, and causing a general
scampering and chasing after the lighter articles of our
equipment, which took flight in the furious wind. Most
exasperating of all, it quickly determined us to break
camp, and in less than half an hour we had all of our
effects stored on the vessel, and were pulling off the
beach, when just as our sail was spread the wind died
down to a zephyr hardly sufficient to keep away the
mosquitoes. At 7 o'clock the lake was as quiet as can
be imagined, and after remaining almost motionless for
another hour we pulled into the steep bank, made our
beds on the slanting declivity at a place where it was
impossible to pitch a tent, and went to sleep only to be

awakened at night by showers of rain falling upon our upturned faces. We congratulated ourselves that we were in a place where the drainage was good.

In the shallow water near the shores of Lake Kluktassi, especially where a little bar of pretty white sand put out into the banks of glacier mud, one could always find innumerable shoals of small graylings not over an

OUTLET OF LAKE KLUKTASSI.
Terminal Butte of the Hancock Hills (on the right).

inch in length, and our Indians immediately improvised a mosquito bar into a fish net, catching hundreds of the little fellows, which were used so successfully as bait with the larger fish of the lake that we finally thought the end justified the means.

Instead of dying down as we spread sail early in the morning of the 9th, the wind actually freshened, upsetting all our prognostications, and sending us along at a rate that

allowed us to enter the river early in the forenoon, and
I doubt if the besiegers of a fortress ever saw its flag go
down with more satisfaction than we saw the rude wall-
tent sail come down forever, and left behind us the most
tedious and uncertain method of navigation an explorer
was ever called upon to attempt—a clumsy raft on a
motionless lake, at the sport of variable winds. Our
joy was somewhat dampened at sticking several times on
the bars, one of which delayed us over half an hour.

In all these rivers just after emerging from the
lakes the current was quite swift, and so shallow in many
places as almost to deserve the name of rapids. This
was particularly the case where the swift stream cut into
the high banks that loomed some forty to sixty feet
above us as we rushed by, a top stratum that rested upon
the stiff yellow clay being full of rounded bowlders,
which, when undermined, were let down into the river's
bed, choking it partially with most dangerous-looking
obstacles.

During the whole day we were passing through burned
districts of heavy timber that looked dismal enough,
backed, as they were, by dense clouds of black smoke
rising ahead of us, showing plainly that the devastation
was still going on. Many of these sweepings of fire were
quite old ; so old, in fact, that the dark rotting trunks
had become mere banks of brown stretched along the
ground, the blackened bark of the stumps being the only
testimony as to the manner of its destruction. Others,
again, were so recent that the last rain had not yet
beaten the white ashes from their blackened limbs,
while late that evening we dashed through the region of
smoke and flame we had discerned earlier in the day.

It is wonderful what great wide strips of river these flames will cross, probably carried by the high winds, when light bunches of dry, resinous matter are in a blaze. We saw one instance which, however, must be a rare one, of a blazing tree that fell into the water, where it immediately found a hydrostatic equilibrium, so that its upper branches continued on fire, blazing and smoking away like a small steam launch. It might readily have crossed the river as it floated down, and becoming entangled in the dry driftwood of the opposite bank, have been the nucleus of a new conflagration, the limits of which would have been determined by the wind and the nature of the material in its path. Of course, in such an intricate wilderness of black and brown trunks and stumps, any kind of game that approaches to black in color, such as a moose or black or brown bear; in fact, any thing darker than a snow-white mountain-goat, can easily avoid the most eagle-eyed hunter, by simply keeping still, since it could scarcely be distinguished at any distance above a hundred yards.

The western banks at one stretch of the river consisted of high precipitous banks of clay, fringed with timber at the summit. In one of the many little gullies that cleft the top of the bank into a series of rolling crescents, a member of the party perceived and drew our attention to a brown stump which seemed to have an unusual resemblance to a "grizzly bear," to use his expression. The resemblance was marked by all to such an extent that the stump was closely watched, and when, as we were from four to six hundred yards away, the stump picked up its roots and began to walk down the slope, there was a general scrambling around for guns, giving the stump an intimation that all was not right, and with one good look from a couple of knots on its side, it disappeared among the rest of the timber before a shot at a reasonable distance could be fired. Thereafter our guns were kept in a more convenient position for such drift timber.

After we had made a good forty miles that day, we felt perfectly justified in going into camp and about seven o'clock we commenced looking for one. The river was uniformly wide, without a break that would give slack water where we could decrease our rapid pace, and that day commenced an experience such as I have treated of in the chapter on rafting. Not knowing the efficacy of this method at the time, we did not find a camp until 8:15, but back of us lay over forty-five miles of distance traversed, which amply compensated us for the slight annoyance. Ahead of us there still hung dense clouds of smoke which seemed as if the whole world was on fire in that direction. An hour or so after camping (No. 24) a couple of miners came into camp, ragged and hungry, the most woe-begone objects I ever saw. They belonged to a party that numbered nearly a dozen and who had started about a month ahead of us. These two had left a third at camp about a mile up the river (from which point they had seen us float by), and were returning to civilization in order to allow the rest of the party food sufficient to enable them to continue prospecting. The party, at starting, had intended to eke out their civilized provisions with large game from time to time, in order to carry them through the summer. They were well armed and had several practical hunters with them, who had often carried out this plan while prospecting in what seemed to be less favored localities for game. Their experience confirmed the Indian reports that the caribou and moose follow the snow-line as it retreats up the mountains in the short summer of this country, in order to avoid the mosquitoes, with the exception only of a few stragglers here and there, on which no reliance can be placed. It was certainly a most formidable undertaking for these ragged, almost barefooted men to walk back through such a country as I have already described, with but a mere pittance of food in their haversacks. Possessing no reliable maps, they were obliged to follow the tortuous river, for fear of losing it, since it was their only guide out of the country. Large tributaries coming in from the west, which was the side they had chosen, often forced them to go many weary miles into the interior before they could be crossed. They hoped to find an Indian canoe by the time the lakes were reached, but from the scarcity of these craft I doubt if their hopes were ever realized. I heard afterward that they had suffered considerably on this return trip, especially in crossing through the Perrier Pass, and had to be rescued in the Dayay Valley by Indians from the Haines Mission.

The country was constantly getting more open as we proceeded, and now looked like the rolling hill-land of old England. By the word open, however, I do not mean to imply the absence of timber, for the growth of spruce and pine on the hills and of the deciduous trees in the valleys continued as dense as ever, and so remained nearly to the mouth of the river, varying, however, in regard to size and species.

Upon the 10th, the current did not abate a jot of its

swiftness, and although we started tolerably late, yet when Camp 25 was pitched, at 8:15 P.M., in a thick grove of little poplars (there being no prospect of a better camp in sight), we had scored 59 miles along the axis of the stream, the best record for one day made on the river. About 10 o'clock, that morning, we again passed through forest fires that were raging on both sides of the river, which averages at this point from 300 to 400 yards in width. A commendable scarcity of mosquitoes was noticed on this part of the river.

Shortly after noon we passed the mouth of a large river, from 150 to 200 yards in width, which my Chilkat Indians told me was called the Tah-heen'-a by them. The resemblance of this name to that of the Tahk-heen'-a made me abandon it, and I called it after M. Antoine d'Abbadie, Membre d'Institut, the French explorer. In regard to Indian names on this part of the Yukon River, I found that a white man labors under one difficulty not easy to overcome. The Chilkats, who are, as it were, the self-appointed masters over the docile and degraded "Sticks," while in the country of the latter, have one set of names and the "Sticks," or Tahk-heesh, have another. Oftentimes the name of a geographical object is the same in meaning, differing only according to the language. More often the names are radically different, and what is most perplexing of all, the Sticks will give the same name as the Chilkats in the presence of the latter, thus acknowledging in the most humble and abject way their savage suzerainty.

For some time before reaching the mouth of the D'Abbadie high hills had been rising on the eastern slope, until near this tributary their character had become truly mountainous. I called them the Semenow Mountains, after Von Semenow, President of the Imperial Geographical Society of Russia. They extend from the D'Abbadie River on the north to the Newberry River (after Professor Newberry, of New York), on the south. Between them and the Hancock Hills is located an isolated and conspicuous butte which I named after M. Charles Maunoir, of the Paris Geographical Society. A very similar hill between the Tahk River and the Yukon was named after Professor Ernst Haeckel, of Jena, Germany. The mouth of the D'Abbadie marks an important point on the Yukon River, as being the place at which gold begins to be found in placer deposits. From the D'Abbadie almost to the very mouth of the great Yukon, a panful of "dirt" taken with any discretion from almost any bar or bank, will when washed give several "colors," to use a miner's phrase. The Daly River comes in from the east some forty miles further on, measured along the stream, forming, with the Newberry and D'Abbadie, a singular trio of almost similar streams. The last-mentioned river I have named after Chief Justice Daly, of New York, a leading patron of my Franklin Search expedition. The frequent occurrence of large tributaries flowing from the east showed this to be the main drainage area of the Upper Yukon, a rule to which the sole exception of the Nordenskiöld River (after Baron von Nordenskiöld, the celebrated Swedish explorer of the Arctic), which comes in from the west, fifty miles beyond the Daly, and is the peer of any of the three just mentioned. Immediately after passing these rivers, the Newberry especially, the Yukon became very much darker in hue, showing, as I believe, that the trib-

utaries drained a considerable amount of what might be
called—possibly inappropriately—" tundra " land, *i. e.*,
where the water, saturated with the dyes extracted from
dead leaves and mosses, is prevented by an impervious
substratum of ice from clarifying itself by percolating
through the soil, and is carried off by superficial drain-

LOOKING BACK AT THE RINK RAPIDS.

age directly into the river-beds. Where we camped on
the night of the 25th I noticed that many of the dead
seasoned poplars with which we built our camp-fire and
cooked our food had been killed in previous winters by
the hares, that had peeled the bark in a circle around the
trunk at such a uniform height of from twenty to twen-
ty-four inches from the ground, measured from the lower

edge of the girdle, that I could not but think that this was about the average depth of the winter snow, upon which the hares stood at the time.   On the 11th we drifted over fifty miles.   Shortly after starting we passed the mouth of the Daly, already referred to, while directly ahead was a noticeable hill named by the Chilkats Eagles' Nest, and by the Tahk-heesh Otter Tail, each in their own language.   I easily saw my way out of the difficulty by changing its name to Parkman Peak, after Professor Francis Parkman, the well-known American historian.

We passed the mouth of the Nordenskiöld River on the afternoon of the 11th, and the same day our Indians told us of a perilous rapid ahead which the Indians of the country sometimes shot in their small rafts ; but they felt very anxious in regard to our bulky vessel of forty-two feet in length, as the stream made a double sharp bend with a huge rock in the center.   We started late on the morning of the 12th, and at 10 o'clock stopped our raft on the eastern bank in order to go ahead and inspect the rapids which we were about to shoot.   I found them to be a contraction of the river bed, into about one-third its usual width of from four to six hundred yards, and that the stream was also impeded by a number of massive trap rocks, thirty to forty feet high, lying directly in the channel and dividing it into three or four well marked channels, the second from the east, being the one ordinarily used by the Indians.   We rejected this, however, on account of a sharp turn in it which could not be avoided.   These rapids were very picturesque, as they rushed between the fantastically formed trap rocks and high towers, two of which were united by a slender nat-

LORING BLUFF.

(Looking up the Yukon River from Von Wilczek Valley)

ural bridge of stone, that spanned a whirlpool, making
the whole look like an old ruined stone bridge with but
one arch that had withstood the general demolition.
We essayed the extreme right-hand (eastern) passage,
although it was quite narrow and its boiling current was
covered with waves running two and three feet high, but
being the straightest was the best for our long craft.
Thousands of gulls had made the top of these isolated
towers their breeding places, for nothing but winged life
could ever reach them, and here, safe from all intrusion,
they reared their young.   As we shot by on the raft they
rose in clouds and almost drowned the noise of the roaring waters with their shrill cries.   This extreme right-
hand channel through which we shot, could, I believe, be
ascended by a light-draft river steamer provided with a
steam windlass, a sharp bend in the river bank just
before it is entered giving a short and secure hold for a
cable rope ; and if I am not too sanguine in my conjectures, the cascades below the Grand Cañon mark the head
of navigation on the Yukon River, as already noted.   I
named this picturesque little rapid after Dr. Henry
Rink, of Christiana, a well-known authority on Greenland.   After the Yukon receives the many large tributaries mentioned, it spreads into quite a formidable
magnitude ; interspersed with many islands, all of which
at their upper ends, are so loaded with great piles of
driftwood, oftentimes fifteen to twenty feet high, as to
make the vista in one of these archipelagoes quite different according as one looks up or down the river, the
former resembling the picturesque Thousand Isles of the
St. Lawrence, while the latter reveals only a dreary
stretch of felled timber, lying in unpicturesque groups,

with the bright green of the island foliage making the dreariness more conspicuous.

From Lake Kluk-tas-si almost to old Fort Selkirk we observed along the steep banks of the river a most conspicuous white stripe some two or three inches in width. After our attention had been attracted to this phenomenon for two or three days, we proceeded to investigate it. It averaged about two or three feet below the surface, and seemed to separate the recent alluvial deposits from the older beds of clay and drift below, although occasionally it appeared to cut into both, especially the alluvium. Occasionally, although at very rare intervals, there were two stripes parallel to each other and separated by a few inches of black earth, while oftentimes the stripe was plain on one side of the river and wholly wanting on the other.   A close inspection showed it to be volcanic ash, sufficiently consolidated to have the consistency of stiff earth, but nevertheless so friable that it could be reduced to powder by the thumb and fingers.   It possibly represents the result of some exceptionally violent eruption in ancient times from one or more of the many volcanic cones, now probably extinct, with which the whole southern coast of Alaska is studded.   The ashes were carried far and wide by the winds, and if the latter then, as now, blew almost persistently from the southward during the summer (and I understand the reverse is the case in the winter), we could reasonably fix the eruption at that time of the year.

The Yukon River as it widens also becomes very tortuous in many places, and oftentimes a score of miles is traversed along the axis of the stream while the dividers on the map hardly show half a dozen between the

INDIAN VILLAGE OF KITL-AII-GON IN THE VON WILCZEK VALLEY.

same points. In the region about the mouth of the Nordenskiöld River a conspicuous bald butte could be seen
directly in front of our raft no less than seven times, on
as many different stretches of the river. I called it Tan-
talus Butte, and was glad enough to see it disappear
from sight.

The day we shot the Rink Rapids, and only a few hours
afterward, we also saw our first moose plowing through
the willow brush on the eastern bank of the stream like a
hurricane in his frantic endeavors to escape, an undertaking in which he was completely successful. When first
seen by one of the party on the raft, his great broad palmated horns rolling through the top of the willow brake,
with an occasional glimpse of his brownish black sides
showing, he was mistaken for an Indian running down a
path in the brake and swaying his arms in the air to attract
our attention. My Winchester express rifle was near
me, and as the ungainly animal came into full sight at a
place where a little creek put into the stream, up the
valley of which it started, I had a fair shot at about a
hundred yards ; took good aim, pulled the trigger—and
the cap snapped,—and I saved my reputation as a marks-
man by the gun's missing fire. This moose and another
about four hundred miles further down the river were the
only two we saw in the Yukon Valley, although in the
winter they are quite numerous in some districts, when
the mosquitoes have ceased their onslaughts.

That same evening—the 12th, we encamped near the
first Indian village we had met on the river, and even this
was deserted. It is called by them Kit¹-ah'-gon (meaning the place between high hills), and consists of one log
house about eighteen by thirty feet, and a score of the

brush houses usual in this country ; that is, three main poles, one much longer than the rest, and serving as a ridge pole on which to pile evergreen brush to complete the house. This brush is sometimes replaced by the most thoroughly ventilated reindeer or moose skin, and in rare cases by an old piece of canvas. Such are the almost constant habitations of these abject creatures. When I first saw these rude brush houses, thrown together without regard to order or method, I thought they were scaffoldings or trellis work on which the Indians, who lived in the log house, used to dry the salmon caught by them during the summer, but my guide, Indianne, soon explained that theory away. In the spring Kit¹-ah́-gon is deserted by its Indian inmates, who then ascend the river with loads so light that they may be carried on the back. By the time winter approaches they have worked so far away, accumulating the scanty stores of salmon, moose, black bear, and caribou, on which they are. to subsist, that they build a light raft from the driftwood strewn along banks of the river, and float toward home, where they live in squalor throughout the winter. These rafts are almost their sole means of navigation from the Grand Cañon to old Fort Selkirk, and the triangular brush houses almost their only abodes ; and all this in a country teeming with wood fit for log-houses, and affording plenty of birch bark from which can be made the finest of canoes. Kit¹-ah-gon is in a beautiful large valley, as its Indian name would imply (I named it Von Wilczek Valley, after Graf von Wilczek of Vienna), and I was surprised to see it drained by so small a stream as the one, but ten or twenty feet wide, which empties itself at the valley's mouth. Its proximity

UPPER END OF THE INGERSOL ISLANDS.

(Looking down the river from Von Wilczek Valley.)

to the Pelly, twenty miles further on, forbids its draining a great area, yet its valley is much the more conspicuous of the two. Photographs of this and adjacent
scenes on the river were secured by Mr. Homan before
departing, and a rough "prospect" in the high bank
near the river showed "color" enough to encourage the
hope of some enthusiastic miner in regard to finding
something more attractive. Looking back up the Yukon a
most prominent landmark is found in a bold bluff that
will always be a conspicuous point on the river, and
which is shown on page 193. I named this bluff after
General Charles G. Loring, of the Boston Museum of Fine
Arts.

From Von Wilczek valley to old Fort Selkirk is but a
little over twenty miles ; and the river is so full of islands
in many places that for long stretches we could hardly
see both banks at a time, while it was nothing unusual
to have both out of sight at points where the islands
were most numerous. This cluster of islands (named
after Colonel Ingersoll, of Washington), is, I think, situated in the bed of one of the ancient lakes of which I
have spoken, although the opinion of a professional
geologist would be needed to settle such a matter.

At 3 P. M. we reached the site of old Fort Selkirk.
All our maps, some half a dozen in number, except one,
had placed the site of Selkirk at the junction of the
Pelly and Yukon between the two, the single exception
noted placing it on the north bank of the Pelly
where the streams unite. Noticing this discrepancy I
asked Indianne for an explanation, and he told me that
neither was correct, but that the chimneys of the old
ruins would be found on the south side of the river about

a mile below the junction, and I found him correct, the chimneys being visible fully a mile before we reached them.   Here we were on land familiar to the footsteps of white men who had made maps and charts, that rough and rude though they were, were still entitled to respect, and accordingly at this point I considered that my explorations had ceased, although my surveys were continued to the mouth of the river ; making the distinction that the first survey only is an exploration, a distinction which I believe is rapidly coming into vogue.   Altogether on the Yukon River, this far, there had been taken thirty-four astronomical observations, four hundred and twenty-five with the prismatic compass, and two for variation of compass.   I have no doubt that these are sufficiently accurate at least for all practical purposes of geographical exploration in this country, until more exact surveys are demanded by the opening of some industry or commerce, should that time ever come.   The total length of this portion of the river just traversed from Haines Mission to Selkirk was five hundred and thirty-nine miles ; the total length of the raft journey from its commencement at the camp on Lake Lindeman being four hundred and eighty-seven miles ; while we had sailed and "tracked" and rowed across seven lakes for a distance aggregating one hundred and thirty-four miles.

RUINS OF OLD FORT SELKIRK.

The sharp bluff across the river, shown between the two right-hand chimneys, is the same figured more closely on page 200 or below at 40.

CHAPTER IX.

THROUGH THE UPPER RAMPARTS.

T the site of old Fort Selkirk commences the Upper Ramparts of the Yukon, or where that mighty stream cuts through the terminal spurs of the Rocky Mountains, a distance of nearly four hundred miles, the first hundred of which, terminating near the mouth of the Stewart River, are almost equal to the Yosemite or Yellowstone in stupendous grandeur.

I was very anxious to determine beyond all reasonable doubt the relative sizes of the two rivers whose waters unite just above old Fort Selkirk, as upon this determination rested the important question whether the Pelly or the Lewis River of the old Hudson Bay traders, who had roughly explored the former, ought to be called the Yukon proper ; and in order to settle this point I was fully prepared and determined to make exact measurements, soundings, rate of current and any other data that might be necessary. This information, however, was unnecessary except in a rough form, as the preponderance of the old Lewis River was too evident to the most casual inspection to require any exactness to confirm it.

The ratio of their respective width is about five to three, with about the ratio of five to four in depth ; the latter, however, being a very rough approximation ; the Lewis River being superior in both, and for this reason I abandoned the latter name, and it appears on the map as the Yukon to Crater Lake at its head.

At old Fort Selkirk nothing but the chimneys, three in number—two of them quite conspicuous at some distance—are left standing, the blackened embers scattered around still attesting the manner of its fate. From the careful and substantial manner in which the rubble stone chimneys were constructed, this Hudson Bay Company post was evidently intended to be permanent, and from the complete destruction of all the wood work, the Chilkat Indians, its destroyers, evidently intended that its effacement should be complete. The fate of this post has been alluded to in an earlier part of the narrative. Here we remained two or three days, making an astronomical determination of position, the mean of our results being latitude 62° 45′ 46″ north, longitude 137° 22′ 45″ west from Greenwich.

No meteorological observations were taken thus far on the river, the party not being furnished with a complete set of instruments, and our rapid passage through a vast tract of territory making the usefulness to science highly problematical. The nearest point to the Upper Yukon at which regular observations of this character are recorded is the Chilkat salmon-cannery of the North-west Trading Company, on Chilkat Inlet. The two regions are separated by the Kotusk Mountains, a circumstance which makes meteorological inferences very unreliable. Climatology is better

LOOKING INTO THE MOUTH OF THE PELLY RIVER.

(The Pelly enters between the black perpendicular bluff and the high hills beyond.)

represented, however, in regard to the subject of botany. Quite a number of botanical specimens were collected on the Upper Yukon, and have since been placed in the able hands of Professor Watson, curator of the Harvard herbarium, for analysis. While only a partial and crude collection made by an amateur, it has thrown some little light on the general character of the flora, as limited to the river bed, which we seldom quitted in the discharge of our more important duties connected with the main object of the expedition. Professor Watson's report on this small collection will be found in the Appendix.

The extent of the Alaskan expedition of 1883 was so great that I deemed it best to divide the map of its route into convenient sections; and the three subdivisions, the second of which this chapter commences, were made wholly with reference to my own travels. It is therefore not intended in any other way as a geographical division of this great river, although it might not be altogether unavailable or inappropriate for such a purpose. The Middle Yukon, as we called it on our expedition, extends from the site of old Fort Selkirk to old Fort Yukon, at *the great Arctic bend of the Yukon*, as it is sometimes and very appropriately termed—a part of the stream which we know approximately from the rough maps of the Hudson Bay Company's traders, who formerly trafficked along these waters, and from information derived from pioneers of the Western Union Telegraph Company and others. This part of the river, nearly five hundred miles in length, had, therefore, already been explored; and to my expedition fell the lot of being the first to give it a survey, which though far from perfection, is the first

worthy of the name, and is, I believe, like that of the
Upper Yukon, sufficient to answer all purposes until
such time as commerce may be established on the river
subservient to the industries, either of mining or of fishing, that may hereafter spring up along its course.

I have just spoken of the comparative sizes of the
Pelly and Lewis Rivers, as showing the latter to be
undoubtedly the Yukon proper; and the view on page
209, taken looking into the mouth of the Pelly from an
island at the junction of the two streams, as well as that
on page 213, looking back up the Yukon (old Lewis
River), from the site of old Selkirk, shows the evident
preponderance of the latter, although in the case of
the Pelly but one of its mouths, the lower and
larger of the two that encircle the island, can be
seen distinctly.

The bars at the mouth of the Pelly are a little richer
in placer gold "color" than any for a considerable distance on either side along the Yukon, creating the
reasonable inference that the mineral has been carried
down the former stream, an inference which is strength-
ened by the reports that gold in paying quantities has
been discovered on the Pelly, and is now being worked
successfully, although upon a somewhat limited scale.
Even the high, flat plateau on which old Fort Selkirk
was built is a bed of fine gravel that glistens with grains
of gold in the miner's pan, and might possibly "pay"
in more favorable climes, where the ground is not frozen
the greater part of the year. Little did the old traders
of the Hudson's Bay Company imagine that their house
was built on such an auriferous soil, and possibly little
did they care, as in this rich fur district they possessed

VIEW LOOKING UP THE YUKON FROM THE SITE OF FORT SELKIRK.

an enterprise more valuable than a gold mine, if an American can imagine such a thing.

The perpendicular bluff of eruptive rock, distinctly columnar in many places, and with its talus reaching from half to two-thirds the way to the top, as shown in the view looking into the mouth of the Pelly, on page 209, and the view on page 205 also, extends up that stream on the north or right bank as far as it was visited, some two or three miles, and so continues down the Yukon along the same (north) bank for twelve or thirteen miles, when the encroaching high mountains, forming the upper gates of the ramparts, obliterate it as a later formation. In but one place that I saw along this extended front of rocky parapet was there a gap sufficient to permit of one's climbing from the bottom, over the rough *débris*, to the level grassy plateau that extended backward from its crest; although in many places this plateau could be gained by alpine climbing for short distances, up the crevices in the body of the steep rock. This level plateau does not extend far back before the foot of the high rolling hills is gained.

In the illustration on page 209 the constant barricades of tangled driftwood encountered everywhere on the upstream ends and promontories of the many islands of these rivers are shown, although the quantity shown in the view falls greatly below the average, the heads of the islands being often piled up with stacks ten or twenty feet high, which are useful in one way, as forming a dam that serves during freshets and high water, to protect them more or less from the eroding power of the rapid river.

A grave or burial place of the Ayan (or Iyan) Indians

probably some three months old, planted on the very edge of the river bank near the site of old Fort Selkirk, was a type of the many we afterward saw at intervals from this point for about two-thirds of the distance to old Fort Yukon, and is represented on page 217. Before burial the body is bent with the knees up to the breast, so as to occupy as little longitudinal space as possible, and is inclosed in a very rough box of hewn boards two and three inches thick, cut out by means of rude native axes, and is then buried in the ground, the lid of the coffin, if it can be called such, seldom being over a foot or a foot and a half below the surface of the pile. The grave's inclosure or fence is constructed of roughly-hewn boards, standing upright and closely joined edge to edge, four corner-posts being prolonged above, and somewhat neatly rounded into a bed-post design represented in the figure, from which they seldom depart. It is lashed at the top by a wattling of willow withes, the lower ends of the boards being driven a short way into the ground, while one or two intermediate stripes of red paint resemble other bands when viewed at a distance. From the grave itself is erected a long, light pole twenty or twenty-five feet in height, having usually a piece of colored cloth flaunting from its top ; although in this particular instance the cloth was of a dirty white. Not far away, and always close enough to show that it is some super-stitious adjunct of the grave itself, stands another pole of about equal height, to the top of which there is fastened a poorly carved wooden figure of a fish, duck, goose, bear, or some other animal or bird, this being, I believe, a sort of savage *totem* designating the family or sub-clan of the tribe to which the deceased belonged.

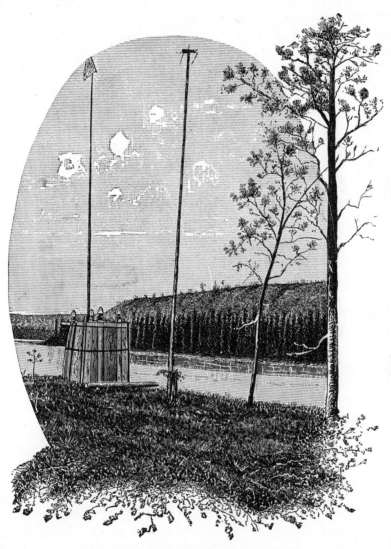

AYAN GRAVE NEAR OLD FORT SELKIRK.

Looking across and down the Yukon River.

This second pole may be, and very often is, a fine young spruce tree of proper height and shape and convenient situation, stripped of its limbs and peeled of its bark. The little "totem" figure at the top may thus be easily placed in position before the limbs are cut off. It is sometimes constructed as a weather-vane, or more probably it is easier to secure firmly in its position by a wooden pin driven vertically, and so as the green wood seasons and shrinks it becomes as it were a sepulcral anemoscope without having been so intended. These poles may be horizontally striped with native red paint, and the outside pole has one or more pieces of cloth suspended from its trunk. These graves are always near the river shore, generally on the edge of a high gravel bank which is in course of excavation by the swift current, and when fresh and the boards white are visible from a distance of many miles. There is no tendency, as far as I could see, to group them into graveyards, beyond the fact that they are a little more numerous near their semi-permanent villages than elsewhere, the convenience of interment being evidently the controlling cause of location. Leaving out the two high poles, there is a rough resemblance to the graves of civilized countries; and no doubt much of their form and structure is due to the direct or indirect contact with civilization. My own Indians (Chilkats) told me that they formerly placed the bodies of their dead on pole scaffoldings in the branches of the trees near the river bank, somewhat after the manner of the Sioux and other Indian tribes of our great western plains ; and in one instance a very old, rotten and dilapidated scaffold in a tree was pointed out to me as having once served that purpose, although there were no indications to con-

firm the story ; but these might have easily been obliter-
ated. They also make small scaffoldings or little
caches in the lower branches of trees to protect their contents, usually provisions and clothing, from bears, wolves,
and possibly from their own dogs, of which they possess
large numbers of a black and brown mongrel breed. In
the summer time these curs are eminently worthless except
as scavengers for the refuse decaying salmon, but
in the winter season they are used to draw the rude
native sledges and to assist in trailing moose and
caribou.

Mr. Homan succeeded in getting a photograph
(page 221), of a group of Ayan or Iyan Indians, with
their birch-bark canoes. We found it very difficult to
keep these nervous fellows still ; and, as far as fine
rendering of features is concerned, the photograph was
not perfect. Their birch-bark canoes are the best on
any part of the long river for lightness, compactness,
and neatness of build and design, and form a most
remarkable contrast to the unwieldy dilapidated "dug-
outs" of the Tahk-heesh Indians above them on the
Yukon. The Ayan canoe paddle, well
shown in outline in the hands of one of
the group, is of the cross-section on this
page, the ridge or rib *r* being always held to the
rear in using it. In addition to the paddle, the canoeman keeps with him two light poles, about as long as
the paddle itself, and as heavy as its handle ; and these
are employed in ascending the river, the pole man
keeping near the shallow shores, and using one in each
hand on either side of the canoe, poling against the
bottom. So swift is the river in these parts (and in fact

CROSS-SECTION AYAN
CANOE PADDLE.

AYAN INDIANS AND THEIR BIRCH-BARK CANOES.

it is extremely rapid during its entire course), that the native canoemen use no other method in ascending it, except for very short distances. The Eskimo method, in use on the lower part of the river, of harnessing dogs to their craft like canal horses and towing them along the banks, I did not see in operation during my stay among the Ayans, although they possessed all the requisites for such an easy and convenient method of navigation. In descending the river the current is the main motive power, especially for long journeys, and the paddle is only sparingly used to keep the canoe in the swiftest part of the stream. When required, however, they can go at a speed that few canoemen in the world, savage or civilized, can equal.

Two species of fish were caught from the banks near the site of Selkirk, the grayling being of the same kind we had caught near the rapids just above and below the Grand Cañon, and had found in varying numbers from Perthes Point in Lake Bove, to the mouth of White River, nearly a hundred miles below Selkirk, averaging a trifle over a pound in weight ; and a trout-like salmon, caught occasionally from Lake Nares to White River, sometimes with an artificial fly, but more frequently on the trout lines with baited hooks that were put out over night wherever we camped. A most disgusting and hideous species of eel-pout monopolized our trout lines whenever they were put out at this point, from which even the invincible stomachs of our Indian allies and visitors had to refrain. Small black gnats, somewhat resembling the buffalo gnats of the plains, were observed near Selkirk in considerable numbers, and our Indians hinted that they indicated the presence of large game, a story which we would gladly have had corroborated, but in this we were disappointed.

We got away from Selkirk on July 15th, shortly after noontime, having waited for a meridian culmination of the sun in order to take an observation for latitude. The country gradually becomes more mountainous as we descend, and this bold character continues with but slight exceptions for over a hundred miles further. The river view reminded me strongly of the Columbia River near the Cascades, the Hudson at West Point, or the Potomac at Harper's Ferry, differing only in the presence everywhere of innumerable islands, a permanent characteristic of the Yukon, and one in which it exceeds any other stream known to me, whether from observation or description.

Although we had understood from the few Indians who had visited us in their canoes, that their village was but a few miles below Fort Selkirk, we had become so accustomed to finding insignificant parties of natives, here and there, that it was a great surprise to us when we suddenly rounded the lower end of an island about four o'clock that afternoon, and saw from a hundred and seventy-five to two hundred wild savages drawn up ready to receive us on the narrow beach in front of their brush village on the south side of the river. Our coming had evidently been heralded by couriers, and all of the natives were apparently half-frantic with excitement for fear we might drift by without visiting them. They ran up and down the bank wildly swaying their arms in the air, and shouting and screaming to the great fleet of canoes that surrounded us, until I feared they might have unfriendly designs, and in fact, their numbers appeared

so overwhelming when compared with our little band that
I gave the necessary orders in respect to arms so as to
give the Indians as little advantage as possible in case
of an encounter at such close quarters. A line was carried ashore by means of these canoes, and every man,
woman and child in the crowd made an attempt to get
hold of it, the foremost of them running out into the
ice-cold water up to the very arm-pits in order to seize
it, and the great gridiron of logs went cutting through
the water like a steam-launch, and brought up against
the shore in a way that nearly took us off our feet.

Immediately after our raft was securely moored, the
crowd of Indians who lined the narrow beach commenced
singing and dancing—men and boys on the (their) left,
and women and girls on the right. The song was low and
monotonous, but not melodious, bearing a resemblance to
savage music in general. Their outspread hands were
placed on their hips, their arms *akimbo*, and they swayed
from side to side as far as their lithe bodies would permit, keeping time to the rude tune in alternate oscilla-
tions to the right and left, all moving synchronously and
in the same direction, their long black masses of hair
floating wildly to and fro, and serving the practical purpose of keeping off the gnats and mosquitoes which otherwise might have made any out-door enjoyments impossible. During all this time the medicine men went through
the most hideous gymnastics possible along the front of
the line, one who had a blue-black blanket with a St.
George's cross of flaming red in its center being especially conspicuous. He excelled in striking theatrical attitudes of the most sensational order, in which the showy
blanket was made to do its part, and he was forthwith

dubbed Hamlet by the men of the party, by way of a substitute for his almost unpronounceable name. Even after the performance, this pompous individual strutted along the banks as if he owned the whole British North-west territory ; a pretension that was contradicted by his persistent begging for every trifling object that attracted his eye, as though he had never owned any thing of value in his life. After the singing and dancing were over, a few trifling presents were given to most of the Indians as a reward for their entertainment. A photograph was attempted by Mr. Homan of this dancing group, but the day was so unfavorable, with its black lowering clouds, the amateur apparatus so incomplete, and the right moment so hard to seize, that the effect was a complete failure. Once or twice we got the long line in position in their best attitudes, " Hamlet " looking his most ferocious, and resembling a spread eagle with the feathers pulled out, but just as the photographer was ready to pull the cap off the camera, some impatient young fellow, inspired by the crowd and the attitude of dancing, would begin to hum their low song of Yi-yi-yi-yi's and it was as impossible to keep the others from taking up the cadence and swaying themselves as it was to arrest the earth's revolution.

From a book written by a previous traveler on the lower river, who pretended to a knowledge of the tribes upon its upper part also, I had been deluded into the idea that useful articles—such as knives, saws, and files, —were the best for trading purposes with these Indians, or for the hire of native help; but I was not long in finding out that this was most gratuitous misinformation; for the constant burden of their solicitations was a request for tea and tobacco, small quantities of which they get by barter with intermediate riparian tribes. These wants I found to extend among the natives throughout the whole length of the river in varying degrees, and, as the former article is very light, I would especially recommend it to those about to enter the country for purposes of scientific research, for which it is such a grand field. Next to tea and tobacco, which we could only spare in small quantities, fish-hooks seemed to be in good demand among this particular tribe ; and the very few articles they had to spare, mostly horn spoons, and birch-bark ladles and buckets were eagerly exchanged. Below White River, fishing on the Yukon with hook and line ceases, and fish-hooks are worthless as articles of exchange. Another article freely brought us was the pair of small bone gambling-tools (shown on this page) so characteristic of the whole north-west country. They have been described when speaking of the Chilkat Indians and I saw no

AYAN AND CHILKAT GAMBLING TOOLS. Scale ½.

material difference in their *use* by this particular tribe.

These Indians call themselves the A-yans—with an occasional leaning of the pronunciation toward I-yan ; and this village, so they said, contained the majority of the tribe, although from their understanding of the question they may have meant that it was the largest village of the tribe. Their country, as they claim it, extends up the Pelly—the Indian name of which is *Ayan*—to the lakes, up the Yukon from this point to the village of Kitˡ-ah-gon, and down that stream to near the mouth of the White and Stewart Rivers, where they are succeeded by a tribe called the *Netch-on'-dees*

or *Na-chon'-des*—the Indian name of the Stewart River
being Na-chon'-de. They are a strictly riparian race
of people and define their country only as it extends
along the principal streams. From the river as a home
or base, however, they make frequent hunting excursions to the interior in the winter time for moose and
caribou. This village, which they called *Kah-tung*,
seemed to be of a semi-permanent character ; the houses
or huts made of spruce brush, over the top of which
there was an occasional piece of well-worn cloth or dirty
canvas, but more often a moose or caribou skin. These
brush houses were squalid affairs, and especially so
compared with the bright intelligent features of the
makers, and with some of their other handicraft, such
as their canoes and native wearing apparel. The little
civilized clothing they possess is obtained by barter with
neighboring tribes, and has generally been worn out by
the latter before they exchange, hence it is tattered and
filthy beyond measure, and in no wise so well adapted
to their purpose as the native clothing of buckskin. One
could hardly stand up in these brush houses, they were
built so low, and any attempt to do so was frustrated by
the quantities of odoriferous salmon hanging down from
the squat roofs, undergoing a process of smoking in the
dense clouds that emanated from spruce-knot fires on
the floor. These ornaments, coupled with the thick
carpeting of live dogs upon the floor, made the outside
of the house the most pleasant part of it. The houses
were generally double, facing each other, with a narrow
aisle a foot or two wide between, each one containing a
single family, and being about the area of a common or
government A tent. The ridge-poles were common to

the two houses, and as both leaned forward considerably
this gave them strength to resist violent winds. The
diagram on this page gives a ground plan of an Ayan
double brush-house. The village of Kah-tung contained
about twenty of these
squalid huts, huddled near
the river bank, and alto-
gether was the largest Indian village we saw on the
whole length of the Yukon
River.

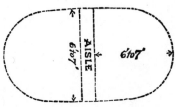

PLAN OF AYAN SUMMER HOUSE OF BRUSH.

There was a most decided Hebrew cast of countenance
among many of the Ayans; more pronounced, in fact,
than I have ever seen among savages, and so much so as
to make it a subject of constant remark.

Their household implements were of the most primitive
type,—such as spoons of the horn of the mountain goat,
very similar to those of the Tlinkits, but by no means so
well carved ; and a few buckets, pans, and trays of birch-
bark, ingeniously constructed of one piece so as not to
leak, and neatly sewed with long withes of trailing roots.
(The finer thread-like spruce roots, well-boiled, are, I believe, generally used by them in sewing their birch-bark
canoes and utensils.)

Their present village was, as I have said, evidently
only of a semi-permanent character, used in the summer
during the time that salmon were ascending the river to
spawn ; the bright red sides of this fish, as they were
hanging around, split open, forming a not inartistic contrast with the dark green spruce boughs of the houses
and surrounding forests; the artistic effect, however, was
best appreciated when holding one's nose. Scattered

around in every direction was a horde of dogs that defied computation, and it must be an immense drain on their commissariat to keep these animals alive let alone in good condition. The amount of active exercise they took, however, would not suffice to reduce them in flesh, for their principal occupation seemed to be unlimited sleep.

KON-IT'L, CHIEF OF THE AYANS.

Although we were not successful in getting a photograph of the long group of dancers, we were more fortunate with a group of the chiefs and medicine-man "Hamlet," from which the portrait on this page, of Kon-it'l, their chief, is taken. It was impossible to get them to face the camera at such short range until one of the members of the exploring party took his position with them, while Mr. Homan secured the photograph.

The Ayan mothers, instead of carrying their babes on their backs with their faces to the front, as is usually done by savage women, unless when using a cradle, turn them around so as to have them back to back, and carry them so low as to fit as it were into the "small of the back."

Most of the Ayan men, and especially the younger members, were armed with bows and arrows, but there was quite a considerable sprinkling of old flint-lock Hudson Bay Company muskets among them, which they

AYAN MOOSE ARROW.

had procured by trade many years ago when Fort Selkirk flourished, or by intertribal barter, and their cost to these poor savages was almost fabulous. The Company's manner of selling a gun was to set it upright on the floor of the trader's store, and then to pile up furs alongside of it until they reached the muzzle, when the exchange was made, many of the skins being those of the black and silver-gray fox, and their aggregate value being probably three to four hundred dollars. Their bows and arrows were of the stereotyped Indian make, with no distinguishing ornament or peculiarity of construction worthy of notice.

The moose arrows used by this tribe, shown in illustration on this page, have at the point the usual double

barb of common arrows, while one side is prolonged for
two or three inches into a series of barbs ; these latter
they claim have the effect of working inward with the
motions of the muscles of the animal if it be only
wounded. Once wounded in this manner these sleuth-
hounds of savages will remain on the trail of a moose for
days if need be, until this dreadful weapon has reached
a vital point, or so disabled the animal that it easily suc-
cumbs to its pursuers.   In hunting moose in the summer
time, while these animals are swimming across the lakes
or broad streams, I was told by one of my interpreters
who had often traded among them, and was well acquainted with their habits and customs, that these Ayans
(and in fact several tribes below them on the river), do
not hesitate to jump on the animals' back in the lake or
river, leaving the canoe to look after itself, and dispatch
the brute with a hand knife, cutting its throat or stab-
bing it in the neck as illustrated on page 261. Of course,
a companion in another canoe is needed to assist in getting the carcass ashore, and secure the hunter's canoe.
They often attack the moose in their canoes while swimming as described by previous explorers on the lower
river, but say that if by any unskillful movement they
should only wound the animal it may turn and wreck
their vessel, which is too great a loss for them to risk.
A flying moose will not turn in the water unless irritated
by wounds.   The knives they use in hunting are great
double-edged ones, with flaring ornamental handles, well
illustrated in the upper left hand corner of the picture
mentioned.   They tell me these knives are of native
manufacture, the handles being wrapped with moose
leather so as to give the hand a good grip. Alto-

gether, they are most villainous and piratical looking things.

Only one or two log-cabins were seen anywhere in the Ayan country, and these had the dilapidated air of complete and permanent abandonment, although this whole district of the river is teeming with timber appropriate for such use. Probably the nomadic and restless character of the inhabitants makes it irksome for them to dwell in such permanent abodes, in spite of the great comfort to be derived in their almost Arctic winters from

CROSS-SECTION THROUGH AYAN WINTER TENT.

such buildings, if well constructed. The severity of the winter is shown by the moist banks of the river, the appearance of which indicates that they have been frozen some six or eight feet in depth. In winter the Ayans live mostly in tents, but by an ingenious arrangement these ordinarily cold habitations are made reasonably comfortable. This winter tent is shown in cross-section above, I being the interior, and P P the tent poles well covered with moose or caribou skins. A second set of poles, p p, are given a wider spread, inclosing an air space, A S, a foot or two across. These, too, are covered with animal skins, and a thick banking of snow, ss, two or three feet deep is thrown over the outside tent during the coldest weather of winter, making a sort of hybrid between the Eskimo *igloo*, or snow house, and the Indian skin lodge.

Many of the Ayans were persistent beggars, and next morning, the 16th of July, we got an early start before many of them were about, for as a tribe they did not seem to be very early risers.

Nearly directly opposite the Kah-tung village the perpendicular basaltic bluffs shown in the view at the mouth of the Pelly cease ; and from this point on, the hills on both sides of the river were higher and even mountainous in character ; "the upper gates of the upper ramparts."

From this point on down through the ramparts small black gnats became annoyingly numerous and pugnacious, while the plague of mosquitoes seemed to abate a little. The mosquito-bars, which were some protection from the latter, were of no use against the former, the little imps sailing right between the meshes without even stopping to crawl through. Veils with the very finest meshes would be needed to repulse their onslaughts, and with these we were not provided.

That day, the 16th, we drifted forty-seven miles, through a most picturesque section of country, our journey being marred only by a number of recurring and disagreeable thunder showers that wet us to the skin.

Everywhere in conspicuous positions near the edge of the river banks we saw straggling and isolated Ayan graves, resembling, in general, the one photographed at Selkirk, and not unlike pretty little white cottages, when seen from the distance projected against the somber green of the deep spruce forests.

About thirty-four miles beyond old Selkirk a small but conspicuous mountain stream came in from the south, which I named after Professor Selwyn, of Ottawa, Canada.

The river was still full of islands, however, many of which are covered with tall spruce, and look very picturesque in the almost cañon-like river-bottom, the steep mountain sides being nearly devoid of heavy forests.

In one of the many open spaces far up the mountain side, we saw a huge black bear, evidently hunting his daily meal among the roots and berries that there abound. Although we passed within half a mile of him, he took no more notice of us than if our raft had been a floating chip, and we did not disturb his search with any long-range shots.

A little further down, and on the same side of the river, the northern, we saw three white mountain goats on the very highest ridges of the hills. Timid as they are, the only notice they deigned to give us was that such as were asleep roused themselves and stood gazing at us until we had drifted well past, when they began grazing leisurely along the ridge.

About this time our attention was quite forcibly called to a singular phenomenon while riding on the raft, which was especially noticeable on quiet sunny days. It was a very pronounced crackling sound, not unlike that of a strong fire running through dry cedar brush, or that of the first rain drops of a thunder storm falling on the roof of a tent. Some of the men attributed it to the rattling on the logs of the raft of a shower of pebbles brought up by

the swift current from underneath, which would have
been a good enough theory as far as the sound was
concerned; but soundings in such places invariably
failed to touch bottom with a sixteen-foot pole, and,
moreover, when we were in shallower and swifter waters,
where the bottom was pebbly, the sounds were not
observed. As the noise always occurred in deep water
of a boiling character, figuratively speaking,—or in that
agitated condition so common in deep water immediately
after a shoal, a condition with which our experience in
prying the raft off shoals had rendered us familiar—I
attempted to account for it upon the theory explained
by the figure just below. The raft x, drifting with the
arrow, passes from a shallow to a deep stretch of water.
The Yukon River is a very swift stream for its size (we
drifted that day, July 16, forty-seven and a half geographical miles in eleven hours and fifty minutes, and
even this rate cannot represent the swiftest current), and
the pebbles, carried forward over the shallows and

reaching the crest a,
are borne along by
their own inertia and
the superficial current,
and literally *dropped*
on a gravel-bank at some point forward, such as b, and,
water being so excellent a conductor of sound, an observer
on a low floating craft, during quiet days, might distinctly
hear this falling, whereas it would not be heard if the
pebbles were simply rolling along the bottom in swifter
and noisier water. The suddenness with which this
crackling commenced and the gradual manner in which
it died out, seem to confirm this idea. A series of

soundings before and after the occurrence of these singular noises would have settled this theory; but the sound recurred so seldom (say twice, or perhaps three times, a day in this part of the river), that it was impossible to predict it in time to put the theory to the test, unless one kept constantly sounding while upon the river. It was observed on the lower river in a much less degree, and probably might there have passed unnoticed if previous experience had not recalled it to our attention.

That evening we camped at 8 o'clock, after trying to conduct our cumbersome vessel to a pretty little spot for the purpose, but our well-used "snubbing" line parted at the critical moment and we drifted down into a most miserable position among the high, rank willow shoots, laden with water from the recent rains. Towing or "tracking" our craft back against the swift current with our small force was plainly out of the question, and as the river bank seemed of the same character, as far as we could see, some two or three miles, we made the best of it and camped, for we were getting used to such experiences by this time.

Next morning, about 7 o'clock, when we were nearly ready to start, we found four Ayan Indians, each in his birch-bark canoe, visiting our camp. They came from the Kah-tung village above, having left it, as they said, shortly after our departure on the preceding day, and had camped for the night on the river just above us. They expressed great surprise at the distance we had made by simple drifting, having until this morning felt certain that they had passed us the day before around some one of the many islands in the broad river. They were going down the river some two or three hundred miles to a white trader's store of which they spoke, and we kept passing each other for the next three or four days. They had spoken at the Kah-tung village of this trading station (which we took to be Fort Yukon), which they said they could reach in three days; kindly adding that we might make the distance with our craft in a week or so. They now changed their minds and thought we might only be a day or two behind them. I found that the progress of the raft, when care was taken to keep in the swiftest current, for twelve or fourteen or perhaps sixteen hours a day, with no unusual detentions, fully equaled the average day's journey of the Indian canoes, which remained in the water not more than six or seven hours a day ; their occupants stopping to hunt every animal that might be seen, as well as to cook a midday lunch at their leisure. In fact my own Indians, who had traded among them, more than hinted that they were hurrying considerably in order to go along with us and to reach the white trader's store as a portion of our party.

These same four fellows, when they met us on the morning of the 17th, had with them the carcass of a black bear, which they offered for sale or barter ; and on our buying one hindquarter, which was about all that we thought we could use before spoiling, they offered us the rest as a gift. We accepted the offer to the extent of taking the other hindquarter, for which we gave them a trifle, whereupon the rest of the carcass was left behind or thrown away on the beach, a circumstance which was explained to us by the fact that all four of these Indians were medicine-men, and as such were forbidden by some superstitious custom from eating bears' flesh. They told us that the animal was the same black bear we had seen on the northern hillsides of the river the day before.

The morning of the 17th and certain other periods of the day were characterized by a heavy fog-bank, which did not quite reach the river bottom, but cut the hillsides at an altitude of from three hundred to five hundred feet above the level of the stream. The fog gave a dismal and monotonous aspect to the landscape, but proved much better for our physical comfort than the previous day, with its alternating rain and blistering heat. We found these fogs to be very common on this part of the river, being almost inseparable from the southern winds that prevail at this time of the year. I suppose these fogs proceed from the moisture-laden air over the warm Pacific which is borne on the southern winds across the snow-clad and glacier-crowned mountains of the Alaskan coast range, becoming chilled and condensed in its progress, and reaching this part of the Yukon valley is precipitated as rain or fog. The reason that we had escaped the fogs on the lakes was that the wind came across tracts of land to the south, and the hygrometric conditions were different. A little further down the Yukon, but within the upper ramparts, we suffered from almost constant rains that beat with the southern winds upon our backs.

Shortly after one o'clock in the afternoon we floated by the mouth of the White River flowing from the southwest, which has the local name of Yú-ko-kon Heena, or Yú-ko-kon River, a much prettier name than the old one of the Hudson Bay traders. The Chilkats call it the Sand River, from the innumerable bars and banks of sand along its course ; and many years ago they ascended it by a trail, which when continued leads to their own country, but is now abandoned. Some forty to fifty miles up its valley the Indian trading trail which leads from the headwaters of the Tanana to old Fort Selkirk crosses its course at right angles; and since the destruction of Fort Selkirk in 1851, the Tanana Indians, who then made considerable use of the trail to reach the fort for trading purposes, employ it but little; and only then as far as the White River, whose valley they descend to reach the Yukon.

This stream resembles a river of liquid mud of an almost white hue, from which characteristic it is said to have derived its name from the old Hudson Bay traders —and no better illustration of its extreme muddiness can be given than the following : One of our party mistook a mass of timber that had lodged on the up-stream side of a low, flat mud-bar, for floating wood, and regarded it as evidence of a freshet, a theory which seemed corroborated by the muddy condition of the water, until the actual character of the object was established by closer observation as we drifted nearer. The mud-bar and adjacent waters were so entirely of the same color that the line of demarcation was not readily apparent, and had it not been for the drift rubbish around the former it might have escaped our scrutiny even at our short distance from it. The Indians say that the White River rises in glacier-bearing lands, and that it is very swift, and full of rapids along its whole course. So swift is it at its mouth, that as it pours its muddy waters into the rapid Yukon it carries them nearly across that clear blue stream ; the waters of the two rivers mingling almost at once, and not running distinct for miles side by side, as is stated in one book on Alaska. From the

mouth of the White or Yu'-ko-kon to Bering Sea, nearly
1,500 miles, the Yukon is so muddy as to be noticeable
even when its water is taken up in the palm of the hand ;
and all fishing with hook and line ceases.

About four in the afternoon the mouth of the Stewart
River was passed, and, being covered with islands, might
not have been noticed except for its valley, which is very
noticeable—a broad valley fenced in by high hills. A
visit to the shore in our canoe showed its mouth to be
deltoid in character, three mouths being observed, and
others probably existing. Islands were very numerous
in this portion of the Yukon, much more so than in any
part of the river we had yet visited, and as the raft had
drifted on while I went ashore in the canoe, I had a very
hard task to find it again and came within a scratch of
losing it, having passed beyond the camp, and being
compelled to return. It was about nine o'clock in the
evening and the low north-western sun shone squarely in
our faces, as we descended the river, eagerly looking for
the ascending smoke of the camp-fire, which had been
agreed upon, before separation, as the signal to be kept
going until we returned. The setting sun throwing its
slanting rays upon each point of woods that ran from
the hillsides down to the water's edge, illumined the top
of them with a whitish light until each one exactly
resembled a camp-fire on the river bank with the feathery
smoke floating off along the tree tops. Even my Indian
canoeman was deceived at first, until half a dozen appearing together in sight convinced him of his error.
All these islands were densely covered with spruce and
poplar, and the swift current cutting into their alluvial
banks, though the latter were frozen six or eight feet

thick, kept their edges bristling with freshly-fallen timber ; and it was almost courting destruction to get under
this *abatis* of trees with the raft, in the powerful current, to avoid which some of our hardest work was necessary. The preservative power of this constantly
frozen ground must be very great, as in many places we
saw protruding from the high banks great accumulations
of driftwood and logs over which there was soil two and
three feet thick, which had been formerly carried by the
river, and from which sprung forests of spruce timber,
as high as any in sight, at whose feet were rotting trunks
that must have been saplings centuries ago. Yet
wherever this ancient driftwood had been undermined and
washed of its dirt and thrown upon the beach along with
the tree but just fallen, the difference between the two
was only that the latter still retained its green bark, and
its broken limbs were not so abraded and worn ; but
there seemed to be no essential difference in the fiber of
the timber.

The evening of the 17th, having scored forty geographical miles, we camped on a low gravel bar, and
bivouacked in the open air so clear and still was the
night, although by morning huge drops of rain were falling on our upturned faces.

On the 18th, shortly after noon, we passed a number of *Tahk-ong* Indians, stretched upon the green
sward of the right bank leisurely enjoying themselves ;
their birch-bark canoes, sixteen in all, being pulled up
on the gravel beach in front of them. It was probably a
trading or hunting party, there being one person for each
canoe, none of whom were women. Already we observed an increase in the size and a greater cumbrousness

in the build of the birch-bark canoes, when compared with the fairy-like craft of the Ayans, a characteristic that slowly increased as we descended the river until the *kiak*, or sealskin canoe of the Eskimo is encountered along the lower waters of the great river. Of course this change of build reflects no discredit upon the skill of the makers, as a heavier craft is required to navigate

MOOSE-SKIN MOUNTAIN, AND CAMP 32 AT THE MOUTH OF DEER RIVER.

the rougher water, as the broad stream is stirred up by the persistent southern winds of the Yukon basin.

About 8.30 P. M. we passed an Indian camp on the left bank, which, from the seeming good quality of their canvas tents as viewed from the river, we judged might prove to be a mining party of whites. From them we learned that there was a deserted white man's store but a few miles beyond, but that the trader himself, had quitted the place several months before, going down to salt-water, as they expressed it. This was evidently the same trader the Ayans expected to meet at a little semi-permanent station of the Alaska Commercial Company dubbed Fort Reliance; and they seemed quite discomfited at his departure, although he had left the preceding autumn, and as we afterward ascertained more from fear of the Indians in his neighborhood than any other reason.

We camped that night at the mouth of a noticeable but small stream coming in from the east, which we afterward learned was called Deer Creek by the traders, from the large number of caribou or woodland reindeer seen in its valley at certain times of their migrations.

At this point of its course the Yukon River is extremely narrow in comparison with the distance from its head— about 700 miles,—and considering its previous mean width, being here only two hundred or two hundred and fifty yards across. It certainly must have great depth to be able to carry the immense volume of water of so swift and wide a river as it is above, for the current does not seem to increase appreciably in this narrow channel.

Directly northward in plain sight is a prominent landmark on this part of the river, viz., a high hill called by the Indians "the moose-skin mountain." Two ravines that converge from its top again diverge when about to meet about half way down the mountain slope, and along these two arms of an hyperbola there has been a great landslide, laying bare the dull red ocherous soil beneath, which contrasts almost vividly with the bright green of the grass and foliage of the mountain flank, and in shape and color resembles a gigantic moose-skin stretched out to dry. That day's drift gave us forty-seven and a half miles, and all our scores were good while passing the ramparts, the delays from sand, mud and gravel bars being very small.

Believing that I was now in close proximity to the British boundary, as shown by our dead reckoning—kept by Mr. Homan,—I reluctantly determined on giving a day (the 19th of July) to astronomical observations,—reluctantly because every day was of vital importance in reaching St. Michael's, near the mouth of the river, in time to reach any outgoing vessels for the United States ; for if too late to catch them, we should have to spend a dismal and profitless year at that place. That day, however, proved so tempestuous, and the prospect so uninviting, that after getting a couple of poor "sights" for longitude, I ordered camp broken, and we got away shortly after eleven o'clock.

A few minutes before one o'clock we passed the abandoned trading station on the right bank of the river, which we surmised from certain maps and from subsequent information to be the one named Fort Reliance. It was a most dilapidated-looking frontier pile of shanties, consisting of one main house, probably the store, above ground, and three or four cellar-like houses, the ruined roofs of which were the only vestiges remaining above ground. The Indians said that Mr. McQuestion, the trader, had left on account of severe sickness, but his own story, when we met him afterward on the lower river, was that he was sick of the Indians, the main tribe of which were peaceful enough, but contained several ugly tempered communistic medicine-men

who had threatened his life in order to get rid of his
competition in the drug business, which resulted greatly
to their financial detriment.

Nearly opposite Fort Reliance was the Indian village
of Noo-klak-ó, or Nuclaco, numbering about one hundred and fifty people. Our approach was welcomed by
a protracted salute of from fifty to seventy-five discharges of their old rusty muskets, to which we replied
with a far less number. Despite the great value of powder and other ammunition to these poor isolated savages,
who are often obliged to make journeys of many hundreds of miles in order to procure them, and must oftentimes be in sore need of them for hunting purposes, they
do not hesitate in exciting times—and every visit of a
stranger causes excitement—to waste their ammunition
in foolish bangings and silly salutes that suggest the
vicinity of a powder magazine. I suppose the expenditure on our visit, if judiciously employed in hunting,
would have supplied their village with meat for probably
a month ; and yet we drifted by with hardly a response.
This method of saluting is very common along the river
from this point on, and is, I believe, an old Russian custom which has found its way thus far up the stream,
which is much beyond where they had ever traded. It
is a custom often mentioned in descriptions of travel further down the river. The permanent number of inhabitants, according to Mr. McQuestion, was about seventy-
five or eighty ; and therefore there must have been a
great number of visitors among them at the time of our
passing. They seemed very much disappointed that we
did not visit their village, and the many who crowded
around the drifting raft in their little fleet of canoes

spoke only of tea and tobacco, for which they seemed
ready to barter their very souls. Their principal diet in
summer and early fall is furnished by the salmon of the
Yukon, while during winter and spring, until the ice
disappears, they feed on the flesh of moose and caribou.
A trader on the upper river told me that the ice of the
stream is removed from the upper ramparts and above
principally by melting, while all that covers the Yukon
below that part is washed out by the spring rise of the
river, there being fully a month's difference in the matter between the two districts. Noo-klak-o′ was a semi-
permanent village, but a most squalid-looking affair,—
somewhat resembling the Ayan town, but with a much
greater preponderance of canvas. Most of the native
visitors we saw were Tanana′ Indians, and I was somewhat surprised to find them put the accent, in a broad
way, on the second syllable, *Ta-nah′-nee*, differing
radically from the pronunciation of the same name by
the Indians at the mouth of the river, and by most white
travelers of the Lower Yukon. From this point a trail
leads south-westward over the mountains to a tributary
of the Tanana, by means of which these Indians visit
Noo-klak-o. The 19th was a most disagreeable day, with
alternating rain showers and drifting fog, which had followed us since the day of our failure in securing astronomical observations, and to vary the discomfort, after
making less than thirty miles we stuck so fast on the
upper point of a long gravel bar that we had to carry
our effects ashore on our backs, and there camp with
only half a dozen water-logged sticks for a camp-fire.
What in the world any mosquito wanted to do out on that
desert of a sand-bar in a cold drifting fog I could never

imagine, but before our beds were fairly made they put in an appearance in the usual unlimited numbers and made sleep, after a hard day's work, almost impossible.

Starting at 8:10 A.M., next morning, from Camp 33, at 11:30 we passed a good sized river coming in from the west, which I named the Cone-Hill River, from the fact that there is a prominent conical hill in the center of its broad valley, near the mouth.

Just beyond the mouth of the Cone-Hill River we suddenly came in sight of some four or five black and brown bears in an open or untimbered space of about an acre or two on the steep hillsides of the western slope. The raft was left to look after itself and we gave them a running volley of skirmish fire that sent them scampering up the steep hill into the dense brush and timber, their principal loss being loss of breath. By not attending to the navigation of our craft in the excitement of the short bear hunt we ran on a submerged rock in a current so swift that we swung around so rapidly as almost to throw a number of us overboard, stuck for a couple of minutes with the water boiling over the stern, and in general lost our faith in the ability of our vessel to navigate itself. In a previous chapter I have mentioned having been told by a person in southern Alaska, undoubtedly conscientious in his statement, and having considerable experience as a hunter, that the black and brown bear of his district never occupied the same localities, and although the sequence of these localities might be as promiscuous as the white and black squares on a checker-board, yet each species remained wholly on his own color, so to speak ; and this led him to believe that the weaker of the two, the black bear, had good reason to be afraid of his more powerful neighbor. This day's observation of the two species living together, in one very small area, shows either an error of judgment on the part of the observer mentioned, or a difference of the ursine nature in different regions.

After leaving the Stewart River, which had been identified by a sort of *reductio ad absurdum* reasoning, I found it absolutely impossible to identity any of the other streams from the descriptions and maps now in existence, even when aided by the imperfect information derived from the local tribes. Indianne, my Chilkat-Tahk-heesh interpreter, got along very well among the latter tribe. Among the Ayans were many who spoke Tahk-heesh, with whom they traded, and here we had but little trouble. Even lower down we managed to get along after a fashion, for one or two of the Ayan medicine-men who came as far as Fort Reliance with us, could occasionally be found, and they understood the lower languages pretty fairly, and although we struggled through four or five tongues we could still make out that tea and tobacco were the leading topics of conversation everywhere. Beyond Fort Reliance, and after bidding adieu to our four Ayans, we were almost at sea, but occasionally in the most roundabout way we managed to elicit information of a limited character.

About the middle of the afternoon of that day, the 20th, we floated past a remarkable-looking rock, standing conspicuously in a flat level bottom of the river on the eastern side, and very prominent in its isolation. I could not but notice the strong resemblance between it and Castle Rock on the Columbia River, although I judge it to be only about one-half or two-thirds the size of the latter, but much more prominent, not being over-shadowed by near and higher mountains. I called it the Roquette Rock, in honor of M. Alex. de la Roquette, of the Paris Geographical Society. The Indians have a legend connected with it, so it is said, that the Yukon River once flowed along the distant hills back of it, and that the rock formed part of the bluff seen in the illustration just below, overhanging the western shore of the river, both being about the same height and singu-

ROQUETTE ROCK.
(As we approached looking down the stream.)

larly alike in other respects. Here the bluff and rock lived many geological periods in wedded bliss as man and wife, but finally family dissensions invaded the rocky household and culminated in the stony-hearted husband kicking his wrangling wife into the center of the distant plain, and changing the course of the great river so that it flowed between them to emphasize the perpetual divorce. The bluff and the rock, so my informant told me, are still known among the Indians as "the old man" and "the old wife." Despite a most disagreeable day, on the 20th we showed a record of forty-five geographical miles, by way of compensation for the dark lowering clouds that hung over us like a pall. The scenery passed that day would have been picturesque enough when viewed through any other medium than that of a wretched drizzle of rain. Just before camping we saw high perpendicular bluffs of what appeared to be limestone, frowning over us from the eastern shore, which were perforated with huge caverns that would have made good dens for bears, but their situation was such that no bears not possessing wings could have reached them. On the map this bluff figures as Cave Rock.

We got a late start on the 21st, the wretched weather being good for late sleeping if for nothing else, the middle of the forenoon finding us just pulling out. At noon we passed a good-sized river coming in from the east, but if it had been mapped we were unable to identify it. A few minutes afterward we swung around a sharp bend in the river and saw a confused mass of brush or logs that denoted an Indian village in the distance, a supposition confirmed by the number of canoes afloat in its front and by a motley crowd of natives on the bank, well mingled with the inevitable troop of dogs that to the eye of the experienced traveler is as sure a sign of an Indian village as both Indians and houses together. This was the first Indian village we had encountered on the river deserving the name of permanent, and even here the logs of which the cabins, six in number, were built, seemed to be mere poles, and by no means as substantially built as it might have been with the material at hand. It was perched up on a high flat bank on the western side of the river, the gable ends of the house fronting the stream, and all of them very close together, there being only one or two places wide enough for a path to allow the inmates to pass. The fronts of the houses are nearly on the same line, and this row is so close to the scarp of the bank that the "street" in front is a very narrow path, where two persons can hardly pass unless one of them steps indoors or down the hill; and when I visited the village the road was so monopolized by scratching dogs that I could hardly force my way through them. This street may have been much wider in times of yore—for it seemed to be quite an old village—and the encroachments of the eroding river during freshets may have reduced it to its present narrowness. If so, it will not be long before the present village must be abandoned or set back some distance. Further up the river we saw a single pole house projecting over the bank about a fourth or a third of its length, and deserted by its occupants. The body of the houses is of a very inferior construction, in which ventilation seems to be the predominating idea (although even this is not developed to a sufficient degree, as judged by one's nose upon entering), and the large door in front is roughly closed by a well-riddled moose or caribou skin, or occasionally by a piece of canvas so dirty that at the distance of a few feet it might be taken for an animal's skin. The roofs are of skins battened down by spruce poles, which, projecting beyond the comb in irregular lengths, often six and eight feet, gave the whole village a most bristling appearance. A

fire is built on the dirt-floor, in the center of the habitation, and the smoke left to get out the best way it can. As the occupants are generally sitting flat on the floor, or stretched out at full length on their backs or stomachs in the dirt, they are in a stratum of air comparatively clear; or, at least, endurable to Indian lungs. The ascending smoke finds ample air-holes among the upper cracks of the walls, while that dense mass of it which is retained under the skins of the roof, making it almost impossible to stand upright, is utilized for smoking the salmon which are hung up in this space. The Indian name of the village is Klat-ol-klin', but it is generally known on the Middle River as Johnny's Village, after the chief's Americanized name. That dignitary was absent on a journey of several days down the river, at the time of our arrival.

A number of long leaning poles, braced on their downhill ends by cross uprights, were noticed on the gravel beach in front of the village ; these serve as scaffoldings upon which to dry salmon in the sun, and to keep them from the many dogs while undergoing this process. While taking a photograph of the town, two or three salmon fell from the poles ; and in a twinkling fully sixty or seventy dogs were huddled together about them in a writhing mass, each one trying to get his share,—and that of several others. The camera was sighted toward them, a hurried guess made as to the proper focus, and an instantaneous view attempted, but the negative looked more like a representation of an approaching thunder shower, and I never afterward printed from it. Occasionally in these rushes a row of scaffolding will be knocked down, and if it happens to be loaded with salmon the consequent feast will be of a more extensive nature. These dogs were of a smaller breed, and noticeably of a darker color, than the Eskimo dogs of the lower river. They are employed by these Indians for the same purposes, but to a more limited extent.

It was at this village that what to me was the most wonderful and striking performance given by any natives we encountered on the whole trip was displayed. I refer to their method of fishing for salmon. I have already spoken of the extreme muddiness of the Yukon below the mouth of the White River; and this spot, of course, is no exception. I believe I do not exaggerate in the least when I say, that, if an ordinary pint tin-cup were filled with it, nothing could be seen at the bottom until the sediment had settled. The water is about nine or ten feet deep on the fishing banks in front of the houses, where they fish with their nets; or at least that is about the length of the poles to which the nets are attached. The salmon I saw them take were caught about two hundred or two hundred and fifty yards directly out from the shore in front of the houses. Standing in front of this row of cabins, some person, generally an old man, squaw or child, possibly on duty for that purpose, would announce, in a loud voice, that a salmon was coming up the river, perhaps from a quarter to a third of a mile away. This news would stir up some young man from the cabins, who from his elevated position in front of them would identify the salmon's position, and then run down to the beach, pick up his canoe, paddle and net, launch the former and start rapidly out into the river; the net lying on the canoe's birch deck in front of him, his movements being guided by his own sight and that of a half dozen others on the high bank, all shouting advice to him at the same time. Evidently, in the canoe he could not judge well of the fish's position, especially at a distance ; for he seemed to rely on the advice from the shore to direct his movements until the fish was near him, when with two or three dexterous and powerful strokes with both hands, he shot the little canoe to a point near the position he wished to take up, regulating its finer movements by the paddle used as a sculling oar in his left hand, while with his right he grasped the net at the end of its handle and plunged it into the water the whole length of its pole to the bottom of the river (some nine or ten feet); often leaning far over and thrusting the arm deep into the water, so as to adjust the mouth of the net, covering about two square feet, directly over the course of the salmon so as to entrap him. Of seven attempts, at intervals covering three hours, two were successful (and in two others salmon were caught but escaped while the nets were being raised), salmon being taken that weighed from fifteen to twenty pounds. How these Indians can see at this distance the coming of a single salmon along the bottom of a river eight or ten feet deep, and determine their course or position near enough to catch them in the narrow mouth of a small net, when immediately under the eye a vessel holding that number of inches of water from the muddy river completely obscures an object at its bottom, is a problem that I will not attempt to solve. Their success depends of course in some way on the motion of the fish. In vain they attempted to show members of my party the coming fish. I feel perfectly satisfied that none of the white men could see the slightest trace of the movements to which their attention was called.   Under the skin roofs of their log-cabins and on the scaffoldings upon the gravel beach were many hundred salmon that had been caught in this curious way. The only plausible theory which I could evolve within the limits of the non-marvelous, was, that the salmon came along near the top of the water, so as to show or indicate the dorsal fin, and that as it approached the canoe, the sight of it, or more likely some slight noise, made with that intention, drove the fish to the bottom without any considerable lateral deviation, whereupon they were inclosed by the net.   But my interpreters told me (and I think their interpretation was correct in this case, roundabout as it was), that this superficial swimming did not take place, but that the motion of the fish was communicated from the deep water to the surface, often when the fish was quite at the bottom.

The nets used have already been partially described. The mouth is held open by a light wooden frame of a

KLAT-OL-KLIN FISHING NETS.
Scale, 1-30.

reniform shape, as shown in the figure on this page, and as one may readily see, this is of great advantage in securing the handle firmly by side braces to the rim of the net's mouth as shown, that being undoubtedly the object sought.   Further down the river (that is, in the "lower ramparts"), the reniform rim becomes circular; thus of course increasing the chances of catching the fish; all the other dimensions, too, are greatly increased.   When the salmon is netted, a turn is immediately given to the

handle, thus effectually trapping the fish below the
mouth of the net, and upon the dexterity thus displayed
no little of the fisherman's success depends. Two salmon were lost upon this occasion after they had actually
passed into the net, owing to lack of agility in this operation. When fully entrapped
and brought alongside, a fish-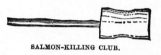
club, as shown, is used to kill
the salmon immediately by a

SALMON-KILLING CLUB.

hard blow over the head, for the struggles of so large
a fish might easily upset a frail canoe.

Up to this time the birch-bark canoes on the river had
been so fragile and "cranky" that my Chilkat Indians,
who were used to the heavy wooden canoes of their country, felt unsafe in employing them for all purposes, but
these were so much larger and stronger in build, and our
old Tahk-heesh "dug-out" so thoroughly worthless,
that we felt safe in buying one at this village, but for a
number of days "Billy" and "Indianne" paddled very
gingerly when making excursions in it.

A few Hudson Bay toboggan sledges were seen on
scaffolds at and near the village ; they seem to be the
principal sledges of this part of the country. The snow
shoes of this tribe differed from those of the Chilkats by
trifling modifications only, being a sort of compromise
between the hunting and packing snow shoes of the
latter.

About a mile or a mile and a quarter below Klat-ol-
klin', and on the same side of the river, is a fairly constructed white man's log cabin, which had once been used
as a trading store, but was now deserted. We afterward
learned that this trading station was called Belle Isle,

and had only been built two years before, having been abandoned the preceding year as not paying. The Indians evidently must have surmised that the trader would return, as they respected the condition in which he left the building, in a manner most creditable to their honesty, no one having entered or disturbed it since he left. They evidently care very 'little for beads as ornaments, for I saw none of them wearing that much coveted Indian adornment, while great quantities were scattered around by the trader's store, having been trampled into the ground. At no place on the river did I find such an eagerness for beads as characterizes the American Indians of milder climes, but nowhere did I see such total disregard for them as was shown here.

Near Belle Isle is a prominent hill called by the Indians *Ta-tot'-lee*, its conspicuousness heightened by the comparative flatness of the country which lies between two entering rivers and a great bend of the Yukon. As our survey showed it to be just within Alaska, bordering on the boundary between it and the British Northwest Territory, I gave it the additional name of Boundary Butte.

The country was now noticeably more open, and it was evident that we had already passed the most mountainous portion of the chain, the intersection of which by the river forms the upper ramparts.

The next day we made thirty-six miles, and as the whole day had been a most disagreeable one when at six o'clock we got drawn into an eddy, near which was a fair place to camp, I ordered the raft made fast and the tents pitched.

That day—the 22d—while under way, we saw a large dead king-salmon, floating belly upwards with the current, and we kept near it for some time. This spectacle became more familiar as we descended, while everywhere we met with the rough coarse dog-salmon strewn upon the beach, frequently in such numbers, and tainting the air so strongly with the odor of their decay, that an otherwise good camp would be spoiled by their presence.

MOUNT TA-TOT'-LEE, OR BOUNDARY BUTTE.

(Also showing Middle Yukon River Indians' methods of killing swimming moose.)

The river rose ten inches that night—a fact easily accounted for by the protracted and often heavy rains. The forenoon of the 23d was very gloomy, but shortly after noon the weather surprised us by clearing up.

At 3:30 that day we came upon another Indian town called Charley's Village; but the current was so swift that we could not get the raft up to the bank so as to camp alongside, but we were successful in making a sand-bar about half a mile below. Charley's Village was an exact counterpart of Johnny's, even as to the number of houses—six—and the side of the river—the western; and considering this and the trouble to reach it, I did not attempt to photograph it. When attempting to reach it with the raft, so anxious were the Indians for our success, that as many as could do so put the bows of their canoes on the outer log of the raft, and paddled forward with as much vehemence as if their very lives depended upon the result. In three or four minutes they had worked themselves into a streaming perspiration, and had probably shoved the huge raft as many inches toward the bank. We found a Canadian voyageur among them of the name of Jo. Ladue, who, as a partner of one of the traders on the lower river, had drifted here in prospecting the stream for precious mineral. "Jo," as he is familiarly known, speaks of the natives of both these villages as Tadoosh, and says they are the best-natured Indians from here till the Eskimo are met with. Ladue had a fairly-made scow over twenty feet long, about half a dozen wide, and three deep, which he wanted to hire us, but as it would not hold all the party and effects we had to decline the tender, despite his emphatic assurances that we could not safely go much further with our raft. It was with Ladue that I first noticed particularly the pronunciation of the name of the great river, on whose waters we were drifting, a pronunciation which is universal among the few whites along its borders, and that sounded strangely at first ; that is with the accent on the first syllable, and not on the second, as I had so usually heard it pronounced in the United States. That night, the 23d, the mosquitoes were perfectly unbearable in their assaults, and if the weather had not turned bitterly cold toward morning I doubt if we could have obtained any sleep at all, for the mosquito-bars seemed to be no protection whatever.

I think I established one mosquito theory of a practical bearing, on a pretty firm basis, while upon this trip "in the land of the mosquito's paradise ;" and that was, if the insects are so thick that they constantly touch each other on the mosquito-bar when crawling over it, it will be no protection whatever, if the meshes are of the usual size, and they will come in so fast that comfort is out of the question, but otherwise there is some chance which increases as their numbers diminish. Even if there are two or three to the square inch of your bar of many square yards, it surprises you how few get through, but the minute they begin crawling over each other they seem to become furious, and make efforts to squeeze through the meshes which are often rewarded with success, until a sharp slap on the face sounds their death knell. The doctor, in a fit of exasperation, said he believed that two of them would hold the legs and wings of another flat against its body, while a third shoved it through ; but I doubt the existence of co-operation among them. I think they are too mean to help one another.

CHAPTER X.

AFTER passing Johnny's village in descending the stream, and more perceptibly after leaving Charley's village, the country opens rapidly, and another day's drift of forty-two and a half geographical miles brought us to what an old trader on the lower river calls the "Yukon flat-lands," an expression so appropriate that I have adopted it, although I have never heard any other authority for its use.

While descending the stream on the 24th, late in the forenoon, we saw a large buck moose swim from one of the many islands to the mainland just back of us, having probably, as the hunter would say, "gotten our scent." I never comprehended what immense noses these animals have until I got a good profile view of this big fellow, and although over half a mile away, his nose looked as if he had been rooting the island and was trying to carry away the greater part of it on the end of his snout. The great palmated horns above, the broad " throat-latch " before, combined with the huge nose and powerful shoulders, make one think that this animal might tilt forward on his head from sheer gravity, so little is there apparently at the other end to counterbalance these masses. When the Russians were on the lower river these moose-noses were dried by them and considered great delicacies. A few winters ago the cold was so intense, and the snow covered the ground for so great a depth throughout the season, that sad havoc was played with the unfortunate animals, and a moose is now a rare sight below the upper ramparts of the river, as I was informed by the traders of that district. It is certainly to be hoped that the destruction has only been partial, so that this noble game may again flourish in its home, where it will be secure from the inroads of fire-arms for many decades to come. Not long since the little river steamer that plies on this stream for trading purposes, owned by the Alaska Commercial Company, could hardly make a voyage to old Fort Yukon and back without encountering a few herds of these animals swimming across the stream, and exciting were the bouts with them, often ending in a victory for the moose with the " Yukon " run aground on a bar of sand or gravel ; but for some years not an animal has been seen by them. Formerly the meat they secured in this way, with what they procured from the Indians along the river, assured them of fresh food during the month or so they were absent from St. Michael's ; but their entire dependence for this kind of fare has been thrown upon the salmon furnished by the natives, which is much more difficult to keep fresh during the short hot summer of the river.

This river steamer, the "Yukon," was daily expected by "Jo" Ladue, and upon it he intended to return to Nuklakayet, his winter station. I also hoped to fall in with it during the next week, as our civilized provisions were at a very low ebb and I wished to replenish them. During a great part of our drift on the 24th, we were accompanied by Jo and his three Indian allies, in their scow, who said they would keep us company until we met the "Yukon" steamer. While we were leisurely floating along, "Jo" saw a "short cut" in the river's bend, into which we could not row our ponderous craft, and down this he quickly disappeared, remarking that he would pick out a good camping place for us for the night.

Although we were well out of the high mountainous country, we could see the chain through which we had passed still bearing off to the left, the summits in many places covered with snow, long fingers of which extended down such mountain gullies as had a northern exposure. As we emerged from the hilly country the soil, for the first time, seemed to be thick and black wherever it was exposed to our eye by the caving in of the banks ; and grass, always good, now became really luxuriant for any climate. In many places we saw grass ready to mow, were it not for the fact that even the largest prairies have an undergrowth of stunted brush which one might not observe at a distance in the high grass, but which is very perceptible in walking through it. The greatest obstacle to cattle raising in the Yukon valley would be the dense swarms of mosquitoes, although I understand that a couple of head of cattle were kept at old Fort Yukon for one or two summers. By burning off all timber and brush from large districts and a little judicious drainage it might be possible to encourage this industry with the hardier breeds of cattle, but at present the case is too remote to speculate upon.

I now remarked in many places along the flat river-bottoms—which had high banks, however—that the ground was covered, especially in little open prairies, with a tough sponge-like moss or peat. If the bank was at all gravelly, so as to give good drainage, and to allow of the river excavating it gradually, as is usual in temperate climes, this thick moss was so interwoven and compacted that it would not break or separate in falling with the river banks, but remained attached to the crest, forming great blankets of moss that overhung the shores a foot thick, as I have endeavored to represent on this page, *a. b.* representing the moss. Some of these banks were from fifteen to eighteen feet in height, and this overhanging moss would even then reach to the water, keeping the shores neatly

MOSS ON YUKON RIVER.

sodded to the water's edge on the inclined banks, and hanging perpendicularly from those that projected over. Great jagged rents and patches were torn out of the hem of this carpet by the limbs and roots of drifting logs, thus destroying its picturesque uniformity. I suppose the reason why it was more noticeable in open spaces was that the trees and underbrush, and especially their roots, would, from the effect of undermining, carry the moss into the water with their heavy weight as they fell.

At half-past five o'clock we sighted a steamer down the river which we thought might be the Alaska Commercial Company's "Yukon" coming up around a low island of sand, but it proved to be a beached boat called the St. Michael's, lying high and dry, about ten or twelve feet above the present water level, on a long, low island of sand and gravel.

Some years before, a rival corporation to the Alaska Company, called, I believe, The Northern Trading Company, tried to establish itself on the Yukon River, (and elsewhere in Alaska, but the Yukon district only concerns us here), and trading houses were built in many places along the stream, most of them within a short distance, perhaps a mile or two, of those established by the Alaska Commercial Company. Fierce competition ensued, and I was told that the Indians got goods at wholesale prices in San Francisco, *i. e.*, at almost infinitesimal prices compared with those they were accustomed to pay. The Alaska Company was finally victorious, but found matters considerably changed when the struggle was over. When they attempted to restore the prices of the old *régime*, and to ask immediate payment —for both companies had given the Indians unlimited credit—such a hornet's nest was stirred up that ultimately the company was obliged to abandon nearly a half-dozen posts, all above Nuklakayet, for fear of the Indians, who required a Krupp steam-hammer to pound into their thick heads the reason why a man might sell them a pound of tobacco for ten cents to-day and to-morrow charge them ten dollars an ounce; especially when they have to pay for the latter from the products of the trap, and the former is put down in the account book in an accommodating way. The Northern Trading Company also put on the Yukon River this boat, the St. Michael's, a clumsily-built stern-wheeler that had wintered at Belle Isle, **and on** going down with the spring freshet had struck **this bar**, then under water, and as the river was falling she was soon left high in the air.

We camped for the night on the same bar, which I called St. Michael's Island, and about an hour afterward "Jo" and his scow came along and pulled up to camp on the opposite shore. He explained his delay—for I really thought he had passed us and was camping further down—by saying that he and his Indians had been hunting, and he produced two or three ducks, in the very prime of their toughness, as corroborative testimony, but I surmised that the true story was that "all hands and the cook" had gone to sleep, whereupon the scow had likewise rested on the soft bottom of some friendly sandspit. The remainder of the journey confirmed this suspicion.

Starting from Camp No. 38, on St. Michael's Island, the river, as the map shows, becomes one vast and wide net-work of islands, the whole country being as level as the great plains of the West, and we were fairly launched into the "Yukon flat-lands." As we entered this floorlike country our Chilkat Indians seemed seriously to think that we had arrived at the river's mouth and were now going out to sea ; and I can readily imagine that even a white person, having no knowledge of the country, might well think so. There was an almost irresistible impression that beyond the low flat islands in front one must come in sight of the ocean.

As we started out into this broad, level tract, the

mountains to the left, or west, still continued in a broken range that was thrown back at an angle from the river's general course, and projected into a sort of spur formed of a series of isolated peaks, rising squarely out of the flat land, and diminishing in size until they disappeared toward the north-west in a few sharp-pointed hillocks just visible over the high spruce trees of the islands. I called them the Ratzel range, or peaks, after Professor Frederick Ratzel, of Munich.

This flat character of the country continues for about three hundred miles further, and the river, unconfined by resisting banks, cuts numerous wide channels in the soft alluvial shores, dividing and subdividing and spreading, until its width is simply beyond reasonable estimation. At Fort Yukon, about a thousand miles from the mouth, its width has been closely estimated at seven miles, and at other points above and below it is believed to be twice or thrice that width. This breadth is measured from the right bank to the left across shallow channels and flat islands, whose ratio to each other is, on the whole, tolerably equal. Some of these islands are merely wide wastes, consisting of low stretches of sand and gravel, with desolate-looking ridges of whitened drift-timber, all of which must be under water in the spring floods, when the river in this region must resemble a great inland sea. In no place does this wide congeries of channels seem to abate its former swiftness a single jot, but the constant dividing and subdividing occasionally brought us to lanes so narrow and shallow that it seemed as though we could not get through with our raft, and more than once we feared we should have to abandon our old companion. For nearly three weeks we were drifting through these terribly monotonous flat-lands, never knowing at night whether or not we were camping on the main bank, and by far the most frequently camping on some island with nothing but islands in sight as far as the eye could see.

On the 25th we got under way quite early, and at 8:30 A. M. passed an Indian encampment of four very fine-looking tents, situated on an island, and here "Jo" Ladue told us he would stop and await the arrival of the Alaska Company's new steamer. I had suspicions that "Jo" did not like the pace we kept up, or rather that he did not relish being awakened whenever his scow sought the quiet of an island shore.

But a few minutes afterward there was a junction of several channels of the river, and we floated out into the lake-like expanse ahead with a vague feeling that so much water could hardly possess any current, but nevertheless we sped along at our old pace. This sheet of water was wider than the majority of the lakes at the head of the stream, and it was hard not to revert to them in thought, and imagine ourselves unable to move without a sail and a good wind abaft. Very soon an ominous line of drift timber appeared in our front, seeming to stretch from shore to shore as we approached it, and the great channel broke up into half a dozen smaller ones that went winding through sand-spits and log-locked débris, down one of which we shot and were just breathing more freely when the same occurrence was repeated, and we slipped down a shallow branch that was not over fifty yards in width, only to bring up on a bar in the swift current, with less than a foot of water ahead over the spit that ran from the bar to the shore.

Near the other shore was a channel so deep that we might have floated with ease, but to reach it again we should have to pry our vessel up stream against water so swift as almost to take us off our feet. Through this deep channel every thing was carried on our backs to the shore, and then commenced a struggle that lasted from ten o'clock in the morning until well past two in the afternoon; our longest and most trying delay on the trip, and which limited our day's travel to thirty-six miles in fourteen hours' work. Half as much would have satisfied us, however, for I think it was the only time on the trip when we made serious calculations regarding the abandonment of the raft and the building of another. There were other occasions when such an event seemed probable, but in some way we had managed to escape this necessity.

Our camp that evening was on a bank so high and solid that we conjectured it must be the main bank (of the eastern side). So steep was it that steps had to be cut in it in order to reach the top with our camping and cooking effects.

At this camp—39—and a few of the preceding ones we found rosebuds large and sweet enough to eat, and really a palatable change from the salt and canned provisions of our larder. They were very much larger than those we are accustomed to see in the United States proper and somewhat elongated or pear shaped; the increase in size being entirely in the fleshy capsule which was crisp and tender, while even the seeds seemed to be less dry and "downy," or full of "cotton," than those of temperate climes.

The mosquitoes were a little less numerous in the flat-

lands, but, at first, the little black gnats seemed to grow
even worse. Mr. Homan, who was especially troubled
by these latter pests, had his hands so swollen by their
constant attacks that he could hardly draw his fingers
together to grasp the pencil with which he recorded his
topographical notes. Dr. Wilson and I experimented
with some oil of pennyroyal taken from the medicine
chest, which is extensively used as an important ingred-
ient of the mosquito cures advertised in more southern
climes. It is very volatile and evaporates so rapidly
that it was only efficacious with the pests of the Yukon
for two or three minutes, when they would attack the
spot where it had been spread with their old vigor.
Mixed with grease it held its properties a little longer,
but would never do to depend upon in this mosquito
infested country.

I noticed that evening that banked or cumulus clouds,
lying low along the horizon invariably indicated mountains or hills stretching under them if all the other parts
of the sky were clear. At that time we recognized
the Romantzoff range by this means, bearing north-
west, a discovery we easily verified the next morning
when the air was clear in every direction. At no time
while we were drifting through the flat-lands, when the
weather and our position were favorable, were hills or
mountains out of view, although at times so distant as
to resemble light blue clouds on the horizon.

Although we were at the most northern part of our
journey while in this level tract, actually passing within
the Arctic regions for a short distance at old Fort Yukon,
yet there was no part of the journey where we suffered
so much from the downpouring heat of the sun, when-

ever the weather was clear ; and exasperatingly enough our greatest share of clear weather was while we were floating between the upper and lower ramparts.

All day on the 26th the current seemed to set to the westward, and we left island after island upon our right in spite of all our efforts, for we wanted to keep the extreme eastern channels so as to make old Fort Yukon, where we had learned that an Indian, acting as a trader for the Alaska Company might have some flour to sell. Our most strenuous efforts in the hot sun were rewarded by our stranding a number of times on the innumerable shoals in the shallow river, delaying us altogether nearly three hours, and allowing us to make but thirty-three miles, our course bringing us almost in proximity to the western bank. I knew that we must be but a short distance from old Fort Yukon, at which point I intended to await the river steamer's arrival so as to procure provisions, for I had only two days' rations left; but this day had been so unfavorable that I almost gave up all hope of making the Fort, expecting to drift by next day far out of sight of it. About eleven o'clock that night " Alexy," the half-breed Russian interpreter for Ladue, came into our camp in his canoe, saying that Ladue had gone on down to Fort Yukon that day, keeping the main right-hand channel which we had missed, and that we were now so far to the west and so near Fort Yukon that we might pass it to-morrow among the islands without seeing it unless we kept more to the right. After receiving this doleful information, which coincided so exactly with our own conclusions, we went to sleep, and " Alexy " paddled away down stream, keeping a strong course to the east, but it would have required Great Eastern's engines on board of our cumbersome raft in order for us to make it.

From the moment of our casting loose the raft, on the morning of the 27th, we commenced our struggle with the current to gain ground, or rather, water, to the eastward, often with double and treble complements of men at both oars. Point after point we successfully essayed, working like pirates after their prey; and fully a half dozen of these, I believe, were so closely passed across their upper ends that a score less of strokes would have allowed us to float down the western channel. Almost at the last minute we got such a straight away course to the right bank that looking backward it seemed as if we had ferried our way directly across the river, and as we rounded the last island Fort Yukon's old dilapidated buildings burst into view, in the very nick of time, too, for that particular island extended well below the site of the old fort, and we passed around it hardly a good hop, skip and a jump from its upper point. We could not suppress a cheer as the hard-earned victory was won, for to verify the old adage that "it never rains but it pours" good luck, there at the bank was the river steamer "Yukon" and from her decks came a rattling volley of shots to welcome us and to which we replied almost gun for gun. A little more hard pulling and we landed the raft just above the buildings and about three or four hundred yards above the steamer, which we at once prepared to visit. The "Yukon" is quite a small affair compared with the river boats of the United States, but quite well built and well modeled. They spoke of it as a ten-ton boat, although I took it to be one of double or treble that capacity, its machinery being powerful enough to drive a vessel of five or six times that tonnage against any ordinary current, but very necessary for a boat of even the smallest size on such a swift stream as the Yukon. The machinery took up the greater portion of her interior and were it not for the upper decks, it would have been difficult to

THE STEAMER " YUKON," (IN A HERD OF MOOSE).
(A scene in the Yukon Flat-lands.)

find room for her large crew. The moment I caught sight of the crew they seemed so like old acquaintances that I was on the point of probing my memory for the circumstances of our former meeting, when a second thought convinced me that it was only my familiarity with the Eskimo face that had produced the effect of a

recognition. These Eskimos had been hired on the Lower
Yukon, and but for their being a little more stolid and
homely than those of north Hudson's Bay, I should
have thought myself back among the tribes of that region.
They make better and more tractable workmen than any
of the Indians along the river, and in many other ways are
superior to the latter for the white men's purposes, being
more honest, ingenious and clever in the use of tools,
while treachery is an unknown element in their character.
The master of the "Yukon" was Captain Petersen, and
the Alaska Company's trader was Mr. McQuestion, both
of whom had been for many years in the employ of that
company on the river. From the former I ascertained
through information which he volunteered, that he had
a large ten or twelve ton river schooner at the trading
station of Nuklakayet, some three hundred miles
further down the river to which I was welcome when I
reached that point with the raft. After the "Yukon"
had ascended the river as far as Belle Isle, he would
return and would pick us up wherever found and tow the
schooner or *barka* as it was called in the local language
of the country, a sort of hybrid Russian vernacular.
From long experience on the river, Captain Petersen
estimated its current at about five miles an hour above
old Fort Yukon for the short distance which he had ascended with the steamer; but probably four from there to
Nuklakayet; three and a half to Nulato; and three below that until the influence of the low tides from Bering's
Sea is felt. Of course this rate of speed varies somewhat
with the season, but is the average during the period of
navigation in July and August. He expected to over-
take me about the 15th of August somewhere near Nul-

ato, as he had orders to pull the St. Michael's off the
gravel bar where she was lying, the Alaska Commercial
Company having bought out all the effects of the rival
concern after the latter had expended between half a
million and a million of dollars without any reasonable
remuneration for the outlay.   This the captain thought
would detain him a week or ten days, and if I could get
as far as Nulato, or Anvik, it would save him towing the
"barka" that far on its way to St. Michael's or " the
redoubt," as they all call it on the river.   Thus we
should be doing each other a mutual favor.   The
"barka," however, had none of its sails, except a jib,
and this circumstance, coupled with the head winds that
we should be sure to encounter on the lower river at this
season, reduced us to find our motive power still in the
current.   Provisions were purchased in sufficient quantity
to last as far as Nuklakayet, where we could select from
a much more varied stock.

Our dead reckoning, as checked by the astronomical
observations, showed the distance from the site of old
Fort Selkirk to Fort Yukon to be four hundred and
ninety miles, and two-tenths, (490.2) ; and the entire distance of the latter place from Crater Lake, at the head
of the river, nine hundred and eighty-nine (989) miles ;
the raft journey having been twelve miles less.   In running from Pyramid (Island) Harbor of Chilkat Inlet, the
last point we had left which had been determined by astronomical instruments of precision, to Fort Yukon, the
next such point, a distance of over a thousand miles,
Mr. Homan's dead reckoning, unchecked the whole distance, was in error less than ten miles ; and from Fort
Selkirk, determined by sextant and chronometer—the

latter regulated between the above two places—to Fort
Yukon, the error was less than six miles. At this point
we connected our surveys with the excellent one given
to the lower river by Captain Raymond in 1869 ; although
we continued our own as far as the Aphoon, or northern,
mouth of the Yukon River.

When Russian America became Alaska, or to be pre-
cise, in 1867, that date found the Russians established as
traders only on the lower river a considerable distance
below the flat-lands, while in 1848 the Hudson Bay Company had established Fort Yukon within their territory,
a port which they were still maintaining. Upon our ac-
cession, it was determined to fix the position of Fort
Yukon astronomically, and if it should prove to be on
Alaskan soil—west of the 141st meridian—the Hudson
Bay Company employes would be notified to vacate the
premises. This was done by Captain Raymond in 1869.
In the course of this occupation a good map of the
Yukon River was made from its mouth to Fort Yukon,
which was published by the War Department, accompanied by a report. With this it may be said that the
results of the expedition ceased, as that department of
the government does not publish and sell maps made under its direction, and they therefore are practically de-
prived of circulation. When I asked Captain Petersen
if he used maps in navigating the river, he said that he
seldom did, as there were no good ones in existence for
the permanent channels of the river, while the temporary
channels were so variable that his old maps were of little service. He had never heard of the Raymond map
being published, and on being shown one, seemed astonished that so good a map was in existence, and asked me

to send him a copy, which I was unable to do, as I could not procure one at the proper department in Washington. The maps he had were those made by the Russians when they were in possession of the country, which are still the best of such as can be procured.

The Indians in and around old Fort Yukon are known to the traders as the Fort Yukon Indians, which is probably as good a name as any, as they are not entitled to be regarded as a distinct tribe (or even as part of one), in the ordinary acceptation of the word. The country of the flatlands is not well stocked with game of the kind that would support any great number of Indians at all seasons, and as the river spreads over so wide an extent, the chances of catching fish are proportionately decreased, and altogether the flat-lands would be rejected by the natives for other locations. I was told by those who ought to know, and whose assertions seem to be borne out by other evidence, that there were no Indians who made this country their home until Fort Yukon was established in 1848, an event which attracted the usual number of Indians around the post who are always seen about a frontier trading station, many of whom made it their home. They came up the river, down the main stream, and down the great tributary, the Rat or Porcupine River which empties itself near the fort, so that the settlement was recruited by stragglers from several tribes, and it was for this reason that I spoke of them as not being a distinct tribe. The Indian who assumed the rôle of chief, Senati, as he is called by the white people, a savage of more than ordinary authority and determination, came from the lower ramparts where there exists a village bearing his name, which he still visits.

Since the abandonment of the post by the Alaska Company, his force of character has done much to hold together the handful of natives that still cling to the old spot ; but with his death and the desertion of the place by white traders this part of the river will soon return to its former wildness. When the Hudson Bay Company came upon the river at the point where they built this fort, they felt safe from the encroachments of the Russians. although trespassing upon Russian soil, as the Yukon was supposed to flow northward, and, like the Mackenzie, to pour its waters into the polar sea. Old maps may still be found bearing out this idea,* the Colville being pressed into service as the conjectural continuation of the Yukon into the Arctic portion of Alaska.

The 27th and 28th were occupied in taking observations to rate and correct the chronometer, much of the first day being spent in company with the officers of the boat, who recounted their interesting adventures on the river and its adjacent regions, in which their lives had been spent. I recall an episode of Mr. McQuestion's early life which so well illustrates the extraordinary vigor of the *voyageurs* of the Hudson Bay Company in the British north-west territory that I shall briefly repeat it. His boyhood was spent in the northern peninsula of Michigan and the states and territories to the westward, until finally he found himself at old Fort Garry, then an important post of the Hudson Bay Company. Here he was brought into constant contact with the restless

---

* As late as 1883, a fine globe bearing that date, costing some hundreds of dollars, was received by the American Geographical Society from a London firm, which still bears this error, corrected over twenty years ago.

voyageurs, and from them he imbibed much of their adventurous spirit, and was imbued with a longing to visit the far north land of which they spoke. He heard of Athabasca as other lads might hear of California and Mexico and Peru, while the Mackenzie and Yukon resembled to his imagination some fabled El Dorado or Aladdin's dream. He longed to see these lands for himself, but he knew the hard work the *voyageurs* were compelled to endure. He had seen the bundles and bags and boxes of a hundred pounds that they were to carry on their backs around rapids too swift to pole or "track," and over the many portages and exchanges on their long journeys. He knew he was not equal to the work required, but with the enthusiasm of youth he determined to make himself equal to it by a course of physical training, and after several months presented himself to an agent of the company as a full-fledged *voyageur.* To his delight he was accepted and entered on their books at a monthly salary, that probably being the least important part to him at the time. The first party which started northward in the spring included young McQuestion in its number, the most enthusiastic of all. Days wore on and much of his enthusiasm was repressed by the hard experiences of the journey, but it was by no means destroyed. In a few days the other *voyageurs* began talking of the great portage, where every thing, canoes included, had to be carried on their backs around the swift rapids, and wishing that their task, the hardest they had to encounter in the northern regions, was well over. McQuestion rather regarded it in the light of variety, as a break from the monotony of weary paddling over still and "tracking" through swift water. At last the lower end of the great portage was reached at a small cascade, and as the great canoe in which the young *voyageur* was paddling was nearly at the lower end of the line, he could plainly see the indications ahead. The canoes came up and landed at the little rocky ledge, their one hundred pound bundles were thrown out on the bank, high and dry, and the canoe itself was dragged from the water to make room for the next. McQuestion saw the chief of the canoe throw a bundle on the first comer's back, and expected to see him start off over the trail to the upper end of the portage, said to be ten or twelve miles across, and running through a tanglewood with all kinds of obstructions occurring the whole way. As the man did not start off, however, McQuestion watched eagerly for the reason, and was astonished to see the chief put a second bundle of a hundred pounds upon the other for the packer to carry, a load under which he expected to see the poor fellow stagger or fall. He did not fall, however, nor even stagger, but wheeled in his tracks and started off at a good sharp run, and disappeared over the hill. In a few minutes he reappeared on the crest of another hill, still maintaining his rapid gait, and with half a dozen others following him on the trail, with each carrying the same weight, and proceeding at the same gait. His heart sank within him, and as he climbed the ledge of rock he felt almost like a criminal on the way to execution. He received his two bundles, started off, and managed to keep up his gait over the crest of the nearest hill, when he fell, spread out at full length over the first log he attempted to cross. He returned to the factor in charge of the expedition, and a compromise was made by which he paid to that functionary the amount per month he was to have received in order to accompany the party as a passenger. At one of the northern posts he obtained a situation more to his liking, and thus drifted into the company's employ, finally crossing over to the Yukon River, and transferring his allegiance to the Alaska Company when it succeeded his old masters.

On the forenoon of the 20th, the Yukon continued her voyage up the stream, having accomplished all the summer trading with the Fort Yukon Indians the day previous. I was present at an afternoon parley with them, and was greatly impressed at the patience exhibited and required by traders among these savages ; a patience such as not one shopman in a thousand possesses, according to my experience, however great a haggler he may be. McQuestion had learned the art of patience from his old employers, probably the most successful bargainers with savages the world has ever seen. Indian No. 1 put in an appearance with a miserable lot of furs, and a more miserable story of poverty, the badness of the winter for trapping, the scarcity of animals and the inferiority of the pelts, his large family in need of support, his honesty with the company in the past, and a score of other pleas, the upshot of which was a request that he might be supplied with clothing and ammunition for another year in return for the pelts at his feet. The trader replies, setting a definite price in trading material for the amount of skins before him, and the "dickering" begins. After half an hour or an hour's talk of the most tiresome description, the discussion ends in the Indian accepting the exact amount the trader originally offered, or about one-tenth of his

own demands. Indian No. 2, who has heard every word
of the conversation, then comes forward with the same
quality of furs and exactly the same story, the trade
lasting exactly the same time, and with exactly the same
result; and so on with all the others in turn. Even
No. 12, of the dozen present, does not vary the stereotyped proceedings any more than an actor's interpretation of a part varies on the twelfth night of the piece.
Then Indian No. 1 comes forward again with a package
of furs of a better quality than the first he displayed,
and solemnly affirms that these are the only ones he has
left, and that if the trader will not give him enough
clothing for himself and family, and enough ammunition
to last through the winter in return for them, they must
all go naked and perhaps starve for want of the means
of procuring food. This story, with its continuation,
lasts about half as long as the first, but ends in the same
way, as the Indian's eloquence has about as much effect
on the trader as it would on the proverbial row of stumps.
The farce is repeated by all the Indians in turn, and is
yet again repeated at least once before the entire trans-
action is over, during all of which time the white trader
sits composedly on his stool, and gives a patient and
unvarying answer to each in his turn, under provocation
that would have put Job in a frenzy before the first
circle was completed.

On the 29th of July we took an early departure, and
about noon passed an Indian village of five or six tents
and ten or a dozen canoes, which might have appeared
uninhabited but for the dogs that surrounded the tents,
nearly a score to every one, proving that their owners
were either asleep or only temporarily absent. The dogs

flocked down the beach and up the bank, and emitted such a chorus of unearthly howls that we were grateful to the current for hurrying us away. That day we drifted 50.5 (geographical) miles in a trifle over thirteen hours, showing but little diminution in the river's rate of speed. It was an exceedingly hot blistering day on the river, almost unbearable, and the heat, coupled with the clouds of mosquitoes, impelled the doctor to remark that it was clear to the casual observer that we were in the Arctic regions. About seven o'clock in the evening, the thermometer marking 80° Fahrenheit in the shade, we saw "sun-dogs," or parhelia, very plainly marked on either side of the western sun, a phenomenon I had so often observed in the Arctic winter and in Arctic weather elsewhere, as to seem incongruous during such tropical heat. A heavy rain shower came up about ten o'clock at night and continued at intervals until late the next morning.

"It is an ill wind that blows no one any good," and if the gnats and mosquitoes did keep us awake all night they allowed us to start two hours earlier than usual, and in spite of a gale in the afternoon that made it very difficult to steer well and to keep off the lee banks, we camped reasonably early and had forty-four miles to our credit in addition. This wind was very cold and disagreeable, with heavy black clouds overhead ; a most decided change in the weather since the day before, but for the better, as the strong wind kept down the mosquitoes and gave us all a good night's rest.

The 31st was uneventful, and in fact it was only in the casual incidents of our voyage that we found any thing to interest us while floating through this region, a flat desert clothed with spruce trees, all of a uniform size, and monotonous in the extreme. We scored forty-five geographical miles and retired at night in a rain shower, which continued with such unabated fury next day that we remained in camp. A stroll that evening disclosed the distal extremity of a mastodon's femur on the gravel beach near camp, Mr. Homan finding a tooth of the same animal near by. For many years the scattered bones of this extinct animal have been found along the Yukon, showing that this region was once its home. When at Fort Yukon an Indian brought the tooth of a mastodon to a member of my party, and receiving something for it, probably more than he expected, told the white man that the entire skeleton was protruding from the banks of one of the islands, about a day's journey up the river. Our limited time and transportation forbade investigating it further. In a few years, I suppose, the bank will be excavated by the undermining river, and the bones swept away and scattered over many bars and beaches, for it is in such places that the greatest numbers are found, while a complete skeleton *in situ* is a rarity.

In spite of slight showers and a general "bad outlook," we started early next morning, and were very soon driven into a slough on the left (southern) bank by a strong north-west wind. Through this spot the current was so stagnant that we were over two hours in making a little less than two miles. At one time the head wind threatened to bring us completely to a standstill, so slight was our motive power. Nor was this our only episode of the same character. Several times the exasperating wind played us this trick, and when we camped for the night after twelve hours spent on the water, we could only reckon twenty-six miles to our credit. The event thoroughly established the fact that the central channels of the many which penetrate this flat district contain the swiftest currents, while along the main banks there are numerous water-ways open at both ends with almost stagnant water in them. About three in the afternoon we passed a double log house on the right bank with two or three small log *caches* mounted high in the air on the corner posts, and two graves, all of which seemed new in construction, although the place was entirely deserted. Indian signs of all kinds now began to appear as we approached the lower ramparts, although no Indians were seen. By noon the blue hills of the ramparts were seen to our left, and by the middle of the afternoon, we could make out individual trees upon them, and at half-past seven o'clock we camped on the last island in the great group of from two to ten thousand through which we had been threading our way so long, with the upper gates of the lower ramparts in full sight, about a mile or two distant.

CHAPTER XI.

INDIAN "CACHE" ON LOWER YUKON.

ERY well defined indeed are the upper gates of the lower ramparts, and one enters them from above with a suddenness that recalls his childish ideas of mountain ranges taken from juvenile geography-books, where they are represented as a closely connected series of tremendously steep peaks, with no outlying hills connecting them with the level valleys by gently rolling slopes, as nature has fortunately chosen to do ; this approach to the lower ramparts being one of the few exceptions. The lower termination is not by any means so well marked as after the rapids at Senati's village are passed ; there is a gradual lowering of the range, broken by many abrupt as well as gradual rises until the delta at the mouth of the river is reached, far beyond the point at which any traveler has placed their western limit. I think I agree pretty well with others in placing it about the mouth of the Tanana or Nuklakayet trading station.

This would give the lower ramparts a length of about one hundred miles along the river, or about one-fourth the length of the upper ramparts.

On August 3d we started at 7:30 A. M., and half an hour afterward our hearts were gladdened by re-entering the hilly country, for the flat and monotonous districts through which we had been drifting for many days induced a peculiar depression difficult to describe as well as to suffer. Our entry was signaled by the killing of three young but almost full-grown gray geese out of a small flock which we surprised as we floated around a point of land near the northern bank. This incident ushered in a hunting season when our shot-guns might have done great service but for our unfavorable condition for hunting, planted as we were upon a raft in the middle of a broad river.

We had supposed that when we entered the ramparts and the widely-scattered waters of the river were united into a single channel, our speed would surely increase ; in fact, we had been told as much by the steamboat men. On the contrary, the current was distinctly slower than that of any main channel of the stream through which we had drifted since leaving the head of the river, and after floating for thirteen hours we could only reckon thirty-six geographical miles to our credit, the poorest record we had made except on days when we had stranded upon a river bar or had been forced down a side channel of slack water.

About one o'clock in the afternoon we passed three canoes hauled up on the right bank, their owners being asleep on the warm sand of the shore, nearly naked. Their clothes were hanging out to dry, and they were evidently remaining over from the heavy rain-storm of the day before. Persistent yelling aroused them, and one of their number put off in his canoe, paddling around the raft, but not understanding each other, he returned to the shore, having uttered but one word that we could comprehend, *chy* (tea).

A half-hour afterward we passed the mouth of the Che-taut, a fair-sized stream coming in from the north. Near this point and for some distance beyond, we saw a number of old Indian signs, such as graves, habitations and *caches*, but the only living representatives of the tribe were the three sleepers we had seen a few miles back. Numbers of large wicker fish-traps were seen along the beach, none of which, however, were set ; and, in general, an air of desolation prevailed. As soon as the early cold snaps of approaching winter along the Arctic coast of Alaska send the reindeer southward on their migrations, these Nimrods of the river hasten northward to meet them, for their skins furnish most acceptable winter clothing, and their meat is a welcome change from the dried salmon of the river. About six o'clock we saw a fair-looking Indian log-house on the right bank of the river, having a *barrabora* (Russian name for log-cabin, half or nearly underground, the "dug-out" of the West), and *cache* attached. All of the Indian *caches* of the lower ramparts, and even further down the river until the Eskimo are encountered, are merely diminutive log-cabins from about four by four to eight by eight, mounted on corner logs so high that one can walk underneath the floor, which is generally made of poles or puncheons. A steep log leans against the door-sill and is cut into steps, to enable the owner to ascend (see initial piece to this chapter). The owner of this particular cabin had displayed much more than the usual energy in the construction of his domicile, there actually being a fence inclosing a small yard on one side of the house, and wooden steps leading up the steep bank from the water's edge to the little plateau upon which the cabin was built. These were roughly but ingeniously constructed of small, short lengths of log, the upper sides being leveled with an adze or ax.

We camped at 8:30 P. M. near several Indian graves, about a mile or two above the mouth of the Whymper River, which comes in from the left, and just on the upper boundary of the conspicuous valley of that stream. There were quite a number of graves at this point, forming the first and only burying place we saw on the river that might be called a family graveyard, i. e., a spot where a number, say six or seven, were buried in a row within a single inclosure. From its posts at the corners and sides were the usual *totems* and old rags flying, two of the carvings representing, I think, a duck and a bear respectively, while the others could not be made out. We had heard, in an imperfect way, on the upper river, that some disease was raging among the natives on the lower part, and that whole villages had been swept away and bodies left unburied, but this proved to be wholly sensational. A mild form of measles had indeed attacked a small town, causing one or two deaths, but this was the only foundation we could find for the report. The Yukon River, however, is a great thoroughfare for contagious disease, and maladies raging among the Chilkats have been known to travel its whole course as rapidly as we had done, and from the river as a base had spread right and left among the native tribes, until the cold weather of approaching winter subdued them, if they were amenable to the influence of temperature. I have never heard of any return ing against the stream, but instances of their descending it are not infrequent. Dr. Wilson tried to get a skull out of the many we assumed were at hand, to send to the Army Museum's large craniological collection, but although several very old-looking sites were opened, the skulls were too fresh to be properly prepared in the brief time at our disposal.

The most welcome change in this hilly country is the diminishing of the gnats and mosquitoes into quite endurable numbers. We found several varieties of berries near this camp, one or two of which were quite palatable; the crisp rosebuds still continuing to appear, although perhaps they were not so large as those we found near old Fort Yukon.

These lower ramparts so closely resemble the ramparts of the Upper Yukon in many particulars that the conviction seemed irresistible that they are one and the same chain of mountains, and if I may be excused the simile, are stretched like a bow-string across the great arc of the Yukon, as it bends northward into the Arctic flat-lands, which latter beyond the timber line become the great Arctic tundra.

The night of August 3d was very cold, only a few degrees above freezing, and besides the chance it gave us for a most comfortable night's rest, it stiffened up the few mosquitoes of the evening before so completely that they had to suspend operations altogether. Just before starting Corporal Shircliff killed a large porcupine near camp, an animal said to be quite numerous along the river, and so abundant in the flat-lands near Fort Yukon as to attach his name to the large tributary which joins the river at that point. It was nearly eight o'clock when we started, and after a mile's drifting we passed the mouth of the Whymper River, which we could not see until after we had got well past it. Its valley, however, is quite noticeable, and one would immediately conjecture that a river of considerable dimensions flowed through it.

A somewhat ludicrous incident took place at a short distance below this point. As we were drifting along a couple of wolves came trotting leisurely around a point of land just ahead of us, and the corporal and the cook picking up their rifles began firing at them with the usual fatal results—to the ammunition—the wolves simply snapping at each shot as it was fired, but not apparently increasing their pace, though they were but seventy-five or a hundred yards away. After fully half a dozen shots had been discharged as fast as the two could load and fire, an Indian house broke unexpectedly into view around the point from which the wolves had come, and in one breath two or three of the amused spectators called out to the sportsmen that they were firing at Indian dogs, as was proved by the tameness of the animals and their proximity to the house; whereupon I told the men to desist. The funny thing was that they really were wolves, and the two men had fired so rapidly and the bullets had struck the bank and torn out the gravel just beyond the animals so fast that all their attention was absorbed in that direction and thus they did not observe us, the reports of the shots and the

THE RAPIDS OF THE LOWER RAMPARTS.

(Looking down stream.)

echoes of the impacts being so confusing. The moment we ceased and they heard our voices and got one look at us out on the river the rapidity with which they sought the woods, left no doubt as to their species. The Indian house and surroundings were deserted and the wolves had been smelling around and investigating some old animal refuse near by.

This part of the river was particularly abundant in Indian signs of a permanent character on both banks of the river, but not a living soul was seen anywhere.

A most exasperating gale of wind raged all day, driving us into areas of slackwater in which we could scarcely move, and keeping us alongside of steep banks in the river bends; and when camp was made shortly after eight o'clock, after being on the water over twelve hours, we had made but twenty-six and a half miles.

During the day we saw a number of places at which the red rocks crop out from the summits of the high hills, resembling those on the eastern side of Lake Lindeman, which had been named the "Iron-Capped Mountains" on that account. The contrast of color was not so great, however, for on the latter range the rocks projected through the snow and blue-ice of the glacier-cap, while in the lower ramparts they were surrounded by brownish-red soil and autumnal foliage. I doubt if I should have noticed them but for their great similarity to those on the headwaters of the river.

Our Camp 47 was near a small stream on the left bank and I observed that all of these little creeks passing through the wet moss and tundra-like carpet underneath the dense timber, were highly colored with a port-wine hue, although their waters were so clear that one

could often see to the bottom in places three and four
feet deep. Probably these streams have their sources
in the iron-impregnated soil and rock of the adjacent
mountains, and if flowing through land where the drain-
ings have absorbed the dyes from decaying leaves and
vegetation, acquire this deep red color, almost verging on purple, forming a sort of natural ink, as it were.
Wherever these streams empty themselves, their waters
make a striking contrast with the white and muddy river,
and often where there was nothing else to indicate that
we were approaching a tributary, we would see ahead a
dark stripe running out from the bank and curving down
stream as it took up the new direction of the river's
course, and this would indicate the presence of a creek
from the hillsides, long before we could reach its mouth.

Two days after entering this hilly country we approached the rapids of the lower ramparts, of which we
had heard and read so much that we felt a little anxiety as
to the danger of approaching them. We had a very good
map, Raymond's, of this part of the river, and knew just
about where to expect them, and this circumstance,
coupled with the instructions received on the upper river
to keep well toward the left bank, reassured us somewhat ;
but still we had double complements of men at both bow
and stern oars to be used in case of emergency. A little
bit uncertain at one point in regard to our position with
respect to the rapids we made hasty inquiries at a small
Indian village near which we drifted, and its occupants
told us that we had passed the rapids about half a mile
back, the natives pointing to an insignificant reef of low
white bowlders that jutted out a short distance from the
right bank. They were certainly the mildest rapids I

had ever seen. During higher water, when the current is swifter and the reef just projects from the swift water, these rapids may appear more formidable, but if this part of the river had been wholly unexplored until our arrival, I doubt seriously whether we should ever have observed them. At this point the river is only about two hundred and fifty yards wide, and although the current noticeably increases, its increase can not, I think, be in any proportional to the vast volume of water the river must carry through such a narrow channel; the stream must, therefore, be unusually deep. This part of the lower ramparts, which may be assumed to be the "backbone" or summit of the chain of high hills through which the river has cut its way, is very picturesque, and had it not been for the squally weather and the black clouds that were lowering over the crests, I should have lingered awhile so as to procure a few photographs of the scenery. Gloster's sketches served our purpose too well in such places to think of delaying very long for this object at any point of the journey, and one of them is shown on page 295. I think it would be a fair estimate to say that the hills of the upper ramparts in their highest elevations are nearly twice the height of the corresponding ones in the lower ramparts.

We passed the rapids of the ramparts at 2:10 P.M., and the Indian village below ten minutes later. This is called Senati's (Senatee's) village upon previous maps, and at the date of our arrival was made up of two well-worn tents and four birch-bark houses, the whole containing from forty to fifty souls. Over half a dozen canoes put off from the village and were soon paddling around us, whereupon a lively competition ensued for supplying

us with dried and smoked salmon. It was at this village
that I first noticed the round-rimmed hand net spoken
of in a former chapter as appearing on the lower
river. Their handles of ten and twelve feet in length
may appear to contradict my conjecture as to the unusual depth of the river here, or the Indians may go further down to fish, as we saw large numbers of their
caches perched along the right bank some distance
below. Our camp was a forced one that evening,—the
5th—as we got stuck on a sandspit at the head of an
island where we had to make "a rubber-boot camp" as
the men designated any place where we grounded in
shoal water so far from the shore that rubber-boots had
to be put on in order to carry the cooking and camping
effects to the selected spot. Cold and stormy as the day
had been the mosquitoes sent a fair representation to
inform us that we had not been deserted by them. From
Camp 47 to Camp 48, Mr. Homan figured the day's run
of nearly twelve hours' uninterrupted drift at but
twenty-seven miles, and this in the narrowest portion of
the ramparts, where we had hoped the current would
increase. I was much inclined to think that our progress had been underestimated four or five miles, and
that a desire to coincide with Captain Raymond's maps
had marred an otherwise almost faultless reckoning.

Shortly after noon on the 6th—having started at half-
past eight—we passed the mouth of the Tanana, having
found one more island on this stretch of the river than
is mapped by Raymond. A half-dozen more islands in
many parts of the wide river or even half a hundred more
or less at any point in the flat-lands might have escaped
detection on any previous map, but here the shores are so

bold and the islands so few and conspicuous that they can hardly escape casual observation, and an error of even one upon the map would attract notice.

The Tanana River, to which I have referred, is the largest tributary of the Yukon, and is fully the peer of the parent stream, at the point of confluence. Were it not for the fact that the geographical features which must necessarily limit the drainage area of each preclude the Tanana basin from equaling that of the Yukon, a casual observer standing at the junction of the two might well be puzzled to know which of the two was entitled to be regarded as the main stream. The Yukon River at this point is a little over thirteen hundred miles in length from its head, and a glance at a map will show that in its great northward bend it has inclosed the Tanana, which would have to make a great many windings within this area in order to equal the Yukon in length, a case which we are not justified in assuming. There is a rough method, however, of arriving at its length, according to the story told me by an old trader on the river, upon whose word I can rely. With one white companion, and some Indians as packers, he crossed from the trading station at Belle Isle, near Johnny's village or *Klat-ol-klin*, in a southwest direction, over the hills that divide the Yukon and Tanana basins, ascending a tributary of the former and descending one of the latter, the journey occupying two or three weeks, after which the Indians were sent back. A boat was constructed from the hide of a moose, resembling the "bull-boat" of the western frontiersmen, and in this they drifted to the river's mouth. At the point where the two travelers first sighted the Tanana, the trader estimated it to be about twelve hundred yards wide, or very nearly three-quarters of a mile, and as they were floating fifteen or sixteen hours a day for ten days, on a current whose speed he estimated at six or seven miles an hour, it being much swifter than the Yukon at any point as high as Belle Isle, my informant computed his progress at from ninety to a hundred miles a day; or from nine hundred to a thousand miles along the Tanana. He estimates the whole length of the river by combining the result of his observation with Indian reports, at from ten to twelve hundred miles. Fear of the Tanana Indians appears to be the motive for the rapid rate of travel through their country, and although in general a very friendly tribe to encounter away from home, they have always opposed any exploration of their country. The trader's companion had suggested and promoted the journey as a *quasi* scientific expedition, and he collected a few skulls of the natives and some botanical specimens, but no maps*or notes were made of the trip, and it was afterward said by the Alaska Company's employes that the explorer was an envoy of the "opposition," as the old traders called the new company, sent to obtain information regarding the country as a trading district. Allowing a fair margin for all possible error, I think the river is from eight hundred to nine hundred miles long, not a single portion of which can be said to have been mapped.* This would probably make the Tanana, if I am right in my estimate, the longest wholly unexplored river in the world, certainly the longest of the western continent.

As we drifted by its mouth we could only form an approximate idea of its width, which was apparently two or three miles, including all channels and islands, which

---

* I have since learned that Mr. Bates made a map and took notes

LOOKING BACK INTO MOUTH OF TANANA.

(Tanana Indians, Male and Female. From Petroff's Government Report on Alaska Census.)

may be of the nature of a delta. It seemed to be very swift and brought down quantities of uprooted drift timber of large dimensions as compared with that brought by the Yukon. Looking back it resembled a suddenly exposed inland lake on the borders of the main stream, and its swift waters so overwhelmed those of the Yukon that a great slackening took place in the latter near their confluence, forming a sluggish pool into which we helplessly drifted. All these circumstances give to the Tanana the appearance of equality with the more important stream. Once in its current we went skimming along at a rapid rate that revealed the force of the new stream.

At 1:40 P.M. we passed an Indian village of four tents and two birch-bark houses, containing from twenty to twenty-five souls. Among the canoemen who visited us was a half-breed Indian, very neatly and jauntily dressed, who spoke English quite well, and whom we hired to pilot us to the trading station at Nuklakayet, the channel to which was very blind, and difficult to follow, as we had been told at old Fort Yukon. An hour later a large native village was passed on the north bank, apparently deserted; and another hour brought us to the "opposition" store of the old Northern Trading Company, around which was grouped quite an extensive collection of Indian cabins, graves, *caches*, and other vestiges of habitation. The old store was nearly demolished, while the once thriving Indian village had hardly a sign of life in it.

At half-past four o'clock we passed two or three small Indian camps on the upper ends of some contiguous islands, upon which they were spending the summer in fishing for salmon. At the upper ends of these islands

they build oblique weirs or wicker-work wing-dams con-
verging to a certain point, at which a large wicker-work
net is placed, and into the latter the salmon are directed
and there caught. These wicker-work nets are similar to
those heretofore spoken of as having been seen scattered
along the beach in front of a small house just after entering the ramparts, and some of them are so large that a
man might walk into their open mouths, while they are
probably a score of feet in length. These, together with
the native hand-nets, already spoken of, are the only
appliances I saw used for catching fish ; but they serve
amply to supply the natives throughout the year, and
to give their numerous dogs a salmon apiece every
day.

A little after six o'clock we sighted the Nuklakayet
trading station, and after much hard labor succeeded in
making a landing there, for the channel was most tortuous, and without our Indian pilot we should probably
have missed the place altogether, so much dodging
through winding ways and around obscure islands was
necessary. Mr. Harper, whom we found in charge, was
the only white man present, although Mr. McQuestion,
and another trader who was down the river at the time
(Mr. Mayo), make the station their headquarters. It is
the furthest inland trading post at present maintained
by the Alaska Commercial Company—or any other corporation on the river—although there were formerly
others of which mention has been made, but an occasional
visit of the river steamer has taken their place. Nuklakayet was once on the flat bottom land at the junction of
the Tanana and the Yukon, and was considered a sort of
neutral ground for the British traders from above and

THE NORTHERNMOST GARDEN IN THE UNITED STATES, NUKLAKAYET, ALASKA.

the Russians below, there being at that time summer trading camps only in existence.

Here Mr. Harper had attempted a small garden, which is certainly the most northerly garden existing in the territory of the United States, if not in the western continent ; it being eighty-five geographical or ninety-eight statute miles from the Arctic circle, or within a couple of days' journey of the polar regions. The garden is shown in the illustration taken from a photograph made by Mr. Homan. Its principal vegetables were turnips, the largest of which raised that year weighed a little over six pounds. They seemed particularly crisp and acceptable to our palates, most of us eating them raw, *à la* Sellers. I never knew before that turnips were so palatable. A few other hardy plants and vegetables completed the contents of the garden. Gardening in this country, however, must be greatly impeded by the swarms of mosquitoes, while agriculture on a considerable scale would be retarded by the wet and mossy character of the soil. Mr. Harper has chosen a south-eastern slope directly on the river bank, and here the immediate drainage has helped him to overcome the latter obstacle to the success of his garden.

We inspected the "barka," or decked schooner of ten or twelve tons, and I decided to take her, although fearing that we might find many more discomforts in her cramped quarters, than upon our old raft.

Here, too, the old raft was laid away in peace, perhaps to become kindling-wood for the trader's stove. Rough and rude as it was, I had a friendliness for the uncouth vessel, which had done such faithful service, and borne us safely through so many trials, surprising us with its good qualities. It had explored a larger portion of the great river than any more pretentious craft, and seemed to deserve a better fate.

THE RAFT AT THE END OF ITS JOURNEY (1303 MILES).

(Looking across and down the Yukon River from Nuklakayet.)

CHAPTER XII.

DOWN THE RIVER AND HOME.

HE 7th of August we remained over pumping out the bilge-water from the "barka" and transferring freight from the raft to the schooner, and making use of our photographic apparatus.

At Nuklakayet the Eskimo dogs begin to appear, forty or fifty being owned by the sta-

INDIAN OUT-DOOR GUN COVERING, ON THE LOWER YUKON RIVER.

tion, the majority of which Mr. Harper feared he should have to kill to save the expense of feeding them through the winter. As each of them ate a salmon a day, it will be seen that this cost was no small item. I remembered the trouble I had once experienced in obtaining even a smaller number of these useful creatures; a difficulty which many another Arctic traveler has encountered, while here was a pack about to be slaughtered that would well suffice for any sledging party. The Eskimo dogs of Alaska are larger, finer-looking, and a much more distinct variety than those of North Hudson's Bay, King William Land country, and adjacent districts; a description of any one Alaska dog answering nearly for all, while among the others I have named, there was the widest difference in size, shape and general appearance.

From all I could learn, and I was careful to inquire of their capabilities, I do not think the Alaskan Eskimo dogs can compare with the others in endurance, whether as regards fatigue, exposure or fasting. For all the purposes of men who are never in fear of starvation, I think it more than probable that the Alaskan Eskimo dog would be found superior on short journeys and trips between points where food is procurable; but for the use of explorers, or of any one who may be exposed to the danger of famine, the others are undoubtedly far superior. When I told some of the Yukon River traders, who had spent much of their lives in the native country of these dogs, of some of the feats of endurance of the Hudson Bay species, they seemed to think, judging from their countenances, that I was giving them a choice selection from the Arctic edition of Munchausen.

Eskimo boats, or those in which the wooden frames are covered with sealskin, are also first noticed at this place; although the Eskimo people themselves are not found as regular inhabitants until Anvik has been passed, some twenty or thirty miles. I saw both kinds, the smaller variety, or *kiak*, in native language, and the large kind, or *oomien*, of the Eskimo. An attempt had evidently been made to fashion the bow and stern of the latter into nautical "lines," with a result much more visible than with those of Hudson's Straits and Bay.

On Wednesday the 8th of August, we got away late, and there being a slight breeze behind us, we set the jib —the only sail with the boat—and were agreeably surprised at the manner in which our new acquisition cut through the water, with even this little help; the sail assisting her probably a couple of miles an hour, and, better than all, making it very easy work to keep in the strongest currents.

Indian villages or camps were seen occasionally on the upper ends of islands, with their fish-traps set above them, and from some of these we obtained fresh salmon. As the trading stations are approached, these Indian camps increase, the largest being generally clustered around the station itself, while a diminution both in numbers and size is perceptible in proportion to the distance from these centers. As many of these camps are but temporary summer affairs, which are abandoned late in the fall, this clustering around the white men's stores becomes more marked at that period. That night's camping, however, plainly showed us that the "barka" was not as good as the raft for the purpose of approaching the shore, it drawing about three feet to the raft's twenty inches, so that "rubber-boot camps" might be quite numerous in the future. Worst of all, our rubber boots were but little protection in three feet of water, and filling to the top, became more of an impediment than otherwise in carrying our effects to the shore. Most of our camping places were now selected with reference to steep banks that had at least three feet of water at their foot, yet were not so high but that a long gang-plank could reach the crest.

On the 9th, we started early with a light wind in our face that within an hour had become a furious gale, with white capped waves running over the broad river and dashing over our boat. We ran into shoal water, dropped anchor, and tried to protect onrselves by crawling in under the leaking decks. Here we remained cooped up until four o'clock in the afternoon, when the gale abat-

ing somewhat we pulled up anchor and drifted for six
or seven miles, going into camp at eight o'clock, having
made eight and a-half miles for the day. After camping,
the gale died down to a calm, and allowed us the full
benefit of the mosquitoes. Either we were getting used
to their attacks, or the season had affected the insects,
for they appeared less numerous than on the upper river.

The 10th was another day starting well with a favorable
breeze and ending with a heavy head-wind. That day
we passed the Newicargut and still saw many Indian
camps where fishing for salmon was going on.

The 11th was an aggravating repetition of the events of
the two preceding days. That day we passed the Melozecargut, and camped opposite the mouth of the Yuko-
cargut. * "Cargut" is the native name for river, and
Sooncargut, Melozecargut, and Tosecargut, have been
changed to Sunday-cargut, Monday-cargut, and Tuesday-
cargut by the English speaking traders of the district.

Another object now influenced our selection of camps
for the night, and that was to choose a spot with few or
no islands in its front, so that the descending river
steamer "Yukon" could not pass us while in camp by
taking a channel hidden from our view.

Shortly after midnight a steamer's whistling was heard
far down the river, and after a great deal of anxiety for
fear it was the "Yukon" that had passed us unnoticed,
we heard the puffing approach nearer and nearer, and
soon saw the light of an ascending river steamer. It
proved to be a very diminutive but powerful little thing
which Mr. Mayo was taking to Nuklakayet for the

---

* Spelled *Chargut* on Mr. Homan's map.

winter. Two brothers of the name of Scheffelin, the
elder of whom is well known in frontier mining history
as the discoverer of the celebrated Tombstone district of
Arizona, having amassed a fortune in that territory,
decided to try the mining prospects of the Yukon and
its tributaries, and the prior year had chartered a vessel
in San Francisco on which they put this little river
steamer, and sailed for the Yukon. Here a year was
spent in prospecting, and although " ounce diggings* were
struck " on or near the Melozecargut, yet all the surroundings made " Ed " Scheffelin think it would not pay
to put capital in such an undertaking, although it might
remunerate the individual effort of the itinerant miner
whose capital is his pick-ax, pan and shovel. Early in
the spring the Scheffelins got a letter from Arizona which
determined their return to the United States, and they
had left the river a few weeks previously, the three
traders at Nuklakayet buying their little river steamer,
which the former owners had named the " New Racket."
The wages of these traders had been reduced by the
Alaska Company in order to contract expenses, so that
the company might make a small percentage on the large
capital invested, until the traders found themselves without sufficient means to live upon, and they had bought
the boat intending to organize a small trading company
of their own upon the river unless their former wages
were restored. The Scheffelin mining expedition was an
expensive one, and remarkably well " outfitted " in every
necessary department. The large number of Eskimo
dogs at Nuklakayet had been selected by him for the

* Diggings that will pay an ounce of gold per man a day, or, as
gold usually runs, from $10 to $20 per day.

purpose of sledging expeditions in winter time. He thought seriously of invading the prospective gold fields of Africa as his next venture, showing plainly the roving spirit which had served him so well in the arid deserts of Arizona. No one could meet him anywhere without wishing him good luck in his wild adventures, for he was the prince of good fellows.

The "New Racket" left us very early in the morning, having tied up alongside of camp the night before, while we started about the usual time, an hour after daylight. About 3:30 P.M. that day—the 12th—we passed a very considerable Indian village called Sakadelontin, composed of a number of birch-bark houses and some ten or twelve *caches*, and containing probably fifty or sixty people. It is one of the few large villages to be found at any great distance from a trading station. Before reaching it we observed a number of native coffins perched up in the trees, the first and only ones we saw so situated on the river. All day on the 12th and 13th a heavy gale from the south made even drifting difficult. Upon a couple of northward-trending stretches of the river that were encountered on the 13th we set the jib, and spun along at the rate of six or seven miles an hour. At one place where we were held against the high banks by the force of the gale, we went ashore, and much to our surprise found a most prolific huckleberry patch, where we all regaled ourselves as long as the wind lasted. These berries were quite common along this part of the river, and nearly every canoe that put off from a camp or village would have one or two trays or bowls of wood or birch-bark full of them, which the natives wanted to trade for tea or tobacco. We camped in what is called

FALLING BANKS OF THE YUKON JUST BELOW NUKLAKAYET.

by the river steamer men the "cut-off slough," just south of the mouth of the Koyukuk River, a northern tributary of considerable dimensions, which empties into the Yukon at a point where it makes a short but bold bend to the north, the "slough" making the route about one-fifth shorter. The mouth of the tributary is marked by the Koyukuk Sopka (hill), a high eminence which is visible for many miles around. This feature is characteristic of this part of the Yukon Valley, isolated hills and peaks often rising precipitously from a perfectly level country.

The 14th saw us make Nulato, quite an historical place on the river. It was the furthest inland trading station of the old Russian-American Fur Company at the time of our purchase of Alaska, and had been used as such by them, under different names, for nearly a quarter of a century. It was occupied by the traders of the Alaska Company until a year or two before my arrival, as well as by traders of the "opposition," when the killing of one of the latter led to trouble with the Indians, so that both companies withdrew.

Many years ago, one cold winter night, the Russians of the station were massacred, along with a number of friendly Indians who had assembled around the station. In this disaster fell an English naval officer, Lieutenant Barnard by name, who was looking for traces of Sir John Franklin, even in this out-of-the-way corner of the earth. A respectable head-board marks his grave, but the high grass and willows have buried it almost out of sight.

Here also lies buried a locally noted Russian character of hard reputation, Kerchinikoff by name, whose

story was told me by more than one of the traders, who
had known him and heard of his doings in his adventurous career.   It was romancingly said by way of illus-
trating his prowess among the native tribes, that if the
skulls of his Indian victims had been heaped together in
his grave they would not only fill it but enough would
have remained to erect a high monument to his memory.   He died at a great age, having been from his very
youth a terror to all the tribes on the lower river, but
wholly in the interests, as he interpreted them, of the
great iron monopoly to which he belonged.   Many
years ago the few Russian traders of the Andreavsky
station had been massacred by the Indians.   Kerchinikoff asked for protection and a sufficient force to punish
the murderers, and those at Nulato transmitted his request to the headquarters of the Russian Fur Company
at far-off Sitka, but did not receive even the courtesy of
an answer.   With one or two companions he put a couple
of old rusty Russian carronades in the prow of his trading
boat,—the identical one on which we were drifting down
the river, and which he himself had built—and in lieu of
proper ammunition, which he was unable to get, he
loaded his guns with spikes, hinges and whatever scraps
of iron and lead he could pick up around Michaeloffski,
and appearing suddenly before the Indian village, demanded the surrender of the murderers.   The natives
gathered in a great crowd on the shore of the river,
laughing derisively at his apparently absurd demands,
having never even heard of such a thing as a cannon.
Spears were hurled and arrows shot at the boat, which
thereupon slowly approached, having its cannon pointed
at the dense crowd.   When an arrow buried itself in

the prow, the terrible report of the two carronades made answer, and about a score of Indians were stretched upon the beach, while the wounded and panic-stricken fled in great numbers to the woods for protection. From that day not a single drop of white man's blood was ever shed by any savages upon the lower river, until Kerchinikoff himself, while lying on his sledge in a drunken stupor, was stabbed to death almost within a stone's throw of the graves of those whom he had avenged.

We landed at Upper Nulato (the "opposition" store), and here encountered a half-breed who spoke tolerable English, and who pointed out the places just mentioned.

"Hello, where you come?" was his first question, to which we briefly replied, one of the members of the party remarking it was quite windy hereabouts, referring to the three or four days' gale we had had.

"Allee time like that now," was his cheerful answer. This neatly-dressed young fellow took me down to his *cache*, and seemed especially delighted in showing me his new "parka," or reindeer coat, for winter wear. It was one of the highly-prized "spotted" *parkas*. The spotted reindeer are bred only in Asia, and their hides— for the tribe owning them will never allow the live animals to be taken away—find their way into Alaska by way of Bering's Straits by means of intertribal barter, while numbers are brought by the Alaska Company from Russian ports on that side, and are used as trading material with such tribes as wear reindeer clothing. I offered a good price for this particular "parka," but the owner would not part with it, as they are especially valuable and tolerably rare at this distance up the river, and only the wealthiest Indians can afford to buy them. He told me this was the only one at Nulato at the time, but I did not know how much faith might be put in the statement. Bad as the weather was, we got a good series of observations on the sun, while at Nulato, on the afternoon of the 14th.

On the 15th the old familiar gale from ahead put in its appearance as we started in the morning, but to every body's great surprise it hauled to the rear in the middle of the afternoon, and when we camped at 8:20 P. M., having used our jib in sailing, an Indian from a village near by told us the place was called Kaltag; so that we had made an extraordinary run under all the circumstances. Indian villages were quite numerous during the day. About Kaltag occurs the last point on the river at which high ground comes down to the water's edge on the left side, and for the rest of the voyage, a distance of some five hundred miles, precipitous banks only are found on the right side, while the country to the left resembles the flat-lands seen further back, but the horizon is much more limited than that of the flat-lands, hills appearing in the background, which finally become isolated peaks, or short broken ranges.

The morning of the 16th ushered in a heavy gale from ahead, accompanied by a deluge of showers, and as the camp, 57, was fortunately situated at a point where all the channels were united, so that the river steamer could not pass unnoticed, I determined to remain over.

It would be as tiresome to my readers as it was aggravating to us, to repeat in detail the old story of our starting with a fair wind, its change to a gale that kept us against the banks, and of our passing a few Indian towns.

This continuous drifting against a head wind taught us one singular thing, however, viz. : that our boat would drift faster against this wind when turned broadside to it and exposing the greatest surface to its action, than when facing it bow or stern on and with a minimum of exposed surface ; this fact being the very reverse of what we had supposed, indeed, we had endeavored to avoid this very position. Thereafter we kept the " barka " broadside to the head wind, a very difficult undertaking, which required hard and constant work at the steering oar ; but the mile or mile and a-half an hour gained over the vessel's drift was well worth it. I spoke of this afterward to the river men and found they had long since anticipated me by a much easier contrivance, viz. : by tying an anchor or a large camp-kettle full of stones and suspending it from the end of the jib-boom so that it would trail in the water. This method, a number of them assured me, would have saved our work at the steering oar which we rigged at the stern.

The 18th and 19th we fought our way down the river, inch by inch, against the wind. The latter night the storm culminated in a perfect hurricane, felling trees in the forest, hurling brush through the air, and raising waves four and five feet high, from whose crests flew great white masses of foam, the wide river resembling a sheet of boiling milk in the darkness. Although we were in a well-sheltered cove, which had remained calm the evening before, even in the high wind, yet this gale sent in such huge waves that our "barka" was on the point of being wrecked, and was only saved by the severest labor of the crew. The little birch-bark canoe was swept from her deck and thrown high up on the beach, where it resembled a mass of brown wrapping paper which the storm had beaten down upon the stones. The gale slowly died down on the 20th, but ceased too late to give us a chance to start, and we remained over night, a heavy fog and rain terminating the day.

On the 21st we saw a couple of *oomiens*, (*bidarra*— Russian) or large skin-boats being hauled up stream by native dogs on the bank, somewhat after the fashion of canal-horses on a tow-path. We had baffling winds most of the day, some few of which we could take advantage of, but at 6 P. M. the wind had settled down to its regular "dead-ahead" gale.

We camped at half-past nine o'clock at Hall's Rapids, (named by Raymond), but found them at the time of our visit to consist only of some rough water along the rocky beach, while the high land mapped by him on the south-eastern bank was wanting. As I said before, the high land on the right bank with low country upon the left is a state of things which continues until the delta is reached, when the whole country becomes level.

About six or seven o'clock in the afternoon we were passing the upper ends or entrances, seven of them altogether, of the Shagelook slough, which here makes a great bend to the eastward and incloses an area larger than some of the New England states before it again meets the Yukon River far beyond. This Shagelook slough receives the Innoka River in its upper portion and when the Yukon is the higher of the two it carries part of its waters into the upper entrances of the slough receiving the waters of the Innoka, and both streams emptying themselves at the slough's lower end. When the Innoka is the higher its waters find an outlet into the Yukon by the upper mouths. We now began to feel anxious about the "Yukon," as she was very much over-due. From this point she could make St. Michael's in three or four days, and although we had received official assurances from Washington that the revenue cutter "Corwin" would not leave St. Michael's before the 15th of September, yet there was fear that the boat might pass us or the "Corwin" find some official emergency to call her elsewhere before this date.

The night of the 21st–22d, was a bitterly cold one, verging on freezing, and we slept soundly after our loss of sleep the night before. We started quite early, how-ever, and a little meteorological surprise in the shape of a favorable wind came to our aid after 10 A. M., and at 1:30 P. M. we landed at the mouth of the Anvic or Anvik. The picturesquely-situated trading station is about a mile or a mile and a-quarter above this point, but the shoals were so numerous, the channel so winding, that this was the nearest point we could make, especially with a foul wind. Right alongside of us was a large Indian village, where we learned to our satisfaction that the "Yukon" had not yet passed ; for one of the party at our last camp had interpreted some Indian information to mean that the boat had passed down two days before.

From this place I sent a courier to St. Michael's, who was to ascend the Anvik River to the head of canoe navi-gation, and thence to make a short portage to a stream emptying near the post, the entire distance being readily covered in three days, or in two if sufficient energy is displayed. He promised to be there without fail in three days, *i. e.*, by the 25th, and I paid him a little extra for the extra exertion.   He arrived about a week after I did and we were ten days in reaching St. Michael's from this point.   My object was to let the "Corwin" know that my party was coming.   The "Leo," an Alaskan trading schooner, was also expected to touch at St. Michael's to exchange some signal officers, and I sent word to her, requesting her to wait for us if the "Corwin" had gone. Mr. Fredericksen was the trader, and a very intelligent person for such a lonely and outlandish spot.   He had been furnished with meteorological instruments by the Signal Service, to which he made regular reports.   He informed me that he has seen ice of such depth by the 4th of September as to cut the thick covering of a *bidarra* or *oomien;* but this, of course, is very unusual.   The year before our arrival—1882—the ice did not form until the 12th of October, and the first of that month may be regarded as the average date of its formation.

Mr. Fredericksen warmly welcomed my arrival at his station, having recently had some serious trouble with the Indians, who were not even yet quieted.   A number of Shagelooks, as he termed them, had come down the river, a short time before, to meet the Greek priest from the mission at Ikogmute, who had come to Anvik in order to baptize them.   While the Shagelooks were waiting for the priest, they arranged a plot to rob the trader. Some one or two of them were to provoke him in some exasperating way, and if he showed any resistance or even annoyance, the others were to side with their fellows, seize the trader and secure him until his store was plundered and the booty removed, when he was to be liberated, or murdered if aggressive.   In some way the Anviks got an inkling of the plot, and prepared to side with Mr. Fredericksen, and when the preliminaries commenced with the cutting open of one of the trader's finest skin-boats—*bidarra*—the Shagelooks saw themselves confronted by such an array of well-armed Anvik Indians, that they were perfectly satisfied to let the business drop. The christening was carried out according to programme, but the baffled Shagelooks vowed vengeance on both the Anviks and the trader whenever an opportunity might occur, and they were not reticent in so informing him at their departure, hinting that their turn might come when the Anviks left to hunt reindeer for their winter supply of clothing. That season would soon be at hand, and the Anviks had the alternative of losing their autumn hunting or of leaving the station in a weakened condition at their departure. The arrival of a body of troops, small in number as we were, was a cause of congratulation, and Mr. Fredericksen intended to make the most out of it with discontented natives by way of strengthening his position.

We could do absolutely nothing for him. When the president withdrew the military forces from Alaska, the executive order had "clinched" the act by providing that the military should exercise no further control whatever in that vast territory, and my orders had emphatically repeated the clause. In fact, it was a debatable point whether my expedition was not strictly an illegal one, and in direct violation of the president's order, since it was simply impossible to send in a military party that might not exercise control over its own members, which is all that soldiers ever do without an order from the president, and as to an attack by Indians we had the universal right of self-preservation. I told Mr. Freder-

icksen, however, to make the most out of my visit, which
I suppose he did.

A foresail was borrowed from him, with which I could
make my way from the mouth of the river to St. Michael's,
should any accident have happened to the "Yukon." It
was too large and would have to be cut to fit, an expe-

ANVIK.
(Looking down both the Yukon and Anvik Rivers.)

dient to which I did not intend to resort until we reached
the mouth of the river.

Mr. Fredericksen's station is on the banks of both the
Yukon and the Anvik, as the streams approach within
about fifty or seventy-five yards of each other at this
point, although their confluence occurs, as I have said,
about a mile below. The illustration above is from
the station looking toward the point of confluence.
When the present trader first came to the station a few

years previously, the two rivers were far apart at this point, but the Anvik has encroached so largely upon its left bank that Mr. Fredericksen expected another year to unite the streams at his place, if the Anvik did not actually sweep him away or force him to change his residence.

Anvik is the last station in the Indian country, and at Makágamute, thirty or forty miles below, the Eskimo begin to appear, and continue from that point to the mouth of the river.

We started again on the 23d, with a fine breeze behind us, passing Makagamute or *moot* (pronounced like boot, shoot), at 1:30 P.M. It was composed of eight or ten houses of a most substantial build, flanked and backed by fifteen to twenty *caches*, and had altogether a most prosperous appearance, impressing a stranger with the superiority of the Eskimo over their neighbors. The doors were singular little circular or rounded holes, very like exaggerated specimens of the cottage bird-houses, which some people erect for their feathered friends. Villages were much more numerous on the 23d, than upon any previous day of our voyage. Everywhere might be seen their traps and nets for catching salmon, of which fish they must capture enormous quantities, for they live upon salmon the year round.

Myriads of geese might be observed in all directions during this fine weather, preparing and mobilizing for their autumnal emigration to the south; and the air was vocal with their cries.

On the night of the 23d we had a severe frost, the heavy sedge grass near camp being literally white with it, and the cook was heard grumbling about the condition of his dishcloth, which was about as flexible as a battered milk-pan, until thawed out by means of hot water. The few musquitoes we saw next morning were pitiable looking creatures, although I doubt very much whether any sentiment was wasted on them. However much the cold spell threatened to hasten the arrival of winter, and to send the ships at St. Michael's flying south, yet the discomfiture of the mosquitoes afforded us a good deal of consolation, and thereafter our annoyances from this source were but trifling.

Starting at 8 A.M. with a head breeze, by ten o'clock the wind had become a gale and we were scarcely making half a mile an hour, when at 2:20 P.M. we saw the steamer "Yukon," with the St. Michael's in tow, coming round a high precipitous point about three miles abaft of us, and there went up a shout of welcome from our boat that drowned even the voice of the gale, and almost simultaneously the flash of a dozen guns went up from both the "Yukon's" decks and our own. The point around which the steamer had been sighted, a conspicuous landmark, I named Petersen Point, after Captain Petersen of the "Yukon," that being the only name I gave on the river below old Fort Yukon. In about half-an-hour the steamer was alongside and we were taken in tow, and once more began cleaving the water, in defiance of the gale.

The captain knew we had started from Anvik the day before, but our progress on the first day had been so great that he had become uneasy for fear he might have passed us. He had kept the whistle going at frequent intervals, but of course knew that it could not be heard far in such a gale. If we had not yet reached the

Mission when he arrived there, he intended to return for us.

We made the Mission that evening at the upper or "opposition" store, which was being torn down, and the best logs of which were to go on board the river steamer to be taken to Andreavsky, the trading station kept by Captain Petersen when not in charge of the boat.

By next morring at nine o'clock we had these securely lashed to the sides and were under way, stopping three miles below at the Mission proper. Here is an old Greek church, presided over by a half-breed priest, which looked strangely enough in this far-away corner of the world. The interior was fitted up with all the ornaments customary in the Greek church, the solid silver and brass of more stately structures in Russia being reproduced in tinsel and trappings of a cheaper kind. The Greek priest is also the Alaska Company's trader, and he came aboard to go to St. Michael's to get a winter's supply of trading material for his store. His handsome little sloop was tied behind the big "barka" to be towed along, while from its stern the line ran to the sloop's yawl, in which an Indian had been allowed to come, he tying his little skin canoe behind the yawl, thus making a queue of vessels of rapidly diminishing sizes, quite ludicrous in appearance. With the St. Michael's alongside in tow, and our guards piled with hewn logs as far as the upper deck, we were a motley crowd indeed when under way. The captain explained his unusual delay on the trip by the fact that the "Yukon" had blown out a cylinder-head just after leaving St. Michael's Bar and while trying to make Belle Isle, for which reason their return voyage had to be made under reduced steam in order to avoid a repetition of the accident.

A serio-comic incident connected with this mishap deserves to be recounted. Among their Eskimo deck-hands was a powerful young fellow, deaf as a post, who always slept in the engine-room when off duty, with his head resting on a huge cross deck-beam as a pillow, at a point in front of the engine that had broken down. Whenever he was wanted, as there was no use in calling him, they would walk up and tap him with the foot, or, as they soon learned, a stout kick on any part of the beam would suffice; whereupon he would sit up, give a great yawn, stretch his arms and be ready for work. When the cylinder-head of the engine blew out, it struck the beam directly opposite his own head, and buried itself until the spot looked afterward as though a chain-shot had struck it; but with no more effect on the deaf Eskimo than to make him rise up and yawn, and begin to stretch himself, when the rush of steam from the next stroke of the engine completely enveloped him, before the engineer could interfere, and he comprehended that he was not being awakened to go to work. He got off with a trifling scald on the back of his neck; but his escape from death seemed miraculous.

All that day we stopped about every couple of hours to take on wood, which fortunately had been cut for us beforehand in most places, so that the delays were not very long. In ascending or descending the river, the steamer finds a considerable quantity of the wood it requires already cut at convenient points, the natives of course being paid for their labor. This is the case between the river's mouth and Nuklakayet, or there-abouts, but above this point, and even at many places below it the captain is obliged to go ashore near a great pile of drift-wood, and send a dozen axmen to do this duty. The greater part of the huge stockade of old Fort Yukon and some of its minor buildings have for several years supplied them with wood when in the neighborhood. We stopped the night of the 25th near a native village, and as we were to start very early in the morning, the doctor and myself, at the captain's invitation, made our beds under the table, on the dining-room floor of the steamer, that being the first time we had slept under a roof since leaving Chilkat; although the doctor made some irrelevant remarks about a table not being a roof, evidently wanting to extend back the period of our claim.

On the 26th, running about twelve hours, less our time at "wooding" places, we made Andreavsky, and nearly the whole of the next day was spent in unloading the logs, mooring the St. Michael's in winter quarters, and washing down decks, for it was to this point that the "Yukon" would return for the winter after making St. Michael's. The hills of the right bank rapidly dimin-ish in height as one approaches Andreavsky, and in the vicinity of that place are only entitled to the name of high rolling ground. Near the river the trees disappear and are replaced by willow-brake, although the up-stream ends of the numerous islands are still covered with great masses of drift timber, containing logs of the largest dimensions. Before Andreavsky is reached we come to the delta of the Yukon, an interminable con-course of islands and channels never yet fully explored.

From the most northerly of these mouths to the most southerly is a distance of about ninety miles, according to local computation.

Late as it was when we started on the 27th, we reached a point half way to Coatlik, where wood was cut by our crew for the morning's start. All semblance of rolling country had now disappeared, except in the distance, and the country was as flat as the lower delta of the Mississippi.

Coatlik, seven miles from the Aphoon or northernmost mouth, was reached next day at 1 P. M., and we spent the afternoon in preparing the boilers for the change to salt water, and in taking on another log house, which was to be transported to St. Michael's, there to be used in completing a Greek church in course of erection.

Starting at early daylight on the morning of the 29th, a steam-valve blew out, and it looked as if we should be delayed two or three days for repairs, but the captain fixed up an ingenious contrivance with a jack-screw as a substitute, and at half-past nine in the morning we again proceeded. Soon afterward we reached the Aphoon mouth of the river, where we commenced the slow and tedious threading of its shallow channels between their mud banks. For untold ages this swift, muddy river has deposited its sediment upon the shallow eastern shores of Bering's Sea, until mud and sand banks have been thrown up for seventy or eighty miles beyond the delta, making it unsafe for vessels of any draft to cross them even in moderate weather. St. Michael's is the nearest port to the mouth at which vessels of any size can enter and anchor. The heavy wind still raging made it difficult to steer the boat through the winding channels, and this, coupled with the heavy load of logs that weighed us to the guards, sent us a dozen times on the low mud flats, to escape from which gave us much trouble. Our delay at Coatlik had also lost us some of the tide, there being about two feet of water on the bar at ebb and nearly as much more at flood tide. So shallow is the stream that the channel is indicated by willow canes stuck in the mud, at convenient intervals, serving the purpose of buoys. Near the Aphoon mouth comes in the Pastolik River, and once across the bar of mud near the confluence, the channel of the latter stream is followed to deep water. This muddy sediment is very light and easily stirred up, and when a storm is raging the whole sea as far as the eye can reach resembles an angry lake of mud. From the Pastolik River on, the westerly wind gradually increased to a gale, the sea running very high and making many of us quite sea-sick. Fearing to round Point Romantzoff, the captain put back and anchored in a somewhat sheltered cove, returning about half way to the Pastolik. A flat-bottomed river boat anchored in Bering's Sea during a gale, loaded with a log-house and towing a number of craft, certainly did not seem a very safe abiding place.

Early on the morning of the 30th we got under way, the weather having moderated considerably during the night, and constantly improving as we proceeded. We rounded Cape Romantzoff about the middle of the forenoon, and as we passed between Stuart and St. Michael's Islands, shortly before noon, nothing was left of yesterday's angry sea but a few long ground-swells, which disturbed us but little. At noon we rounded the point that hid the little village of St. Michael's, and were received by a salute of three discharges from as many ancient Russian carronades, to which we responded vigorously with the whistle. All eyes swept the bay for signs of the "Corwin," but a boat putting off from shore told us that she had left on the 10th of August, nearly three weeks before.

The "Leo," which was due about the 15th of the month, had not yet arrived, and although it was known that she had a signal observer on board to take the place of the one now at St. Michael's, it was not positive that she would arrive there at all, if hampered with heavy gales. She had been chartered by the government to proceed to Point Barrow, on the Arctic coast of Alaska, and take on board Lieutenant Ray's party of the International Meteorological Station at that point, and it was not altogether certain that she might not have been wrecked in the ice while engaged in this somewhat hazardous undertaking; the chances varying considerably each season according to the state of the ice and the weather. The state of the latter might be inferred from the fact that the day of our arrival was the first fine one they had had at the redoubt (as St. Michael's is called here and in the Yukon valley), for over six weeks, during which there had been an almost continuous storm.

There was also a vessel, the "Alaska," at Golovnin Bay, about sixty miles north of St. Michael's, across Norton Sound, which was loading with silver ore for San Francisco, and was expected to depart about the 1st of October. It was possible that she might call here, *en route*, as the mining company to which she belonged had a considerable quantity of material stored at this point.

DOWN THE RIVER AND HOME.

The evening of the 30th we spent at a dance in the Eskimo village near by, after which we went on board the "Yukon" to sleep, which however was almost impossible on account of the boat's heavy rolling while at anchor.

I was a little surprised to find that I could carry on even a very limited conversation with the Eskimo of this locality, the last of that tribe I had lived among being the natives of the north Hudson's Bay regions, of whose existence these Eskimo knew nothing.

On the 31st I sent a couple of Eskimo couriers to the "Alaska" at Golovnin Bay, asking her to call at this port in order to take my party on board, after which I sat down to await results. Meantime we had moved on shore into Mr. Leavitt's house, which was kindly put at our disposal. Mr. Leavitt was the signal observer, and had been stationed here over three years, and he was as anxiously awaiting the arrival of the "Leo" as ourselves.

St. Michael's, Michaelovski, or "the redoubt," as it is variously called—St. Michael's Redoubt being the official Russian title, translated into English—is a little village on an island of the same name, comprising about a dozen houses, all directly or indirectly devoted to the affairs of the Alaska Commercial Company. Mr. Neumann was the superintendent, and a very agreeable and affable gentleman we found him, doing much to make our short stay at the redoubt pleasant. There are no fresh water springs on the island near the post, and every few days a large row-boat is loaded with water-barrels and taken to the mainland, where four or five days' supply is secured. The "opposition" store, three miles across

the bay, seems much better situated in this and other
respects, but when St. Michael's was selected by the
Russians over a third of a century previously, the idea
of defensibility was the controlling motive. The passage
between the island and the mainland is a river-like
channel, and was formerly used by the river steamer
until Captain Petersen became master, when he boldly
put out to sea, as a preferable route to "the slough," as
it is sometimes called, there being a number of dangerous rocks in the latter.

On the evening of the 31st we again visited the Eskimo
village, in company with most of the white men of the
redoubt, in order to see the performance of a noted
"medicine-man" or *shaman* from the Golovnin Bay
district. He was to show us some savage sleight-of-hand
performances, and to foretell the probability and time
of the "Leo's" arrival. In the latter operation he took a
large blue bead and crushing it to fragments threw it out
of doors into the sea, "sending it to the schooner," as
he said. After a long and tiresome rigmarole, another
blue bead was produced which he affirmed to be the same
one, telling us that it had been to the vessel, and by
returning whole testified her safety. A somewhat similar
performance with a quarter of a silver dollar told him that
the "Leo" would arrive at St. Michael's about the next
new moon. There was nothing remarkable about these
tricks; and another of tying his hands behind him to a
heavy plank, and then bringing them to the front of his
body, and lifting the board from the floor of the medicine
house, was such a palpable deception as to puzzle no one.

This polar priest, however, had a great reputation
among the natives all about Norton Sound. He had

predicted the loss of the *Jeannette* and the consequent death of the two Eskimo from this point. For his favorable news Mr. Neumann rewarded him with a sack of flour; and I suppose he would have been perfectly willing to furnish more good news for more flour.

The next day I took a genuine Russian bath in a house erected many years ago for that purpose by the Russians. It may be more cleansing, but it is less comfortable than the counterfeit Russian bath as administered in American cities.

The 2d of September was the warmest day they had had that summer, the thermometer marking 65° Fahrenheit. Late in the afternoon the "Yukon" set out on her return to Andreavsky amidst a salute from the carronades and the screaming of the steam-whistle.

On the 3d my Golovnin Bay couriers, who I supposed had started on the preceding day, and were then forty or fifty miles away on their journey, came nonchalantly to me and reported their departure. I bade them good-by, and told them not to delay on the idea that I wanted the "Alaska" next year and not this, and promising me seriously to remember this, they departed. The next day—the 4th—they returned, having forgotten their sugar, an article of luxury they had not enjoyed for months previously, and again departed. I expected to see them return in two or three days for a string to tie it up with, but their outfit must have been complete this time, for I never saw or heard of them again; but I could not help thinking what valuable messenger service the telegraph companies were losing in this far-away country.

Sure enough, on the 8th of the month the "Leo" bore down in a gale and was soon anchored in the bay, where we boarded her. Although already overcrowded for a little schooner of about two hundred tons, Lieutenant Ray kindly made room for my additional party, there being by this addition about thirty-five on board and seventeen in the little cabin. While trying to make Point Barrow, the "Leo" had been nipped in the ice and had her stem split and started, sustaining other injuries the extent of which could not be ascertained. She was leaking badly, requiring about five or ten minutes at the pumps every hour, but it was intended to try and make San Francisco, unless the leaking increased in a gale, when she was to be repaired at Oonalaska, and if matters came to the worst she would be condemned.

A few days were spent in chatting of our experiences, getting fresh water on board and exchanging signal observers, and on the morning of the 11th, at 6 A.M., under a salute of six guns, we weighed anchor and started, with a strong head wind that kept constantly increasing. This gale was from the north-west, and as we had to beat a long distance in that direction in order to clear the great mud banks off the delta of the Yukon, so little progress was made that after an all day's fight we ran back to St. Michael's in an hour's time and dropped anchor once more, to await a change in the weather. Next day we got away early and managed to beat a little on our course. The 13th gave us an almost dead calm until late in the afternoon, when we caught a fine breeze abaft and rounded the Yukon banks about midnight. This favorable breeze increased to a light gale next day and we pounded along at the rate of ten or eleven knots an hour.

On the 15th the gale continued and so increased the

next day that evening saw us "hove to" for fear of running into Oonalaska Island during the night. This run across Bering's Sea in less than three days was stated by our master, Captain Jacobsen, to be the best sailing record across that sheet of water.

The morning of the 17th opened still and calm, with a number of the Aleutian islands looming up directly ahead of us in bold relief. A very light breeze sprang up about noon, and with its help at 6 P.M. we entered the heads of Oonalaska harbor, and at nine o'clock we dropped anchor in the dark about half a mile from the town. Most of us visited the place that night and had a very pleasant reception by Mr. Neumann, the agent of the Alaska Company. Here we found that company's steamer the "Dora," and the revenue-cutter "Corwin," which had been lying here since leaving St. Michael's. These two vessels and everybody generally were waiting for the Alaska Company's large steamer "St. Paul" from San Francisco, upon whose arrival the "Dora," was to distribute the material received for the various trading stations on the Aleutian Islands and the mainland adjacent; the "Corwin" would sail for some point or other, no one could find out where, and the residents would settle down for another year of monotonous life.

The last day's gale on Bering Sea had left no doubt on the minds of those in charge that the "Leo" would have to be repaired, accordingly she was lightened by discharging her load, and on the morning of the 20th she was beached near by, the fall of the tide being sufficient to reveal her injuries, and to allow of temporary repair.

We passed our time in strolling around examining the

islands, while some of the party got out their fishing tackle and succeeded in securing a few fine though small trout from the clear mountain streams.

This grand chain of islands jutting out boldly into the broad Pacific receives the warm waters of the Japanese current—Kuro Siwo—a deflected continuation of a part

OONALASKA.

of the Pacific equatorial current corresponding to our gulf stream. From this source it derives a warmer climate than is possessed by any body of land so near the pole, although it lies in about the same parallels as the British Islands. The cold of zero and the oppessive heat of summer are equally unknown to this region. Grasses grow luxuriantly everywhere, upon which the reindeer used to graze in numerous herds, their keen sight and the absence of timber protecting them from the rude weapons of the native hunters until the introduction of firearms, after which they were rapidly exterminated. In a few days we heard with pleasure that the "Leo" was ready and we soon quitted Alaska for good. The northwest winds sang a merry song through our sails as the meridians and parallels took on smaller numbers, and in a very few days, the twinkling twin lights of the Farallones greeted our eyes, and anchored safely within the Golden Gate, our journey ended.

DISCOVERY AND HISTORY.

The actual discovery of the great northwestern peninsula of the American continent cannot be dated further back than the middle part of the eighteenth century. Its remoteness from the centres of European settlement and from the lines of trade and travel, and its inhospitable climate made Alaska one of the latest regions to yield to the advances of the explorer, surveyor and settler. At a date when the colonies on the North Atlantic coast of America numbered millions of prosperous people, already preparing to take independent rank among the nations of the world, the very existence of this enormous country was unknown. At a very early date, however, voyagers from many lands began their advances toward the far Northwest, and the story of the discovery of Alaska must naturally include a brief outline of these.

As early as 1542 the Spanish adventurers Coronado and Juan Rodriguez de Cabrillo went up the Pacific coast of Mexico, and sailed for some distance along the coast of what is now the State of California. The memory of the former has been locally honored in California in the name of Coronado Beach. At this time the Spanish considered themselves sole masters of the South Sea, as the Pacific was called, and of all lands bordering upon it. But their supremacy there was soon disputed by the intrepid Sir Francis Drake. He not only ravaged their South American seaports, but, in

1579, sailed far to northward in a little schooner of two hundred tons, entered the Golden Gate, and refitted his vessel in what is now the harbor of San Francisco. Thirteen years later the Spaniards pressed still further up the coast. Apostolos Valerianos, best known as Juan de Fuca, sailed from Mexico and passed through the straits that bear his name, and discovered Puget Sound. There adventure from the south made pause for many years, still a weary distance from the Alaskan peninsula.

More than a hundred years after the voyages of Coronado, a different people, from a different direction, began to move toward the same goal. These were the Russians, who had already taken possession of the greater part of Siberia, and who were now persistently pushing on to the occupation of the whole realm between the Baltic and the Pacific. They had already gone eastward as far as the Kolyma River, and possessed the town of Nijni Kolymsk, in about 160° degrees east longitude. In 1646 they advanced still further. Isai Ignatieff, with several small vessels, sailed from the Kolyma, and effected a landing on Tchaun Bay, in the country of the Tchukchees. He found the trade in walrus ivory so profitable that his example was soon followed by others. The very next year the Cossack Simeon Deshneff, with four vessels, sailed eastward, to take possession of all the land in the name of the Russian crown. The Anadyr River, of which reports had been heard from the natives, was his goal. At the same time, Michael Stadukin led an expedition overland in the same direction. But both these enterprises failed. The year 1648, however, saw Deshneff's venture repeated. Three ships sailed for the Anadyr, commanded respectively by Simeon Deshneff, Gerasim Ankudinoff, and Feodor Alexieff. They reached Behring Strait, not knowing it was a strait, and Ankudinoff's vessel was wrecked on East Cape. He and his men were taken on the other vessels, and the expedition kept on. Deshneff made his way around Cape Navarin and Cape Olintorski to the coast of Kamtchatka. There his vessel was wrecked and he and his men made their way home overland, surveying, as they went, the Anadyr River. Again in 1652 Deshneff explored the Anadyr, in a boat, and the next year planned a trade-route, by sea, from that river to Yakutsk, on the Lena.

Many other expeditions to Kamtchatka and the western part of Behring Sea were soon thereafter made. Taras Stadukin in 1654 discovered the westernmost Kurill Islands, and sailed round Kamtchatka into Penjinsk Bay. In 1696, Lucas Simeonoff Moroscovich explored Kamtchatka by land, and during the next year the Cossack Vladimir Atlassoff followed him thither and by force of arms made the Kamtchatdales subjects of the Czar. This conquest was marked by wholesale butcheries of the helpless natives, and confiscation of their goods. The conquest of the Tchukchees was attempted in 1701, but failed, as did a second expedition against them ten years later. This latter, however, under the Cossack Peter Iliunsen Potoff, in 1711, had one highly-important result. It brought back definite reports of the narrowness of Behring Strait, of the location of the Diomedes Islands, and of the proximity of the American continent. Then, for some years, all further advance was stayed.

The next movement was undertaken by no less a personage than Peter the Great,

" ——that Czar
Who made of tribes an Empire."

It was at the end of his reign and life. Two passions moved him. One was the zeal for scientific exploration and knowledge of the world ; the other, the desire to extend his dominion across the Arctic borders of another continent. Accordingly in 1725 he planned a great expedition, drew up full instructions with his own hand, and delivered them to Admiral Apraxin ; then died. His widow, who became Autocrat in his stead, ordered the plan fulfilled, and it was done promptly. On February 5th, 1725, the chief members of the expedition set out from St. Petersburg, their leader and commander being the illustrious Captain Vitus Behring.

The explorers made their way by slow stages to Okhotsk. There they built two ships, the "Fortuna" and the "Gabriel," and on July 20th, 1728, set sail on their adventurous voyage. On this occasion they contented themselves with traversing Behring Strait, and returned without seeing the American coast or even the Diomedes Islands. A second voyage, in 1729, was altogether fruitless, and in the spring of 1730 Behring returned to St. Petersburg without having achieved a single work of importance or won the first fraction of his later fame. But one of the objects of his expedition was presently attained by others, accidentally. The Yakutsk Cossacks, under Athanasius Shestakoff, had been for years fighting to subdue the indomitable Tchukchees, with little success. A party of them took the ship "Fortuna," abandoned by Behring, to make a war-like cruise along the Tchukchee coast. They were soon wrecked in Penjinsk Bay, and were routed in battle with the Tchukchees. But the engineer and navigator of the expedition, Michael Gwosdeff, made a boat from the wreck of the " Fortuna," and with his surviving comrades sailed to the Anadyr River. Thence they sailed to Cape Serdze, expecting there to meet a Cossack expedition from overland. In this they were disappointed. And presently a great storm arose from the eastward and dove them, helpless, before it. Right across the strait they were driven, to the American coast. Upon the latter, however, they could make no landing. The shore was inhospitable and the storm was furious. For two days they cruised along the coast, and then, the storm abating, made their way back to Asia.

Despite the failure of his first expedition, Behring was received with honors and promotion at the Russian capital, and preparations were pressed for another venture under his command. For several years he was engaged in voyages along the Siberian coast, and to Japan. But in 1741 the great achievement of his life began. His pilot, Ivan Jelagin, had gone to Avatcha with two ships, the "St. Peter" and the "St. Paul." On Niakina Bay he had founded the town of Petropaulovsk, named for the vessels. Thither went Wilhelm Steller, the Franconian naturalist, and Louis de Lisle de la Croyere. Thither, finally, ent Behring, and on June 4th, 1741, sailed for America. On June 20th the two vessels were parted by a storm, and did not come together again ; nor did Behring and Chirikoff, their commanders, ever meet again in this world. Chirikoff, in the "St. Paul," made quickest progress. On July 15th he reached the

American coast, and anchored in Cross Sound. His mate, Dementieff, and ten armed men, in the long boat, went ashore. They did not return, and on July 21st Sidor Saveleff with other armed men went after them, in the only other boat of the "St. Paul." They did not return either. But the next day two canoes filled with savages came from the shore toward the ship, showing only too plainly what had become of the landing parties. The savages did not venture to attack the ship, but Chirikoff had no more boats in which to effect a landing. So on July 27th he weighed anchor and sailed back for Kamtchatka. He passed by numerous islands, and on October 9th re-entered the harbor of Petropaulovsk. Twenty-one of his seventy men had perished; among them Louis de Lisle de la Croyere, the French naturalist, who died of scurvy on the day of their return.

The "St. Peter," with Behring and his comrades on board, meanwhile, was driven blindly through tempest and fog toward the Alaskan coast. On Sunday, July 18th, he reached the land and disembarked. He was at the foot of some low, desolate bluff which skirted the shore for a long distance, and beyond which rose the savage splendors of Mt. St. Elias and the Arctic Alps. The spot was near what is now called Kayak Island. For six weeks Behring tarried in that neighborhood, refitting his storm-strained ship, laying aboard supplies of water and food, and making a few explorations of the coast. The two capes between which he landed he named St. Elias and Hermogenes. Here the naturalist Steller found many interesting traces of the natives. Going further north, into Prince William's Sound,

Behring became confused by the number of islands and the difficulties of navigation, and abandoned the direction of the vessel to Lieutenant Waxel. They kept on, past the Kenai Peninsula, past Kadiak Island, and down the coast of the slender Alaska Peninsula, to the southwest, until they reached a group of islands which they named Shumagin, for a member of the company who died and was buried there. This was on August 29th. On September 3d a terrific storm arose, before which they were driven, helpless, far out into the North Pacific, southward to latitude 48°. Scurvy broke out among them with fatal force, and the disheartened men resolved to return to Kamtchatka.

Thenceforward for weeks they suffered almost incredible hardships. Every one was suffering from scurvy. So weakened were they by disease and famine that it took three men to hold the helm. Only a few sails were used, for the men were not able to hoist and manage more. When these were torn away by the storms, the helpless craft drifted under bare poles. The weather was a chaos of wind and fog and snow. For weeks they drifted blindly, now eastward, now westward, scarcely hoping to see land again, and utterly ignorant of the part of the ocean into which they had been borne. But on November 4th a particularly furious gale drove them ashore on an unknown coast. They were in the southeastern part of Behring Sea, on one of the Kommandorski group of islands. The vessel was completely wrecked, and the men built huts on the shore for winter quarters. Waxel was still in command. Behring was a victim to natural stupidity, constitutional cowardice, and scurvy. All through the dreadful voyage from

Prince William Sound he had remained in his cabin, shivering in abject terror. A few weeks after landing, on December 8th he died. In honor of him his men named the island Behring Island, and the group the Kommandorski, while Behring Strait and Behring Sea in their names give immortality to one of the least worthy of men. Waxel, Steller, and the others remained on Behring Island all that winter, feeding on the flesh of sea-lions and the monster Arctic manatee or sea-cow, now extinct. They collected a considerable store of furs of the sea-otter, blue fox and other animals, which they took back to Russia and thus greatly stimulated the zeal of further conquest. In the summer of 1742 they made their way to Petropaulovsky in a boat constructed from the wreck of their ship. Waxel reached St. Petersburg with the official report of the expedition in 1749.

Thenceforward the greed of gain led many Russian adventurers to the waters and shores of Behring Sea. Emilian Bassoff discovered Attoo Island, the westernmost of the Aleutian chain, in 1745, and Michael Novodtsikoff, in the same year, discovered other islands near by, and got a rich cargo of furs. Other explorers, who followed up the Aleutian chain were Ribinski, in 1748; Trapesnikoff, in 1749; Yagoff, in 1750; and Ivan Nikiforoff, who reached Unimak Island in 1757. Simon Krasilnikoff, Maxim Lazeroff and others kept up the work of discovering islands, getting furs, and massacreing the natives. The Andreanoffsky Islands were discovered in 1761, and named in honor of Andrean Tolstoi, who fitted out Lazeroff's expedition. In the winter of 1761–2, Pushkareff and his men lived

on the shore of False Pass. They were the first to
spend a winter on the mainland of Alaska. The atroci-
ties committed by them excited the hostility of the
natives, and they were glad to get away in August,
1762. They took with them thirty natives, mostly
women, as prisoners and slaves; but on the voyage
home they wantonly murdered them all except two.

War to the knife thereafter prevailed among the
natives and the Russians. The latter waged it with the
most ferocious energy, but were by no means always
victors. A whole expedition of fifty men was destroyed
on Unimak Island in 1762; and a similar party met
the same fate in 1763, on Ounalaska. Indeed, for years
the history of Russian progress in Alaska was one of
unrelieved horror, an inferno of lust, torture and
death.

And now the advance of the Spanish and others from
the southward was resumed. Juan Perez sailed from
Monterey in 1774, and discovered Queen Charlotte
Island and Nootka Sound. The next year Bruno
Heceta discovered the mouth of the Oregon or Columbia
River. Then the famous English navigator, James
Cook, came upon the scene. In 1778 he reached
Nootka Sound; saw and named Mount St. Elias; explored Cook's Inlet; stopped for a time at Ounalaska;
sailed up Behring Sea, through Behring Strait, to Icy
Cape; explored Norton Sound and the adjacent waters;
touched again at Ounalaska; and then sailed away to
the Sandwich Islands, where he was killed in February,
1779. In these few months this immortal Yorkshire
man and his Connecticut and Virginia comrades had
done more active work of discovery and survey than

all the Russian pillagers who had frequented that part of the world for seventy-five years before.

The first permanent industrial and commercial settlement was effected by the Russians under Shelikoff on Kadiak Island in 1783. Three years later the ill-fated La Perouse visited the Alaskan coast and saw Mt. St. Elias. In 1787, two Russians, Lastochkin and Pribyloff, discovered two islands in the southeast part of Behring Sea, which have since become of enormous value. They named them St. Paul and St. George, and called them together the Suboff Islands. They are now known, however, as the Pribyloff Islands, and are famous as one of the chief homes of the fur seals.

The Russian Government, about 1788, formally laid claim to all the Alaskan lands and waters, and even to the northern part of the Pacific Ocean. At the same time the Spanish and English laid conflicting claims to the region about Nootka Sound, and in 1789 came into violent conflict there. United States expeditions were also busy with explorations in that region, but the Spaniards made no objection to their presence. Captain Gray, of the " Washington," Captain John Kendrick, of the "Columbia," Captain Metcalf, of the "Fair American," Captain Ingraham, of the " Hope," Captain Crowell, of the " Hancock," Captain Roberts, of the "Jefferson," and Captain Magee, of the " Margaret," were among the Americans conspicuous in exploration and trade, chiefly about Nootka Sound and the Straits of Juan de Fuca. Captain George Vancouver, already mentioned as a member of Cook's expedition, also spent much time in exploring the coast, from the island which bears his name northward to the Prince of Wales Islands, in the

British service; and Alexander Mackenzie traveled across the continent from Canada and explored the great river which has been named for him. The surveys of Vancouver were the most thorough and accurate that had been made.

To return, however, to the Russians. In 1782, Gregory Shelikoff, of Rylsk, Siberia, a man of great ability and energy, of remarkable brutality, and of unsurpassed unscrupulousness, entered upon an important campaign for the establishment of trading posts. In this he was accompanied by his wife, Natalie Shelikoff, a woman of extraordinary ability. In 1787, the Czarina Catherine II, gave him a medal in recognition of his services; and in 1790, by an imperial ukase, that notorious but brilliant sovereign gave to a company, of which Shelikoff was the head, the practical monopoly of the Alaska fur trade. Alexander Baranoff, one of Shelikoff's subordinates, was soon made Chief Director of Affairs in the Russo-American colonies. He, like his chief, was a man of consummate executive ability, and utterly destitute of humane feelings or moral sense. In the summer of 1793 he prevailed upon the Czarina to issue another ukase, authorizing the sending of missionaries to America to convert the natives to the Orthodox Greek faith, and also the sending thither of Russian convicts to teach them agriculture. Thirty convicts were thus settled by Baranoff on the Kenai peninsula, and the Archimandrite Joasaph, elder of the Augustin friars, also went thither. Many other convicts and their families, and monkish missionaries, were in 1794 landed at Kadiak and Cape St. Elias. As soon as they were landed, Shelikoff refused to support them, and they were compelled to work for their living. In consequence the missionaries sent bitter complaints to the Czar; and these were accompanied by still more bitter complaints from the natives, who were being subjected to such brutalities as cannot be described in print. These had little effect, however. In 1795, Shelikoff died, and his wife succeeded him as president of the company. At this time the population of Kadiak was more than 3,600 adults. The next year the first Greek church was erected there, and Father Joasaph was made Bishop. In 1799 the Czar Paul chartered anew the Shelikoff company, re-organized as the Russian-American Company, for a term of twenty years. He gave it absolute control of all the American coast-lands and waters north of latitude 55°. The Company was required to survey the region, plant settlements, promote agriculture, commerce and other industries, propagate the Greek faith, and extend Russian influence and possessions as widely as possible. As for the natives, they were by the same decree made the slaves of the Company. Baranoff was made practically the supreme head, the autocrat of the entire realm, on whose word were suspended the issues of life and death.

Under this new *régime* the old policy of cruelty and outrage toward the natives was pursued with added intensity. Generally the Russians worked their will with impunity, though sometimes the natives rose against them with vengeful might, and on several occasions the Russians were glad to flee to British and American ships for shelter. Meanwhile explorations went on. The American ship "Atahualpa" in 1802 discovered the mouth of the Stikine River. Baranoff explored the lower part of the Copper River.   In 1804 Baranoff took Sitka from the natives, after a hard battle; renamed it New Archangel, gave the island on which it stood his own name, and made it thenceforth the chief station in the colony.   About this time an attempt was made to plant trees on the Aleutian islands. The Imperial Chamberlain, Count Nicolas Petrovich Resanoff, founded a school at Kadiak, and effected some valuable administrative reforms, especially in the colonial courts and in the financial system.   Then he went back to Russia to get the Czar's consent to his marriage with the daughter of Don Luis de Arguello, the Spanish governor of San Francisco.   As soon as he was gone, Baranoff undid all his reforms.   Resanoff died on his way to Russia.   His betrothed never believed he was dead, and never would marry another; but waited patiently for his return until she became very old and died.

John Jacob Astor, having formed a company for the Pacific fur trade, sent a vessel to Sitka in 1809, and in 1811 an agent to St. Petersburg to negotiate with the Directory of the Russian-American Company.   The negotiations were successful, and in October, 1811, were approved by the Czar,   Mr. Astor was to furnish provisions and supplies at stated prices, and to take pay therefor in furs from the Company.   They were to assist each other against smugglers, respect each other's hunting-grounds, and not to sell intoxicating liquors to the natives.   In 1817 Baranoff, having grown old and weary of his toil, resigned the Chief Directorship of the colonies, and was succeeded by Captain Leontius Hagenmeister.   He resigned within a year, and was succeeded by Lieutenant Janoffsky. At this time an Imperial Commissioner, Vasili Golofnin, was sent to investigate and report on the abuses of administration. As a result, in July, 1819, the Czar made sweeping changes in the regulations of the colonies, which effected some substantial reforms.

There were now Russian settlements on five of the Aleutian islands, four on the shores of Cook's Inlet, two on Chugach Gulf, and one at Sitka. The last named was a large and handsome place, surrounded by gardens and wheat fields. In 1821 the charter of the Company was renewed for twenty years. The profits of the enterprise, however, were now declining. Not one of Baranoff's successors had a tithe of his ability, and the result of his loss was seen in shrinking dividends. Explorations, however, were pushed vigorously. A two years' expedition surveyed the coasts of Norton Sound, Bristol Bay, and Nunivak Island. The Alexander Archipelago also was thoroughly explored. The Russian Government in 1821 issued a proclamation of sovereignty over the whole Pacific Ocean north of the 51st parallel, and forbidding vessels of other nations to approach within one hundred miles of the shores thereof, save in cases of extreme distress. Against this the United States and England vigorously protested, and with effect. In 1824 a convention was signed between the United States and Russia, by which the North Pacific was opened to American ships, and latitude 54° 40′ was recognized as the southern boundary of the Russian possessions; and a similar treaty was made with England the next year.

Kotzebue Sound was explored by the English Cap-

tain Beechey in 1826. Captain Staninkovich explored
much of the northern coast of Alaska in 1828. In
1830 Chernoff examined the harbor of Nuchek and the
mouth of the Kaknu River; and Kolmakoff surveyed
the bay and river of Kuskoquim. In this year the
Company took formal possession of all the Kurile Is-
lands. The next year Baron von Wrangell became
Director of the Colonies, and an era of progress began.
The colony was opened for settlement to all Russians.
Fort St. Michael's, on Norton Sound, was established.
Measures were taken to check the destruction of seals
and other sea animals. An observatory was founded at
Sitka. In 1835 Glasunoff explored the deltas of the
Kuskoquim and Yukon rivers, ascending the latter
stream as far as Anvik. Small-pox now broke out at
Sitka, and for several years ravaged all the settlements,
nearly depopulating some of them. In 1838 Malakoff
went up the Yukon River to Nulato, and Kushevaroff
thoroughly explored the northeastern coast as far as
Point Barrow. The next year Mt. St. Elias was observed for the first time to emit smoke, but no further
eruption occurred. In 1843 Lieutenant Zagoskin ascended the Yukon as far as Nowikakat, Malakoff explored the Suchitna, Gregorieff the Copper River, and
Kashevaroff the shores of Behring Sea.

The second charter of the Company expired in 1841,
and strong efforts were made to have it renewed at once.
The Government hesitated, but finally, in 1844, renewed it on even more liberal terms than before. In
the summer of 1848 the first whaling vessel passed
through Behring Strait. It was the American ship
"Superior," commanded by Captain Roys. The ex-

periment was highly successful, and in the next season no less than one hundred and fifty-four American whalers followed the example, all making great catches, and the industry was thus established in those waters. English and American explorers continued to visit to northern coasts of Alaska, and surveyed almost every portion of it.

As the ending of the third charter of the Company approached, efforts were made to secure still another renewal. A complete report on the operations of the Company was made at the end of 1861. According to it, the original capital was $73,500. In 1818 it was "watered," and the shares were made $100 instead of $112.50 each. In 1844 the Company had accumulated a surplus of $337,500. At the end of 1861 the capital was $495,000, and the surplus $553,000. The original investment had paid from six to ten per cent. net annually, besides the enormous peculations of the officers and employés. Despite the earnest endeavors of the Company, however, the Czar finally refused to renew its charter, and the Company began to wind up its business. In 1864 there was a great increase of American interests in the colony. The Western Union Telegraph Company, of New York, doubting the practicability of operating a cable under the Atlantic, planned to construct a telegraph line to Europe by way of Alaska and Siberia. In this the Russian Government agreed to co-operate. A surveying expedition was accordingly sent to Alaska, and much exploring work was done at a cost of more than three million dollars. The incident, though without practical result in itself, drew so much attention to Alaska and its resources that an American syndicate

was formed to purchase for itself the charter which the
Czar refused to grant to the old Russian Company. This
came to the ear of Mr. Seward, the American Secretary
of State, and he soon concluded that it would be a good
bargain for the United States to buy the whole country
outright from Russia. This was done in 1867. The
United States paid Russia $7,200,000 for the whole
Territory of Alaska. Nearly all of this went, at St.
Petersburg, to satisfy old debts and obligations incurred
by Alaskan enterprises. The treaty of sale was agreed
upon on March 30th; it was ratified by the United
States Senate on May 28th; proclaimed by the President on June 20th; General Jefferson C. Davis was
appointed to take command of Alaska on September
6th; and on October 18th the United States took formal
and actual possession of the country.

This new Territory was looked upon as an Indian
country and General Davis was really a military commander. His headquarters were at Sitka, where he had
a garrison of about 250 men. A number of enterpris-
ing business men accompanied General Davis to Sitka,
and immediately began erecting storehouses and offices,
and purchasing the property of the old Russian Company. In less than a week several new stores were
erected and two drinking saloons, two bowling alleys
and a restaurant were in operation. All sorts and conditions of men began flocking in, including pioneers
and squatters, and aspirants for political honors in the
Territory. There was talk of framing a city charter,
and of creating numerous lucrative offices. The usual
amount of crime and disorder of a frontier settlement
occurred, and soon all respectable inhabitants were com-

pelled to lock their doors at nightfall and not venture out again until daylight. Difficulties with the Indians also soon began, and for many years the Territory was in a state of disorder and confusion, lacking any organized government.

In February, 1868, the Russians began to return home and to abandon the Territory to its new owners. In this year many serious troubles with the Indians occurred on the Yukon River, and on the first of January, 1869, there was some disturbance at Sitka itself. In April, 1869, the publication of a newspaper was begun at Sitka by a man who also followed the avocations of lawyer and tailor. This paper passed out of existence after about a year and was not revived. In 1870 the withdrawal of the military garrisons occurred, excepting those at Sitka and Wrangell. In 1874 an attempt was made to colonize Alaska with Icelanders, who were at that time leaving their own country in large numbers. Several of them visited Alaska and were pleased with the appearance of the country. An offer was made to transport thither five hundred Icelanders free of charge, but it was not accepted, and the scheme of colonization was finally abandoned. In 1878 a serious outbreak of Indians occurred at Sitka, and the inhabitants of that town were compelled to appeal for protection to the commander of an English war-ship. In 1884 a regular territorial government was established and a civil governor appointed, the military garrisons having been withdrawn.

THE PEOPLE AND THEIR INDUSTRIES.

The United States census of 1890 definitely enumerated 21,929 inhabitants of Alaska, and estimated the existence of about 8,400 more. Of those enumerated there were 3,922 white males and 497 white females; 82 black males; 770 "mixed" males, and 798 "mixed" females; and 2,125 male Chinese; while the native population included 7,158 males and 6,577 females. According to the same census there were in Alaska 11 organizations of the Orthodox Greek Church; with 22 edifices with a seating capacity of 2,900 and a value of $180,000. The communicants numbered 13,004. The Roman Catholic Church had 6 organizations, with 6 buildings, seating 540 persons, and valued at $9,700. There were 559 communicants. No less than 27 fire insurance companies were doing business in the Territory, and in 1889 the risks written and renewed by them aggregated $1,710,184.

The people of Alaska have been spoken of as Americans, Russians, Hydahs, Tsimpseans, Thlinkets, Aleuts, Innuits or Eskimos and Tinneh, or Athabascan Indians. Eight distinct languages and several dialects are spoken. The Tsimpseans embrace only the settlement at Metlakahtla, about one thousand people who came over from British Columbia. The Hydahs have some five or six villages on the south end of Prince of Wales Island with about nine hundred people. The Thlinkets reside in from forty to fifty villages in the Alexander Archipelago and along the coast from Cape Fox to Copper River. All these have become partly civilized by contact with the whites and through the influence of schools and missions, and there is a large number of those who can speak English and have become excellent citizens. The Aleuts are also partly civilized, but with a civilization conforming more nearly to that of the Russians than our own. These reside upon the islands of the Aleutian chain, the Shunagin and Kodiak groups, the Aliaska Peninsula and the islands of St. Paul and St. George in Behring Sea.

There are a few Aleut half-breeds in Sitka. Many of these people talk the Russian language. The Innuits and Tinnehs cannot be said to be civilized, though their barbarism has been modified by contact with white people. The Innuits reside along the coast from Nushegak, in Behring Sea, to the eastern limit of our dominion in the Arctic region. Lieutenant Ray speaks of them as living in a state of anarchy, making no combinations, offensive or defensive, having no punishment for crimes and no government. Given to petty pilfering, they make no attempt to reclaim stolen property. They are social in their habits and kind to each other. These people are obliged to devote all their energies to procuring the necessary food and clothing to maintain life. Their intelligence is of a low order and the race is apparently diminishing. Physically they are strong and possess great powers of endurance.

The Tinnehs occupy the interior, the Yukon valley, except the portions near its mouth, and come down to the seashore only at Cook's Inlet. They are called "Stick" Indians by the Thlinkets. These people have many traits of the North American Indians elsewhere, and may properly be designated as Indians. The other natives of Alaska are not true Indians and have not generally been treated as such by the government. They have no real tribal relations, though formerly the heads of families were recognized as chiefs and called such.

At the present time, among the Hydahs, Tsimpseans, Thlinkets and Aleuts, the so-called chiefs have very little, if any, power or influence, as such. Among the Eskimos it may be doubted if the office ever amounted to anything.

The progress of the natives of Southeastern Alaska toward civilization is steady and certain, though it must not be supposed that these people yet take high rank in learning, intelligence or morality. The educating and elevating influences of the schools and missions, though doing much, perhaps more than we should expect under the circumstances, must be continued a long time in order to effect anything like satisfactory conditions.

In some respects the physical condition of the different native tribes is alike and in others not. All are strongly built, rather short, and by their habits of living inured to hardship and endurance. The men have very light or no beards, and frequently trim the scattering hairs on their chins closely or pluck them out. The average height is less than that of Europeans. They have an Asiatic cast of features and the coast people are generally thought to have originated from Japanese stock. The Eskimos have a language very similar to the Eskimos of Labrador and almost identical with a small population upon the Asiatic side of Behring Strait. Physically they differ from the Eskimos of Greenland and Labrador, being more robust and healthy. All of the natives of Alaska have small and delicately-formed hands and feet and rather a massive head, straight black hair, dark eyes, high cheek bones and nut-brown complexion. All are to a large extent fish eaters, though the Tinnehs, living in the interior, or Ingalik tribes of the Yukon, are compelled to subsist to a greater extent upon game and land products.

Their dwellings, not so unlike originally, have now become quite different in style and manner of construction. Those residing in Southeastern Alaska have frame or block houses wholly above ground, with sleeping apartments partitioned off from the main or living-room where the central fireplace is located, like the state-rooms of a river steamboat, and many of the Thlinkets have substituted the modern cooking-stove and pipe for the fireplace and open chimney-hole in the roof.

These people are all self-supporting; the Hydahs, Tsimpseans, Thlinkets and Aleuts living comfortably with plenty of food and blankets. The Eskimos, especially those of the Arctic region, have a hard time of it to keep from starvation and death by freezing. The Tinnehs, or Ingaliks, have less of the conveniences, not to say luxuries of life, than any of the coast tribes. The last-named two tribes have small, poorly built, partly underground houses, and their winter dwellings are entirely covered with earth.

Mention has already been made of the town of Sitka, the capital of the Territory. It is beautifully situated, sheltered by a range of snow-covered mountains on the one side and on the other protected from the broad expanse of the Pacific Ocean and its storms by a numerous group of thickly-wooded islands. The waters of the harbor are singularly clear, so that in looking over the side of a vessel one can see the bottom at a depth of many fathoms. A warm equatorial current bathes this shore and bears into these Arctic regions many sponges, coral branches and other growths of warmer latitudes. The town itself lies clustered near the shore and presents a pleasing picture to the visitor as he approaches it from the sea. Its most conspicuous feature is the old weather-beaten and moss-grown castle which crowns a rocky hill. This structure is 140 feet long and 70 feet wide, and is built of huge cedar logs. It was for many years the official residence of the Russian governors and was at times the scene of splendid social gatherings. In its upper story were arranged a ball-room and a theatre, and the building throughout was as richly furnished as a palace in St. Petersburg or Moscow. Some of these rich furnishings still remain, though as a whole the building is in a most dilapidated condition. Another prominent building is the old Greek Church with its emerald green dome, Byzantine spire, fine chime of bells and richly decorated interior. It is liberally maintained, as indeed are all the other Greek Churches in the Territory, by the Russian Government. Most of the houses in Sitka are built of heavy logs, some of them being also clapboarded outside. During the winter about 1,000 Indians live there and the white population is composed of the government officials and agents, a few store-keepers and traders, and perhaps four or five hundred miners and prospectors from the inland regions. In mid-winter there are only about six hours of daylight in each day, and in mid-summer there is for a time practically no night at all. Rain is the principal feature of the climate, and this abundance of moisture causes all vegetation to grow luxuriantly. There is an abundance of vegetables and some fruit, and domestic cattle are kept successfully. Nowhere outside of the tropics is a more luxurious natural vegetation to be found than in these islands of southern Alaska. Sitka is a neat and clean city, and as a rule is now quiet and orderly. It contains a large industrial school, attended by 200 native boys and girls, the course of study including nearly all useful industries. Twenty miles south of Sitka, on the same island, hot springs are to be found, the water of which is rich in sulphur and iron. For many generations these have been a sanitary resort of the natives, and it is not unlikely that in the near future they will be greatly visited by tourists from the United States and elsewhere. The temperature of the water is about 155° Fahrenheit, and the springs are surrounded by tropical vegetation.

After Sitka, the most important settlement in the Territory, is Fort Wrangell. It is beautifully situated at the mouth of the Stickhin River, where there is an excellent and capacious harbor, surrounded by imposing mountains. The town consists of rather more than 100 houses, and includes about 500 permanent inhabitants. There are two or three large stores for the sale of goods to the natives and for the purchase of furs and other natural products, as well as the quaint manufactures of the Indians. There is also a flourishing industrial school for the Indian girls. A leading native industry here is the manufacture of jewelry from silver and ivory. In this the natives are very expert, producing most elaborate patterns and copying any designs given to them with the most patient and unfailing fidelity.

When the United States took possession of Alaska a great many active and ambitious men on the Pacific coast were imbued with the idea that much that was really valuable in Alaska in the line of furs and the precious metals would be developed to their great gain and benefit if they gave the subject the attention which it deserved. Accordingly, many expeditions were fitted out at San Francisco, Puget Sound, and other points on the Pacific coast, and directed to an examination of these reputed sources of wealth in that distant country. Many years have now rolled by, and in that time we have been enabled to judge pretty accurately of the relative value of this new territory in comparison with that of our nearer possessions, and it is now known that the fur-trade of Alaska is all and even more than it was reputed to be by the Russians.

In this connection the most notable instance, perhaps, of the great value of these interests may be cited in the case of the seal islands. It will be remembered that at the time of the transfer, when the most eloquent advocates of the purchase were exhausting the fertility of their brains in drumming up and securing every possible argument in favor of the purchase, though the fur trade of the mainland, the sea-otter fisheries, and the possible extent of trade in walrus oil and ivory were dwelt upon with great emphasis, these fur-seal islands did not receive even a passing notice as a source of revenue or value to the public.   Yet it has transpired, since the government has been wise enough to follow out the general policy which the Russians established of protecting the seal life on the Pribylof Islands, that these interests in our hands are so managed and directed that they pay into the treasury of the United States a sum sufficient to meet all the expenses of the government in behalf of Alaska, beside leaving a large excess every year.

Of other resources, such as the adaptation of the country for settlement by any considerable number of our people as agriculturists or husbandmen, and its actual value as a means of supplying gold and silver, coal or timber, it must be said that as yet no very remarkable gold or silver mines have been discovered, nor have there been any veins of coal worked that would in themselves sustain any considerable number of our people or give rise to any volume of trade.

The timber of Alaska in itself extends over a much larger area of that country than a great many surmise.   It clothes the steep hills and mountain sides, and chokes up the valleys of the Alexander Archipelago and the contiguous mainland; it stretches less dense, but still abundant, along that inhospitable reach of territory which extends from the head of Cross Sound to the Kenai peninsula, where, reaching down to the westward and southwestward as far as the eastern half of Kadiak Island, and thence across Shelikof Strait, it is found on the mainland and on the peninsula bordering on the same latitude; but it is confined to the interior opposite Kadiak, not coming down to the coast as far eastward as Cape Douglas. Here, however, it impinges on the coast or Cook's Inlet, reaching down to the shores and extending around to the Kenai peninsula. From the interior of the peninsula, above referred to, the timber-line over the whole of the interior of the great area of Alaska will be found to follow the coast-line, at varying distances of from 100 to 150 miles from the seabord, until that section of Alaska north of the Yukon mouth is reached, where a portion of the coast of Norton Sound is directly bordered by timber as far north as Cape Denbigh. From this point to the eastward and northeastward a line may be drawn just above the Yukon and its immediate tributaries as the northern limit of timber of any considerable extent. There are a great number of small water-courses rising here that find their way into the Arctic, bordered by hills and lowland ridges on which some wind-stunted timber is found, even to the shores of the Arctic Sea.

In thus broadly sketching the distribution of timber over Alaska it will be observed that the area thus clothed is very great; yet when we come to consider the quality of the timber itself, and its economic value in our markets, we are obliged to adopt the standard of the lumber-mills in Oregon and Washington. Viewed in this light, we find that the best timber of Alaska is the yellow cedar, which in itself is of great intrinsic value; but this cedar is not the dominant timber by any means; it is the exception to the rule. The great bulk of Alaskan timber is that known as Sitkan spruce, or balsam fir. The lumber sawed from this stock is naturally not of the first quality. These trees grow to their greatest size in the Sitka or Alexander Archipelago. An interval occurs from Cross Sound until we pass over the fair-weather ground at the foot of Mount St. Elias, upon the region of Prince William Sound and Cook's Inlet, where this timber again occurs, and attains very respectable proportions in many sections of the district, notably at Wood Island and portions of Afognak, and at the head of the Kenai peninsula and the two gulfs that environ it. The abundance of this timber and the extensive area clothed by it are readily appreciated by looking at the map, and are rendered still more impressive when we call attention to the fact that the timber extends in good size as far north as the Yukon Valley, clothing all the hills within that extensive region and to the north of Cook's Inlet and Kenai peninsula, so that the amount of timber found therein is great in the aggregate. The size of this spruce timber at its base will be typified in trees on Prince of Wales Island 50 feet and over in height, with a diameter of at least three feet. They have not grown as fast as they would have grown in a more congenial latitude to the south, such as Puget Sound or Oregon; hence when they are run through the saw-mill the frequent and close proximity of knots mar the quality and depress the sale of the lumber. Spruce boards are not adapted to nice finishing work in building or in cabinet-ware, or, indeed, in anything that requires a finish and upon which paint and varnish may be permanently applied, for under the influence of slight degrees of heat it sweats, exuding minute globules of gum or rosin, which are sticky and difficult to remove.

The other timber trees in southeastern Alaska, Kadiak and Cook's Inlet may be called exceptional. But one very valuable species of yellow cedar (*C. nutkanensis*) is found scattered here and there within the Alexander Archipelago and on the thirty-mile strip. Here this really valuable tree is found at wide intervals in small clumps, principally along shoal water-courses and fiords, attaining a much greater size than the spruce, as frequently trees are found 100 feet high, with a diameter of five and six feet. The lumber made from these is exceedingly valuable, of the very finest texture, odor and endurance, and is highly prized by the cabinet-maker and the ship-builder.

Thus it will be seen that the forests of Alaska are altogether coniferous, as the small bodies of the birch and the alder and willow thickets on the lower Yukon and Kuskokvim Rivers can scarcely be considered to come under this head. Aside from the yellow cedar, which is rare, the timber wealth of Alaska consists of the Sitka spruce, which is not only abundant and large (trees of from three to four feet in diameter being quite common in southeastern Alaska and Prince William Sound), but also generally accessible.

To give even an approximate estimate of the area of timbered lands in Alaska is at present impossible, in view of our incomplete knowledge of the extent of mountain ranges, which, though falling within the timber limits, must be deducted from the superficial area of forest covering.

A few small saw-mills, of exceedingly limited capacity, have been erected at various points in southeastern Alaska, to supply the local demand of trading-posts and mining-camps, but finished building lumber is still

largely imported even into this heavily-timbered region.
In all western Alaska but one small saw-mill is known
to exist, which is on Wood Island, St. Paul Harbor,
Kadiak. This mill was first set up to supply saw-dust
for packing ice, but since the collapse of that industry
its operations have been spasmodic and not worth men-
tioning. Lumber from Puget Sound and British Col-
umbian mills is shipped to nearly all ports in western
Alaska for the use of whites and half-breeds, while the
natives in their more remote settlements obtain planks
and boards by the very laborious process of splitting logs
with iron or ivory wedges. On the treeless isles of the
Shumagin and Aleutian groups, as well as in the southern settlements of the Aliaska peninsula, even fire-wood
is imported from more favored sections of the territory
and commands high prices.

The fisheries cover a very large area, but their value
and importance, in consequence of the limited market
afforded for exportation on the Pacific coast, has not
been fully developed. The supply certainly is more
than equal to any demand.

The soil of Alaska is not sterile, being at many points
of the requisite depth and fertility for the production of
the very best crops of cereals and tubers. The difficulty
with agricultural progress in Alaska is, therefore, not
found in that respect. It is due to the peculiar climate.

Glancing at the map the observer will notice that
hydrographers have defined the passage of a warm
current, sufficient in volume and high enough in temperature to traverse the vast expanse of the North
Pacific from the coast of Japan up and across a little to
the southward of the Aleutian Islands, and then deflect-

ing down to the mouth of the Columbia River, where it turns, one branch going north up along the coast of British Columbia by Sitka, and thence again to the westward until it turns and bends back upon itself. The other grand arm, continuing from the first point of bifurcation, in its quiet, steady flow to the Arctic, passes up to the northeastward through the strait of Behring. This warm current, stored with tropical heat, gives rise naturally, as it comes in contact with the colder air and water of the north, to excessive humidity, which takes form in the prevalent fog, sleet and rain of Alaska, as noted and recorded with so much surprise by travelers and temporary residents from other climes. Therefore, at Sitka, and, indeed, on the entire seaboard of South Alaska and the Aleutian Islands, instead of finding a degree of excessive cold carried over to the mainland across the Coast range, which the latitude would seem to indicate, we find a climate much more mild than rigorous; but the prevalence of fog clouds or banks, either hanging surcharged with moisture or dissolving into weeks of consecutive rain, so retard and arrest a proper ripening of fruits and vegetables in that climate that the reasonable certainty of success in a garden from year to year is destroyed.

When we look at Alaska we are impressed by one salient feature, and that is the remarkable distances which exist between the isolated settlements. It is not at first apparent, but it grows on the traveler until he is profoundly moved at the expenditure of physical labor, patience and skill required to traverse any considerable district of that country.

The Sitkan district is essentially one of rugged inequality, being mountainous on the mainland to the exclusion of all other features, and equally so on the islands. It is traversed here, there and everywhere by broad arms of the sea and their hundreds and thousands of lesser channels.

Land travel is simply impracticable. Nobody goes on a road ; savages and whites all travel by the water. Perhaps the greatest humidity and the heaviest rainfall in the Alaskan country occur here. The equable and not rigorous climate permits of free navigation at all seasons of the year, and it is seldom, indeed, that the little lakes and shallow lagoons near the sea-level are frozen so firmly as to allow of a winter's skating.

The Aleutian and Kadiak districts are quite as peculiar in themselves and as much individualized by their geological age and formation as is the Sitkan division. They hold within their boundaries a range of great fire-mountains—grumbling, smoking, quaking hills ; some of these volcanic peaks being so lofty and so impressive as to fix in the explorer's eye an image superb and grand, and so magnificent as to render adequate description impossible. Like the Sitkan district, the Aleutian and Kadiak regions are exceedingly mountainous, there being very little low or level land compared with the sum total of their superficial area ; but in that portion extending for 1,100 miles to the westward of Kadiak, nearly over to Asia, bare of timber, a skeleton, as it were, is presented to the eye and strikes one with a sense of an individuality here in decided contrast with that of the Sitkan country. The hills not clothed with timber are covered to their summits in most cases with a thick crop of circumpolar sphagnum, interspersed with grasses, and a large flora, bright and beautiful in the summer season. To thoroughly appreciate how much moisture in the form of fog and rain settles upon the land, one cannot do better than to leave the ship in the harbor, or the post where he is stationed, and take up a line of march through one of the narrow valleys near by to the summit of one of the lofty peaks. He will step upon what appeared from the window of the vessel a firm greensward, and sink to his waist in a shaking, tremulous bog, or slide over moss-grown shingle, painted and concealed by the luxuriant growth of cryptogamic life, where he expected to find a free and ready path.

"Passing from this district," says Mr. Petroff, "a very remarkable region is entered, which I have called the Yukon and the Kuskokvim divisions. I have during two summers traversed the major portion of it from the north to the south, confirming many new and some mooted points. This region covers the deltoid mouth of a vast river, the Yukon, and the sea-like estuary—the Amazonian mouth of another—the Kuskokvim, with the extraordinary shoals and bars of Bristol Bay, where the tides run with surprising volume. The country itself differs strikingly from the two divisions just sketched, consisting, as it does, of irregular mountain spurs planted on vast expanses of low, flat tundra. It is a country which, to our race, perhaps, is far more inhospitable than either the Sitkan or Kadiak divisions; yet, strange to say, I have found therein the greatest concentrated population of the whole Territory. Of course, it is not by agricultural, or by mining, or any other industry, save the aboriginal art of fishing and the traffic of the fur trade that the people live; and, again, when the fur-bearing animals are taken into account, the quality and volume of that trade are far inferior to those of either of the previously named divisions, and we find the natives existing in the greatest number where, according to our measure of compensation, they have the least to gain.

"This country, outside of these detached mountain regions and spurs, is a great expanse of bog, lakes, large and small, with thousands of channels between them, and sluggish currents filled with grasses and other aqueous vegetation, indicated to the eye by the presence of water-lilies.

"The traveler, tortured by mosquitoes in summer, blinded, confused and disturbed by whirling 'purgas,' snow and sleet in winter, finding the coast rendered almost inaccessible by the vast system of shoaling which the current of the great Yukon has effected, passes to the interior, whose superficial area comprises nearly five-sixths of the landed surface of the Territory.

"Here is an immense tract reaching from Behring Strait, in a succession of rolling, ice-bound moors and low mountain ranges for 700 miles, an unbroken waste, to the boundary line of British America. Then, again, from the crests at the head of Cook's Inlet and the flanks of Mount St. Elias northward over that vast area of rugged mountain and lonely moor to the east—nearly 800 miles—is a great expanse of country, over and through which not much intelligent exploration has been undertaken. A few traders and prospectors have gone up the Tennanah and over the old-established track of the Yukon; others have passed to the shores of Kotzebue Sound overland from the Koyukuk. Dog-

sled journeys have been made by these same people
among the natives of the Kuskokvim and those of the
coast between Bristol Bay and Norton Sound.   But the
trader as he travels sees nothing, remembers nothing,
but his trade, and rarely is he capable of giving any
definite information beyond the single item of his losses
or his gains through the regions he may traverse.   We
know, however, enough to say now, without much hesitation, that this great extent which we call the interior
is by its position barred out from occupation and settlement by our own people, and the climatic conditions are
such that its immense area will remain undisturbed in
the possession of its savage occupants."

The fur trade, which is at present the most important Alaskan industry, consists of two general branches,
the trade in land furs and that in the furs of marine
animals.   The former has not, in late years, decreased
in volume, though a decline has been noticed in the
supply of certain sections.   The land furs now exported
from Alaska consist of the skins of bears, brown and
black, three or four kinds of foxes, including the very
valuable silver and blue foxes, otters, martens, beavers,
minks, muskrats, lynxes, wolves and wolverines.   The
sea-otter and the fur-seal supply the pelagic furs, the
seal being by far the more important of the two.   Indeed, at present the fur-seal constitutes wholly one-
half of Alaska's natural wealth.   The value of the seal-
skins shipped from the Territory and sold in European
markets during the twenty-three years of American
occupancy down to 1890 aggregates about $33,000,000.
In the same period the value of other furs was
$16,000,000, and of all other exports only about

$14,000,000. The canned salmon product, which dates only from 1884, has amounted to nearly $7,000,000, and the value of the cod-fish taken since 1868 has been fully $3,000,000. The supply of fish of various kinds in Alaska is practically inexhaustible, but the stores lavished upon the natives of that country by bountiful nature could not be more wastefully used than they are now. Any development in the fishing industry must necessarily be an improvement, causing a saving in the supply. The proportion of Alaskan fish brought into the markets of the civilized world, when compared with the consumption of the same articles by the natives, is so very small that it barely deserves the name of an industry of the country. The business, however, shows a decided tendency to increase in magnitude, and within the last few years the shipments of salted salmon in barrels from the Kadiak-Aleutian divisions have been steadily increasing.

Next in importance to furs and fish are to be ranked gold and silver. The first gold mines of real importance were opened at the end of 1880, near the present settlement of Juneau. At present there are three or four gold producing quartz mines which ship the precious metal to the United States, the largest of them being the Treadwell or Paris mine, which supplies a mill with 240 stamps. There are also paying mines in the Yukon region which have produced for some years past gold dust to the value of from $40,000 to $90,000 a year. The total value of the gold found in Alaska since 1867 is about $4,000,000, but probably as large a sum has been expended in the same time in prospecting and opening and equipping the mines. The annual output of silver is insignificant, amounting to only about $3,000.

Coal has been discovered in various parts of the Territory, but it is all of the lignite variety.   Only one of the veins is at present operated, and it is situated on Herendeen Bay, on the north side of the Alaska peninsula.   Other veins near Cape Lisburne are utilized by the ships which visit that region every year, but are not otherwise systematically worked.   Large deposits of copper and of cinnabar are known to exist, but they are far inland and not readily accessible.

Fourth in importance among the resources of Alaska must be ranked timber.   It is not at present, however, an actual source of wealth, since its exportation is prohibited by the United States Government and even the utilization of the forests for local use for lumber and fuel is much restricted.

The whaling industry is conducted by New Bedford and San Francisco firms, chiefly north of Behring Strait, but cannot properly be included among the resources of Alaska.   During the season of 1890 the product of this industry amounted to 14,567 barrels of oil, 226,402 pounds of whalebone, and 3,980 pounds of walrus ivory, besides considerable quantities of beaver, bear and white fox furs.

" In this survey of the wealth and resources of Alaska the observer is struck," says Mr. Petroff, in the census report, " with one rather discouraging feature: that all these vast resources, the products of land and sea, are taken out of the country without leaving any equivalent to the inhabitants.   The chief industries, such as salmon canneries, cod fisheries, mines, and the fur trade, are carried on with labor imported into Alaska and taken away again, thus taking out of the country the wages earned. Every pound of subsistence for these laborers, as well as all of the clothing they use, is carried by them into Alaska. The shipping of Alaska, which has become of considerable value, is also carried on wholly by non-residents of the Territory, and this state of affairs extends even to the important tourists' travel to the southeastern district of Alaska. Not only the passage-money, but the whole cost of subsistence of these tourists during their stay in Alaska goes to the California owners of the steamship lines. To give an idea of the magnitude of this traffic it is only necessary to state that the number of tourists' tickets sold each season exceeds 5,000, each ticket representing an expenditure of not less than $100, making a total of $500,000.

"The insignificant payments for furs and labor to natives are absorbed entirely in the purchase of small quantities of food and raiment. The spectacle of so vast a tract of country being thus drained continually for twenty-three years without receiving anything to speak of in return, cannot probably be equalled in any other part of the United States and perhaps of the world. At the same time the only prospect for a change in these circumstances by immigration and settlement of people who could supply the demand for labor and develop the industries as residents of the country would appear to be still in the far-distant future."

The fur-gathering industry still holds the foremost rank in Alaska, and the most important of its products are the pelts of the sea-otter and the fur-seal. It is among the Aleutian Islands that these animals are chiefly taken. The otter is widely distributed throughout the archipelago. But the fur-seal is taken almost exclusively upon the Pribyloff or Fur-seal Islands, where they resort in incredible numbers. The taking of these interesting animals is controlled by the Alaska Commercial Company, which has enjoyed a monopoly of the lucrative trade since Alaska came into the possession of this country. The actual work of killing the animals and removing the skins is done by the native Aleutians, in the Company's employ, and the operation, albeit sanguinary, is highly picturesque.

In former times, says Mr. Ivan Petroff, the Aleutian hunters prepared themselves for sea-otter expeditions by fasting, bathing and other ceremonies. The sea-otter was believed to be possessed of a very strong aversion to the female sex, and consequently the hunter was obliged to separate himself from his wife for some time prior to his departure, and also to prepare the garments he was to wear, or at least to wash with his own hands such of his garments as had been made by women. On his return from a successful hunt the superstitious Aleut of former times would destroy the garments used during his expedition, and before entering his hut dress himself anew from head to foot in clothing prepared by his faithful spouse during his absence. The hunting garments were then thrown into the sea. One old man stated, in explanation of this proceeding, that the sea otters would find the clothing and come to the conclusion that their late persecutor must be drowned, and that there was no further danger. With the spread of the

Christian religion among the sea-otter hunters most of these superstitious ceremonies were abolished, but even at the present day the sea-otter hunter occupies a prominent position in the community and enjoys great social advantages. Anything he may want which is not in the possession of his own family will be at once supplied by his neighbors, and weeks, and even months, are spent in careful preparation of arms, canoes and implements.

The mode of hunting the animal has not essentially changed since the earliest times. A few privileged white men located in the district of Ounga employ fire-arms, but the great body of Aleutian hunters still retain the spear and in a few instances the bow and arrow. The sea-otter is always hunted by parties of from four to twenty bidarkas, each manned by two hunters. From their village the hunters proceed to some lonely coast near the hunting-ground, either in their canoes or by schooners and sloops belonging to the trading firms, a few women generally accompanying the party to do the housework in the camp. In former times, of course, this was not the case. The tents of the party are pitched in some spot, not visible from the sea, and the hunters patiently settle down to await the first favorable day, only a smooth sea permitting the hunting of sea-otter with any prospect of success. In the inhospitable climate of Alaska weeks and months sometimes pass by before the patient hunters are enabled to try their skill. A weatherwise individual, here yclept "astronome," generally accompanies each party, giving due notice of the approach of favorable weather and the exact time when it is best to set out, and few Aleuts are bold enough to begin a hunt without the sanction of this individual. At last the day arrives, and after a brief prayer the hunters embark fully equipped, and in the best of spirits exchange jokes and banter until the beach is left behind; then silence reigns, the peredovchik or leader assumes command, and at a signal from him the bidarkas start out in a semicircle from fifty to one hundred yards distant from each other, each hunter anxiously scanning the surface of the water, at the same time having an eye upon the other canoes. The sea-otter comes up to the surface to breathe about once in every ten minutes, the smooth, glossy head remaining visible but a few seconds each time.

As soon as the hunter spies an otter he lifts his paddle as a signal and then points it in the direction taken by the animal, and the scattered bidarkas at once close in a wide circle around the spot indicated by the fortunate discoverer. If the animal comes up within this circle the hunters simply close in, gradually beating the water with their hands to prevent the escape of the quarry; but very often the wary animal has changed his direction after diving, and the whole fleet of canoes is obliged to change course frequently before the final circle is formed. As soon as the otter comes up within spear's throw one of the hunters exerts his skill and lodges a spear-head in the animal, which immediately dives. An inflated bladder is attached to the shaft, preventing the otter from diving very deep. It soon comes up again, only to receive a number of other missiles, the intervals between attacks becoming shorter each time, until exhaustion forces the otter to remain on the surface and receive its death wound. The body of the animal is then taken into one of the bidarkas and the hunt continues if the weather is favorable. On the return of the party each animal killed is inspected by the chief in the presence of all the hunters and its ownership ascertained by the spear-head that caused the mortal wound, each weapon being duly marked. The man who first struck the otter receives from two to ten dollars from the owner. The skins of the slain animals are at once removed, labelled and classified according to quality by the agents of the trading firms and carefully stored for shipment. It frequently happens that a whole day passes by without a single sea-otter being sighted, but the Aleut hunters have a wonderful patience and do not leave a place once selected without killing some sea-otters, be the delay ever so long. There are instances where hunting parties have remained on barren islands for years, subsisting entirely on "algæ" and mussels cast from the sea. On the principal sea-otter grounds of the present time, the Island of Sannakh and the neighborhood of Belkovsky, the hunting parties seldom remain over four or five months without securing sea-otters in sufficient number to warrant their return. Single hunters have sold sea-otters to the value of eight hundred dollars as their share of such brief expeditions, but payment is not made until the return of the party to their home station.

As soon as the result of a day's hunt has been ascertained, the chief or leader reminds the hunters of their duty toward the Church, and with their unanimous consent some skin, generally of a small animal, is selected as a donation to the priest, all contributing to reimburse the owner. The schools also receive donations of this kind, and the skins thus designated are labelled accordingly and turned over to the trading firms, who place the cash value at the disposal of the priest. Rivalry in the business of purchasing sea-otter skins has induced the various firms to send agents with small assortments of goods to all the hunting-grounds, as an inducement to the members of parties to squander some of their earnings in advance.

The method of killing the sea-otter is virtually the same in all sections frequented by it.

The killing of fur-seals is accomplished entirely on land, and has been reduced almost to a science of the greatest dispatch and system. The able-bodied Aleuts now settled upon the two islands of Saint Paul and Saint George are, by the terms of the agreement between themselves and the lessees, the only individuals permitted to kill and skin the seals for the annual shipment as long as they are' able to perform the labor efficiently within a given time. For this labor they are remunerated at the rate of forty cents per animal. Life-long practice has made them expert in using their huge clubs and sharp skinning-knives, both implements being manufactured expressly for this use. These men are as a class proud of their accomplishments as sealers, and too proud to bemean themselves in doing any other kind of work. For all incidental labor, such as building, packing, loading and unloading vessels, etc., the lessees find it necessary to engage laborers from the Aleutian Islands, these latter individuals being generally paid at the rate of one dollar *per diem.*

The work connected with the killing of the annual

quota of fur-seals may be divided into two distinct features, the separation of the seals of a certain age and size from the main body and their removal to the killing-ground forming the preliminary movements; the final operation consisting of another selection among the select, and killing and skinning the same. The driving as well as the killing cannot be done in every kind of weather, a damp, cool, cloudy day being especially desirable for the purpose.

As it is the habit of the young male seals up to the age of four years to lie upon the ground back of the so-called rookeries or groups of families that line the seashore, the experienced natives manage to crawl in between the families and the "bachelors," as they were named by the Russians, and gradually drive them inland in divisions of from 2,000 to 3,000. It is unsafe to drive the seals more than five or six miles during any one day, as they easily become overheated and their skins are thereby injured. When night comes on the driving ceases, and sentries are posted around each division, to prevent the animals from straying during the night, occasional whistling being sufficient to keep them together. In the morning, if the weather be favorable, the drive is continued until the killing-ground is reached, where the victims are allowed to rest over night under guard, and finally, as early as possible in the morning, the sealers appear with their clubs, when again small parties of twenty to thirty seals are separated from their fellows, surrounded by the sealers, and the slaughter begins. Even at this last moment another selection is made, and any animal appearing to the eye of the experienced Aleut to be either below or above the specified age is dismissed with a gentle tap of the club, and allowed to go on its way to the shore, rejoicing at its narrow escape. The men with clubs proceed from one ground to the other, immediately followed by the men with knives, who stab each stunned seal to the heart to insure its immediate death. These men are in turn followed by the skinners, who with astonishing rapidity divest the carcasses of their valuable covering, leaving, however, the head and flippers intact. Only a few paces behind the skinners come carts drawn by mules, into which the skins are rapidly thrown and carried away. The wives and daughters of the sealers linger around the rear of the death-dealing column, reaping a rich harvest of blubber which they carry away on their heads, the luscious oil dripping down their faces and over their garments.

The skins, yet warm from the body, are discharged into capacious salt-houses and salted down for the time being like fish in bins. This treatment is continued for some time, and after the application of heavy pressure they are finally tied into bundles of two each, securely strapped, and then shipped.

GEOGRAPHICAL FEATURES.

According to the terms of the treaty between the United States and Russia, the boundaries of Alaska are as follows:

" Commencing from the southernmost point of the island called Prince of Wales Island, which point lies in the parallel of 54° 40′ north latitude, and between the 131° and 133° west longitude (meridian of Greenwich), the said line shall ascend to the north along the channel called Portland Channel, as far as the point of the continent where it strikes 56° north latitude ; from this last mentioned point, the line of demarcation shall follow the summit of the mountains situated parallel to the coast as far as the point of intersection of the 141st degree of west longitude (of the same meridian) and finally from the said point of intersection the said meridian line of the 141st degree in its prolongation as far as the frozen ocean.

" With reference to the line of demarcation laid down in the preceding article it is understood :

" 1st. That the island called Prince of Wales Island shall belong wholly to Russia (now by this cession to the United States).

" 2d. That whenever the summit of the mountains which extend in a direction parallel to the coast from the 56th degree of north latitude to the point of intersection of the 141st degree of west longitude shall prove to be at the distance of more than ten marine leagues from the ocean, the limit between the British possesssion and the line of coast which is to belong to Russia as above mentioned (that is to say, the limit to the possessions ceded by this convention), shall be formed by a line parallel to the winding of the coast, and which shall never exceed the distance of ten marine leagues therefrom."

The boundry, in 1825, when this description was made, was a theoretical one based on the charts placed before the negotiators, which they doubtless assumed to be a substantially correct expression of geographical facts. The country through which the line passes was then substantially unexplored.

Much survey work has been done in recent years, with the object of determining more accurately the boundary between Alaska and the British possessions in North America ; but the task is not yet complete. The general outlines of the country, however, are familiar to all, and recent maps indicate its boundaries on all sides with substantial accuracy. The whole territory may be roughly divided into six parts, as follows :

1. The Arctic division, containing 125,245 square miles, and comprising all that portion of the North American continent between the one hundred and forty-first meridian in the east and Cape Prince of Wales, or Behring Strait, in the west, the Arctic Ocean in the north, and having for its southern boundary a line indicating the watershed between the Yukon River system and the streams emptying into the Arctic and impinging upon the coast of Behring Sea just north of Port Clarence.

2. The Yukon division, containing 176,715 square

miles, and comprising the valley of the Yukon River as far as it lies within our boundaries and its tributaries from the north and south. This division is bounded by the Arctic division in the north, the one hundred forty-first meridian in the east, and Behring Sea in the west. The southern boundary lies along a line indicating the watershed between the Yukon and the Kuskokvim, Sushetno, and Copper Rivers, and runs from the above-mentioned meridian in the east to the coast of Behring Sea, in the vicinity of Hazen Bay, in the west. The island of St. Lawrence, in Behring Sea, is included in this division.

3. The Kuskokvim division, containing 114,975 square miles, bounded on the north by the Yukon division, and comprising the valleys of the Kuskokvim, the Togiak, and the Nushegak Rivers, and the intervening system of lakes. The eastern boundary of this division is a line running along the main Alaskan range of mountains from the divide between the Kuskokvim and Tennanah Rivers down to the low, narrow isthmus dividing Moller Bay from Zakharof Bay, on the Alaska peninsula. Behring Sea washes the whole west and south coasts of this division, which also includes Nunivak Island.

4. The Aleutian division, containing 14,610 square miles, and comprising the Alaska peninsula westward of the isthmus between Moller and Zakharof Bays and the whole chain of islands from the Shumagin group in the east to Attoo in the west, including also the Pribylof or fur-seal islands.

5. The Kadiak division, containing 70,884 square miles, and comprising the south coast of the Aliaska

peninsula down to Zakharof Bay, with the adjacent islands, the Kadiak group of islands, the islands and coasts of Cook's Inlet, the Kenai peninsula, and Prince William Sound, with the rivers running into them. The main Alaskan range bounds this division in the north and west. Its eastern limit is the one hundred and forty-first meridian, which intersects the coast-line in the vicinity of Mount St. Elias, while the south shores of the division are washed by that section of the North Pacific named the Gulf of Alaska.

6. The southeastern division, containing 28,980 square miles, and comprising the coast from Mount St. Elias in the north to Portland Canal, in latitude 54° 40', in the south, together with the islands of the Alexander Archipelago between Cross Sound and Cape Fox. The eastern boundary of this division is the rather indefinite line established by the Anglo-Russian and Russian-American treaties of 1824 and 1825 respectively, following the summits of a chain of mountains supposed to run parallel with the coast at a distance not greater than three marine leagues from the sea between the head of Portland Canal and Mount St. Elias.

The Arctic division is situated almost entirely above the Arctic circle and is known to explorers only from observations made along the seacoast. The interior consists doubtless of frozen plains and low ranges of hills, intersected by a few shallow and sluggish streams. The only rivers known to emerge from this part of Alaska are the Colville, the Kok, the Inland or Noatak, the Kooak, the Selawik and the Buckland. There are many villages scattered along the coast and others are reported to exist further up on all these rivers. The coast settlements are visited every year by many vessels engaged in whaling, hunting and trading. Their inhabitants possess great commercial genius and energy, and carry on an extensive traffic with the natives of the Asian coast, their common trading-ground being at Behring Strait.

The only mineral of any value that is found on this coast is coal, of which there are several good veins at Cape Lisburne. The chief attraction for the navigators who visit the coast are furs, oil and walrus ivory. The whaling industry is already beginning to decline here as it has done in every other region of the world. Many seals are found here and polar bears are numerous. A few reindeer are found on the coast and moose and mountain sheep are said to be numerous in the interior. Muskrats and squirrels abound everywhere and their skins are offered for sale in large quantities. Foxes also are plentiful, especially the white variety, and their skins are much sought for by the American and European markets. Aquatic birds of all kinds are found in countless hosts. The only fish of value is the salmon.

About thirty villages are known in this region, their total population being a little over 3,000.

The Yukon division is the largest and in many respects most important of all. As this volume is so largely devoted to a description of the great river and the country it traverses little need be said regarding it here. Numerous trading posts have been established and the waters of the river are plied by steamboats. No mineral deposits in large paying quantities have yet been discovered, but it is believed that important gold mines will yet be found. The river abounds in fish and the forests which border it in game. High as the latitude is the summers are very warm and the vegetable growths of the country are luxuriant. The coast line of this division is particularly dreary. It is inhabited by a hardy race of seal and walrus hunters, who occupy numerous small villages. At Port Clarence, just south of Cape Prince of Wales, three or four villages are clustered around a fine harbor. King's Island or Oukivok is a small, high island, surrounded by almost perpendicular cliffs of basalt. On it is a village composed of about forty houses, which are simple excavations in the side of the cliffs. The inhabitants live almost entirely by walrus and seal hunting. On the shores of Golovin Sound small deposits of lead and silver have been found. The most important point on the coast is St. Michael, where there are several trading agencies. The Island of St. Lawrence belongs properly to this division. It had originally a population of about 1,000, but famine and disease have diminished it to one-half that number. The people are Asiatic Esquimaux. There are in all this division of Alaska about seventy-five known settlements, with a total population of nearly 7,000, of whom perhaps about twenty-five are white, 2,500 Athabaskan and the rest Esquimaux.

The Kuskokvim division is, on the whole, poor in such natural products as white men desire, and it has therefore been little visited. It contains a few mineral deposits, however, including cinnabar, antimony and silver. Game and fur-bearing animals are not as numerous as in other parts of Alaska, but there are many seals in the sea and river, and minks and foxes are quite numerous. Many salmon are also found in the river and they form a leading article of food for the natives. There are nearly a hundred villages in this division with about 9,000 inhabitants, nearly all of them being Esquimaux.

The Aleutian division comprises the western part of the Alaska peninsula and the long range of islands extending toward the Asiatic coast. These islands appear to be merely a continuation of the Alaskan range of mountains. Many of them contain volcanic peaks, some of which are still active, and all the islands are mountainous. The soil is altogether treeless save for some dwarf willows, but there is a luxuriant growth of grass. On this account it was once thought that cattle could be successfully raised here, but the long and stormy winters made the experiment a failure. The people of these islands are doubtless of Esquimau origin, although distinct in language and in habits from the remainder of that race. Their twenty-five or thirty villages are inhabited by about 2,500 people, perhaps 100 of the number being white. Their principal industry consists in fishing and taking seals, sea-otters and other marine animals.

The Kadiak division comprises the southern side of the Alaska peninsula, numerous adjacent islands and the coast of the mainland eastward to Mount St. Elias. Its inhabitants are of Esquimau stock and resemble greatly those of the Kuskokvim division. The coast is frequented by great numbers of walrus, which animal provides the inhabitants with food, material for their canoes and ivory, which is used for money and as an

object of trade. Many whales are also taken here. On
the land there are numerous reindeer, brown bears and
foxes, otters and minks. The island of Kadiak has for
a century and a quarter been one of the most important
portions of this division of Alaska. It was here that
some of the earliest Russian settlements were made, and
the population at the present time is considerable.
There are several villages devoted almost entirely to
the building of ships and boats.

North of the Kadiak group is the great estuary
known as Cook's Inlet, which was first visited by the
Russian traders a hundred years ago and was the scene
of many desperate conflicts between rival settlers as
well as between the Russians and the natives. The
natives here are almost giants in size and are strong,
active and warlike. Their houses are superior to those
of the Esquimaux, being constructed above ground of
logs and bark. They are expert fishermen, and the
waters in this region abound in salmon and other fish,
and the land in huge bears, moose, mountain sheep,
wolves and numerous smaller animals, while geese and
ducks and other wild birds are found by the million.
Timber exists here in great abundance, especially in the
valley of the Copper River. There are about fifty villages in the Kadiak division with a population of 4,500.

The Southeastern division consists of the narrow
strip of coast-land from Mount St. Elias southward to
Portland Canal. It is densely wooded and exceedingly
mountainous. The coast is deeply indented with bays
and sheltered by islands. The principal trees are
spruce and yellow cedar. On many of the islands of
the Alexander Archipelago coal has been discovered

Copper and gold have also been found. The fur trade is not now nearly as valuable as in former years, although it is still large and profitable. The waters swarm with salmon, halibut, herring and other fish. The climate is not nearly as cold as might be expected in this latitude, but the rainfall is very heavy, an average of 250 days in the year being stormy. The fifty or more villages contain a total population of nearly 8,000, including about 300 whites.

We know, says Dr. Grewgink, the eminent Russian scientist, of no more extensive theatre of volcanic activity than the Aleutian Islands, the Alaska peninsula, and the west coast of Cook's Inlet. Here we have confined within the limits of a single century all the known phenomena of this kind: the elevation of mountain chains and islands, the sinking of extensive tracts of the earth's surface, earthquakes, eruptions of lava, ashes and mud, the hot springs and exhalations of steam and sulphuric gases. Not only does the geological formation of most of the islands and a portion of the continent point to volcanic origin or elevation, but we have definite information of volcanic activity on twenty-five of the Aleutian Islands. On these islands forty-eight craters have been enumerated by Veniaminof and other conscientious observers, and in addition to these we have on the Alaska peninsula four volcanoes, two on Cook's Inlet, one on Prince William Sound, one on Copper River, and one in the vicinity of Sitka (Mount Edgecombe); three other peaks situated between Edgecombe and the Copper River have not been definitely ascertained to be volcanic. The distance from the Wrangell volcano, in the vicinity of Copper River, to the Sitkan

Island is 1,505 nautical miles. We have every reason
to believe that the Near Islands (the westernmost of the
Aleutian group) are also extinct craters ; and thus we
find one continuous chain of volcanoes from Wrangell
to the Commander Islands (Behring and Copper),
pointing to the existence of a subterranean channel of
lava finding its outlet or breathing-hole through the
craters of this region. The nearest volcanoes to the
south of this line are Mount Baker on the American
continent, in latitude 48° 48′, and the craters of the
Kurile chain of islands on the coast of Asia. That a
subterranean connection exists between this long line of
craters is indicated by the fact that whenever volcanic
activity grows slack in one section of the chain it increases in violence at some other point, an observation
which has been confirmed by all observers.

From all information on the subject at our disposal it
appears that the craters of Mount Fairweather, Cryllon,
and Edgecombe, and Mount Calder (Prince of Wales
Island), have not been active since the middle of the
last century, and as the universal law of volcanic activity seems to place the frequency of eruptions in an
inverse ratio to the height of the volcanoes, we might
reasonably expect that the season of rest for these
craters will be a prolonged one ; but how terrible and
devastating must be the awakening of the sleeping
furnaces when it occurs. With regard to Mount St.
Elias, we have many authentic data as to its volcanic
nature. Belcher and Wrangell consider that the black
ridges descending from the summits of the mountains,
and the fact that the glaciers on Copper River exhibit
a covering of vegetation, as proof of the volcanic char ·

acter of the mountain. The first phenomena may rest
entirely upon an optic delusion, as it is not at all certain
that the black streaks consist of lava or ashes, while the
appearance of vegetation on the surface of glaciers on
Copper River is very probably due to the fall of volcanic ashes; the latter phenomenon may be traced as
easily and with far more probability to the Wrangell
volcano.

One of the most impressive physical features of the
whole Territory is the stupendous glacier at Muir Inlet.
This ice-field, says a recent writer, enters the sea
with a front two or three hundred feet above the water
and a mile wide. Fancy a wall of blue ice, splintered
into columns, spires and huge crystal masses, with
grottoes, crevices and recesses higher than Bunker Hill
Monument and a mile in width! It is a spectacle that
is strangely beautiful in its variety of form and depth
of color, and at the same time awful in its grandeur.
And not alone is the sight awe-inspiring. The ice-
mountain is almost constantly breaking to pieces with
sounds that resemble the discharge of heavy guns or
the reverberations of thunder. At times an almost
deafening report is heard, or a succession of them, like
the belching of a whole park of artillery, when no out-
ward effect is seen. It is the breaking apart of great
masses of ice within the glacier. Then some huge berg
topples over with a roar and gigantic splash that may
be heard several miles, the waters being thrown aloft
like smoke. A great pinnacle of ice is seen bobbing
about in wicked fashion, perchance turning a somersault
in the flood before it settles down to battle for life with
the sun and the elements on its seaward cruise. The

waves created by all this terrible commotion even rock the steamer and wash the shores miles away. There is scarcely five minutes in the whole day or night without some exhibition of this kind. There are mountains each side of the glacier, the one upon the right, or south shore, being the highest. High up on the bare walls are seen the seoriated and polished surfaces produced by glacial action. The present glacier is retrograding quite rapidly, as may be seen by many evidences of its former extent, as well as by the concurrent testimony of earlier visitors. On either side is a moraine half a mile in width, furrowed and slashed by old glacial streams which have given place in turn to others higher up the defile as the glacier recedes. These moraines are composed of earth and coarse gravel, with occasional large boulders. On the north side the material is more of a clayey sort, at least in part, and the stumps of an ancient forest have been uncovered by the action of a glacial river, or overwhelmed by the icy flood. Some scientists claim these forests are in reality pre-glacial, and many thousands of years old. The interior of the great moraines is yet frozen, and at the head of one of the little ravines formed by former glacial river discharges, a little stream still trickles forth from a diminutive ice cavern. Notwithstanding the contiguity of the ice itself, and the generally frigid surroundings, blue-bells and other flowers bloom on the moraine. In the centre of the glacier, some two miles from its snout, is a rocky island, the top of some ancient peak the great mill of ice has not yet ground down.

It is interesting to see how the massive stream of ice

conforms itself to its shores, separating above the obstacle and reuniting below. On approaching or departing from Muir Inlet, the voyager may look back upon this literal sea of ice and follow its streams up to the snow-fields of the White Mountains, which form the back-bone of the peninsula between Glacier Bay and Lynn Canal. The following facts relating to the Muir glacier, its measurement and movement, are derived wholly from Professor Wright's notes. Roughly speaking, the Muir glacier may be said to occupy an amphitheatre which has the dimensions of about twenty-five miles from north to south, and thirty miles from east to west. The opening of this amphitheatre at Muir Inlet is toward the south southeast. It is two miles across from the shoulder of one mountain to the other at the outlet. Into the amphi-theatre pour nine glaciers, and the sub-branches that are visible make the affluents more than twenty in number. Four of the main branches come in from the east, but these have already spent their force on reaching the focus of the amphitheatre. The first tributary from the southwest also practically loses its force before reaching the main current. The main flow is from two branches coming from the northwest and two from the north. The motion is here much more rapid. Observations made upon three portions of the main glacier, re-spectively 300, 1,000 and 1,500 yards from the front, showed the movement to be 135 feet at the first point, 65 at the second and 75 at the third, per day. The summit of the lower point was a little over 300 feet above the water, the second 400 feet and the third con-siderably more, probably 500 feet. The motion rapidly decreased on approaching the medial moraines brought down by the branches from the east. Along a line moving parallel with that of the greatest motion, and half a dozen miles east from it, the rate observed at two points was about 10 feet per day. Thus we get an average daily motion in the main channel of the ice flow, near its mouth, of about 40 feet across a section of one mile. The height of the ice above the water in front, at the extreme point, was found to be 226 feet. Back a few hundred feet the height is a little over 300 feet, and at a quarter of a mile 400 feet. A quarter of a mile out in front of the glacier the water is 85 fathoms, or 510 feet deep. Thus Professor Wright estimates that a body of ice 735 feet deep, 5,000 feet wide and 1,200 feet long passed out into the bay in the thirty days he was there, this movement and discharge taking place at the rate of 149,000,000 cubic feet per day. He says that after the fall of a large mass of ice from the glacier into the bay, the beach near his camp two and one-half miles distant from the glaciers, would be wrapped in foam by the waves. One of many large masses he saw floating about projected some 60 feet out of water, and was some 400 feet square. Estimating the general height of the berg above the water to be 30 feet, and its total depth 250 feet, the contents of the mass would be 40,000,000 cubic feet.

APPENDIX NO. 1.

PROFESSOR SERENO WATSON'S "NOTE ON THE FLORA OF
THE UPPER YUKON."

(From the *Science*, of Cambridge, Mass., February 29, 1884.)

Lieut. Schwatka was able to make a small botanical
collection from about the head waters of the Yukon,
which is of considerable interest as an indication of the
climate of the region, and as showing the range northward into the Yukon valley, of some species previously
known scarcely beyond the British boundary. Lieut.
Schwatka, ascending from the head of Chilkoot Inlet,
crossed the main coast-range by the Perrier Pass, at an
altitude of 4,100 feet, coming at once upon the source of
the Yukon River, in latitude 59° 40'. A descent of
twelve miles brought him to Lake Lindeman ; and upon
the borders of this and other lakes within a distance of
twenty-five miles, nearly equally on both sides of the
sixtieth parallel, the larger part of the collection was
made, between the 12th and 15th of June. The specimens gathered at even this date were in full bloom,
excepting a few indicated in the following list by paren-
theses, and the sedges and grasses, which were well
developed.

Anemone parviflora,
Aquilegia formosa,
Aconitum Napellus, var.,
Barbarea vulgaris,
Arabis petraea,
Cardamine hirsuta, var.,
Viola cucullata,
Lupinus Arcticus,
Rubus Chamæmorus,
(Poterium Sitchense?),

Arctostaphylos Uva-ursi,
Bryanthus empetriformis,
Kalmia glauca,
Ledum latifolium,
(Moneses uniflora),
Pyrola secunda,
Dodecatheon Meadia, var.,
Polemonium humile,
Mertensia paniculata,
Polygonum viviparum,

Saxifraga tricuspidata,   (Betula glandulosa),
Saxifraga leucanthemifolia, (Alnus viridis),
Parnassia fimbriata,   Salix glauca,
Ribes rubrum,   Salix Sitchensis,
Epilobium spicatum,   Habenaria dilatata,
Epilobium latifolium,   Streptopus roseus,
(Heracleum lanatum),   Carex (2 sp.),
Cornus Canadensis,   Deyeuxia Langsdorffii,
Antennaria alpina,   Festuca ovina,
Arnica latifolia,   Lycopodium complanatum,
(Senecio triangularis),   Lycopodium annotinum.
Vaccinium parvifolium,

The rest of the collection was made as opportunity offered, during the descent to Fort Selkirk, in latitude 62° 45', which point was reached on the 13th of July. It included the following species:—

Anemone multifida,   Galium boreale,
Ranunculus Flammula, var., Aster Sibiricus,
Erysimum parviflorum,   Achillea millefolium,
Cerastium arvense,   Artemisia vulgaris,
Arenaria laterflora,   Arnica alpina,
Arenaria physodes,   Arnica Chamissonis,
Montia fontana,   Pyrola rotundifolia, var.,
Linum perenne,   Primula Sibirica,
Hedysarum boreale,   Myosotis sylvatica, var.,
Rubus arcticus,   *Pentsemon confertus,*
Fragaria vesca (?),   *Pentsemon glaucus* (?),
Potentilla fruticosa,   Pedicularis flammea,
Amelanchier alnifolia,   Chenopodium album,
Parnassia palustris,   Polygonum aviculare,
Bupluerum ranunculoides, Zygadenus elegans.
Hordeum jubatum,

The species new to so northern a latitude are marked by italics. The season appears to have been as forward as I found it in 1868 in the lower mountain ranges rising from the plateau of western Nevada in latitude 40°.   SERENO WATSON.

APPENDIX NO. 2.

COMPARISON OF THE MOST IMPORTANT RIVERS OF THE WORLD.

(Prepared for " Along Alaska's Great River " by William Libbey, Jr., Professor of Physical Geography in Princeton College, N. J)

River.	Length in miles.	Their order in the				Length in navigable miles.	Drainage area, sq. miles.
		World	W. Hemis.	N.Amer.	U. S.		
Nile..........	3834	1					1,425,000
Amazon......	3750	2	1			3623	2,275,000
Obi..........	3400	3					1,420,000
Yenesei.......	3330	4					1,180,000
Mississippi....	3184	5	2	1	1	2354	1,244,000
Yang-tse-kiang	3088	6					950,000
Amoor........	3066	7					786,000
Missouri......	2900	8	3	2	2	2400	518,000
Lena.........	2780	9					1,000,000
Congo........	2609	10					1,933,000
Niger..... ..	2585	11					1,023,000
Mekong	2500*	12					400,000
St. Lawrence.	2384	13	4	3		2300	400,000
Hoangho	2305	14					714,000
La Piata......	2300*	15	5				1,242,000
Madeira.......	2200*	16	6				345,000
Yukon.	2044	17	7	4	3†	2036	2(0,000
Mackenzie....	2000*	18	8	5		1750	590,000
Brahmapootra	2000*	19					450,000
Indus	1850	20					373,000

* Estimated, but closely known.

† Estimating whole length 2,044 miles. Taking only the amount in the United States (1,260 miles, all of which is navigable), it is the fifth river therein, the Mississippi, Missouri, Arkansas and Ohio rivers being longer.

Authorities consulted : Bates, Chavanne, Guyot, Hayden and Selwyn, Humphreys and Abbott, Keane, Kloeden, Peterman, Royal Geographical Society of England (proceedings), Stanley, Wallace.

APPENDIX NO. 3.

ITINERARY OF THE ROUTE FROM THE HAINES MISSION
IN THE CHILKOOT INLET TO FORT YUKON.

Statute Miles

Haines Mission to the mouth of the Dayay River	16.1
Head of canoe navigation on " "	9.9
Mouth of the Nourse River (west)	2.3
The Perrier Pass in the Kotusk Mountains (4,100 ft.)	11.0
The Crater Lake (head of the Yukon River) .	0.6
Camp on Lake Lindeman	12.1
(Length of Lake Lindeman, 10.1)	
Cape Koldewey	3.7
North end of Lake Lindeman	5.8
South end of Lake Bennett over the Payer Portage	1.2
Prejevalsky Point (mouth of Wheaton River, west)	18.1
Richard's Rock (east)	1.2
North end of Bennett Lake (Watson Valley, west)	10.0
(Length of Lake Bennett, 29.3)	
West end of Lake Nares (through Caribou Crossing)	1.7
East " " " (or length of the lake) .	3.2
Perthes Point (or length of Lake Bove) . .	8.8
Mouth of Tahko River	7.8
North end of Lake Tahko	10.3
(Length of Lake Tahko, 18.1)	
South end of Lake Marsh (or length of connecting river)	9.1
North end of Lake Marsh (or length of that lake)	28.8
Upper end of the Grand Cañon of the Yukon .	50.9
(Length of the Grand Cañon and Rapids, 4.6)	
Mouth of the Tahk-heen'-a (west) . . .	23.1
North end of Lake Kluk-tas'-si	17.8
Richthofen Rocks (and river)	14.4

North end of Lake Kluktassi 22.1
    (Length " " 36.5)
Maunoir Butte (east) 16.2
Red Butte (west) 3.2
Grizzly Bear Bluffs (west) 9.4
Mouth of the Newberry River (east) . . . 8.9
    " " D'Abbadie " (east) . . 38.0
    " " Daly " (east) . . . 41.6
Parkman Peak (east) 10.7
Nordenskiöld River (west) 39.1
Rink Rapids 25.4
Hoot-che-koo Bluff (east) 25.8
Von Wilczek Valley (east) 17.0
Fort Selkirk (west) (through Ingersoll Islands) . 21.3
    (Total length of river explored, 486.8).
(All of the above are in the 1st Part of the Map, Page 55).
Mouth of the Selwyn River (south) . . . 33.6
    " " White " " . . . 62.1
    " " Stewart " (east) . . . 9.7
    " " Deer " (east) . . . 65.6
Fort Reliance 6.5
Mouth of the Chandindu River 12.0
    " " Cone Hill " (west) . . 27.5
Roquette Rock (east) 13.0
Klat-ol-klin (Johnny's) Village (west) . . 33.0
Belle Isle Station 1.1
Boundary line between Alaska and British America
    (141° W. 20.3
      (Total length of Yukon River in British
      North-West Territory, 783.5).
      (Total length of Yukon River in Alaska, 1260).
Mouth of Totondu 10.0
    " Tahkandik 22.4
Charley's Village (west) 29.0
St. Michael's Bar or Island 47.4
Fort Yukon 97.0
(See Part 2d Map for above).
    (Total length explored and surveyed) . 977.0

Chetaut River (north)	196.0
Rapids in th e Ramparts (Senati's Village) . .	59.0
Mouth of Tananá River, south, (Old Nuklakayet)	28.0
Nuklakayet (north)	18.0

(Total length of raft journey on Yukon
River, 1303.2).

Newicargut (south)	70.0
Melozecargut (north)	38.0
Yukocargut (south)	22.0
Sakadelontin (north)	10.0
Koyukuk River (north)	37.0
Nulato (north)	22.0
Kaltag (north)	37.0
Hall's Rapids	100.0
Anvik (west)	22.0
Makágamute (west)	14.0
Ikogmute Mission (north)	77.0
Andreavsky (north)	100.0
Aphoon Village (north)	105.0
Coatlik	7.0
Aphoon mouth of Yukon River . . .	5.0

(Total length of Yukon River from Aphoon
mouth to Crater Lake, 2043.5).

All the above are in Part 3d of the Map, in pocket
of book.

DISTANCES ON THE COAST (FROM RAYMOND).

Mouth of Aphoon Outlet to Pikmiktalik . .	46.0
Pikmiktalik to anchorage off Redoubt St. Michael's	27.0
Distance from Redoubt St. Michael's to Fort Yukon	1039.0

INDEX.

A

Agriculture, 57.
Ainsworth, J. C., 29.
Alaska Commercial Company, 243, 265, 268, 274, 277, 278, 281, 284, 306, 317, 321, 323, 333, 339, 343.
" Alaska " (ship), 338, 339, 341.
Aleutian Islands, 343.
Alexander Archipelago, 31
" Alexy " (half-breed Russian interpreter), 274.
Amazon (River), 143, 349.
Amoor River, 118, 349.
Andreavsky, 322, 333, 335, 341, 352.
Anvik (or Anvic), 278, 314, 327, 328, 330, 332, 352,
Anvik Indians, 327, 328, 329.
Anvik River, 327, 330, 331.
Aphoon Mouth (of Yukon River), 163, 169, 177, 279, 336, 337, 352.
Arctic (references) 14, 75, 87, 91, 142, 143, 180, 211, 233, 273, 281, 286, 291, 293, 309, 313, 314, 338.
Army, The, 10.
Arrows (see bows also), 231, 232,
Astoria (Oregon), 11.
Avalanches, 17, 22.
Ayan (or I-yan) Indians, 215, 216, 217, 220, 221, 223, 224, 225, 226, 227, 228, 230, 231, 232, 233, 234, 237, 243, 244, 247, 249.
Ayan River (see Pelly also), 227.

B

" Barka, The " (or trading schooner), 277, 278, 309, 313, 315, 325, 333.

Barnard, Lieut. R. N., 321.
" Barraboras," 291.
Barrow, Point, 338.
Bates, Mr. (exploring Tanana), 302.
Baths and bathing, 125, 341.
Bears, 24, 25, 34, 67, 91, 220, 251.
Bears, black, 24, 25, 41, 62, 68, 88, 99, 109, 130, 186, 200, 235, 238, 239, 248.
Bears, brown, (or "grizzly" or " barren-ground "), 25, 41, 99, 173, 174, 186, 248.
Bella Bella, (Indian village), 18.
Belle Isle (trading station), 259, 260. 269, 301, 302, 333, 351.
Bennett, Lake, 100, 101, 103, 107, 108, 109, 111, 350.
Bering's Sea, 118, 241, 277, 336, 337, 343.
Bering's Straits, 117. 323.
Berries, 41, 54, 130, 173, 235.
Birch, (trees or timber), 72.
Boca de Quadra Inlet, 18, 23.
Boundary Butte, 260, 261.
Boundary, The, 245.
Bove, Lake, 114, 115, 116, 223, 350.
Bows and arrows, 129, 231.
British Columbia, 12, 13, 14, 23, 26, 117.
British North - West Territory, frontispiece, 25, 226, 260, 281, 351.
British, The, 306.
Byrnes, Mr., 117, 118.

C

Cable, The Atlantic, 117, 118.
Canadian Pacific Railway, 15, 22.
Candle-fish, (see Smelt).
Canneries, Salmon, (see Salmon canneries).

411